THE NEW
HOMEMADE
KITCHEN

The Institute of
Domestic Technology Presents

THE
New Homemade
KITCHEN

JOSEPH SHULDINER

Photography by REN FULLER
Illustrations by HARRY BATES

Archival Illustrations by Roman Jaster,
Guanyan Wu, and Jessica Kao

CHRONICLE BOOKS
SAN FRANCISCO

Library of Congress Cataloging-in-Publication Data available.

ISBN 978-1-4521-6119-8

Manufactured in China.

FSC
www.fsc.org

MIX
Paper from
responsible sources
FSC™ C008047

Design by **VANESSA DINA**.
Food styling by **MARIAN COOPER CAIRNS**.
Prop Styling by **STEPHANIE HANES**.
Typesetting by **FRANK BRAYTON**.
Typeset in Adobe Caslon, Brandon Grotesque, Bistro Serif.

10 9 8 7 6 5 4 3 2 1

Chronicle books and gifts are available at special quantity
discounts to corporations, professional associations, literacy
programs, and other organizations. For details and discount
information, please contact our premiums department at
corporatesales@chroniclebooks.com or at 1-800-759-0190.

Chronicle Books LLC
680 Second Street
San Francisco, CA 94107
www.chroniclebooks.com

FOR BRUCE:
the love of my life,
my husband,
my champion

INTRODUCTION

The Institute of Domestic Technology was originally conceived in 2011 as an educational adjunct to a renegade backyard farmers' market in sleepy Altadena, California, an unincorporated township nestled against the foothills of the San Gabriel Mountains just northeast of Los Angeles.

Originally billed as the Altadena Urban Farmers' Market University—one of many purposely verbose titles to come—I conceived this market activity as a value-added contribution to the monthly, under-the-radar, guerrilla gathering of thirty backyard farmers and home foodcrafters. While the market took place on the front lawn of market organizers Gloria Putnam and Stephen Rudicel's private residence, I assembled a group of gifted presenters to speak at a makeshift "University" in the house's solarium: Rudicel, who demonstrated making fresh chèvre from his and Gloria's own goat herd's milk; Alex Tarr, a professor of human geography, who gave a lecture on Los Angeles's early Small Farm Home movement; and Erik Knutzen, coauthor of *The Urban Homestead*, who talked about making bread at home.

These pioneers spoke about the budding urban farm movement and the modern resurgence of foodcrafting: sweet preserve making, canning, homemade condiments, cheesemaking, and bread made with wild yeast starters, as well as

new flavor compositions that would stand Grandma's "old-fashioned" recipes on their heads. (Homemade Guinness Stout–Cardamom–Espresso Mustard, anyone?)

An enraptured audience of close to a hundred market-goers occupied every chair we had scrounged together for the day. People who couldn't find a chair sat on the floor, spilling out onto the garden pathway outside the solarium. They stayed for hours. *Wow, I'm good at this!* I thought, with my inside voice. I didn't even know that the farmers' market outside had been so well attended that every single vendor had sold out within the first hour. Regardless, these market-goers refused to leave. Putnam and Rudicel's Urban Farmers' Market had ignited a spark, and our little makeshift academy had fed one of the flames.

Where did all these people come from? I wondered. *And why did they want to learn how to make something they could so easily purchase premade at any supermarket?* I would get the answer to these questions over time, from the Institute's students, many of whom told strikingly similar stories. Without fail, a handful of students in almost every class would reminisce about their rural childhood canning rituals and describe the "how-to" they had lost along with the matriarchal branch of their family tree. Other students expressed their dissatisfaction with being subjected to the marketing of corporations. I also heard a lot about students' newly discovered desire for self-expression, and observed a kind of growing curiosity I now refer to as the Deconstruction Effect: More and more people, it seemed, wanted to know how a commercial product could be broken down into its component parts, analyzed, and re-created by hand using better ingredients.

I share this fascination with "where things come from." In fact, it predates my founding of the Institute by decades. Most ten-year-old boys beg their parents for the latest popular toy or whatever the cool kids are wearing at school. I, on the other hand, wanted a Corona-brand hand-cranked flour mill and a Salton electric yogurt-maker. I pleaded with my mother to help me learn to make sun-dried fruit leather, solar tea, and dandelion wine. (I had, admittedly, read too much Ray Bradbury.) My poor mother tried, but she had no idea how to make these things, nor could she help me find the resources I would need to learn how to make them myself. Libraries were useless and online resources were still another few decades away. I started to imagine running away to a commune where, I had heard, counterculture hippies had gone back to nature and were relearning how to make things from scratch.

One day my mother took me to a handmade craft gallery in the progressive neighborhood in which we lived. It was there that I finally found my bible—Alicia Bay Laurel's *Living on the Earth*. Based on her years living on the Wheeler Ranch commune in Sonoma, California, *Living on the Earth* is a hippie earth-mother's almanac that tells you how to live off the land. It is handwritten in journal form, complete with wonderful illustrations and how-to diagrams. I was transfixed. Here, at last, were seemingly all the secrets that had eluded me.

But as I grew older, I learned to put my unconventional interest in how things were made behind me in order to "fit in." Only as an adult did I begin to rediscover my childhood fascination with what food really is and the way in which it ends up in our pantries and on our plates. During the recession years of the late 2000s, I started to meet people who had set their Plan B's in motion after losing their jobs, along with careers that were supposed to see them through retirement. These Plan B's were mostly food-related: jam making, bread baking, pickling, all of which seemed intentionally nourishing. It was as if these newly unemployed people had chosen to do something that was the opposite of what they had done in their previous lives as newspaper editors, school administrators, and other high-pressure careers that didn't have as much room for self-expression or innovation. I also began to meet other disaffected dropouts who had recently reinvented themselves by turning into urban homesteaders, backyard farmers, hippie-come-lately DIYers, and other food activists. They all shared an interest in disrupting the corporate hold on how we consume. Although it wasn't necessarily apparent to me at first, a movement had begun, a fact that was confirmed in that moment in the solarium. I had finally found my kindred spirits.

Looking to the Past to Discover the Future

Home food preservation and other domestic sciences have a long and colorful history, having evolved from the early development of drying, curing, fermenting, and infusing techniques to the "refined" household rituals of the genteel Victorian family. The domestic sciences, which had been popular in the United States throughout the nineteenth century, became home economics in the early twentieth century. Home economics was mostly centered on the concept of good household management through thrift and strict budgeting. When I was in middle school, girls were still required to take "home ec" classes, and boys had to take a shop class. I remember the girls making fun of home ec, with its cake mixes, Jell-O molds, and sewing, all of which were hopelessly outdated concepts in the women's liberation years of the early 1970s.

By the mid-twentieth century, the food preservation skills and knowledge that had once been a necessity were rendered obsolete by the advent of frozen, processed, and prepackaged convenience foods. Home economics became a kind of punch line. As a result, an entire generation has now grown up without their parents' or grandparents' kitchen skills. Modern technology and access to seasonal ingredients at any time of the year have allowed corporations to convince most consumers that their products are superior to their grandmother's or their own cooking—and safer. But as we have relinquished our self-sufficiency to corporations, the quality of our food has suffered, losing flavor and nutrients. We have also seen large-scale industrial food safety recalls as well as increased rates of obesity, diabetes, and heart disease from our new, highly processed food diet.

Making commonly available ingredients yourself also allows you to know what goes into them, avoiding laboratory-made preservatives, stabilizers, thickeners, and other unnecessary additives used to extend shelf life or boost profits. Making *homemade* also empowers you as a human being. Korean culture has a word for this, *son-mat*, which translates loosely to "the taste of one's hands." It is different from "tongue taste," which is a literal experience when food touches your tongue. "Hand taste" is what makes your food taste like you, and not like someone else. Author Michael Pollan puts it this way: it's the "unmistakable signature of the individual who made it."

It must be said that the rise of industrial food also liberated women from the kitchen in the postwar years, just as they began entering the workforce in larger numbers. Being able to rely on processed foods was a huge time-saver. My feminist mother taught school full time, coming home every night to make dinner for a family of five. I don't think she would have appreciated my suggesting she should spend an hour shelling fresh fava beans, then pickle them after fighting traffic at the end of an exhausting day at work.

However you may feel about the motivation or politics of the modern food-crafting movement, the truth is that today, with the internet, we can find out how almost any food or ingredient is made. What I discovered as I began to revisit my childhood interests was that the information I found online was full of discrepancies, vague references to quantities, and incomplete instructions. Plus, there was virtually no mention of food safety or how to properly store home-processed goods. As a cookbook author, I believe strongly in the importance of testing a recipe and making sure that the instructions are clear and easy to follow. That is why I wrote this book.

Using This Book

The Institute of Domestic Technology Presents The New Homemade Kitchen is a compendium, a handbook meant to serve not only as a reference guide, but also as an inspiration, with something to stimulate the inquisitive ten-year-old in all of us. Divided into Departments based on the Institute's most popular areas of study, each chapter includes step-by-step instructions, helpful tips, equipment reviews, instructor spotlights, and delicious recipes that feature the ingredient you just learned how to make. Also included are "historical" documents (From the Institute Archives) highlighting the story of the "original" Institute of Domestic Technology— a long-forgotten cooking school that apparently opened in Los Angeles in 1911. Dedicated to preserving and promulgating "the domestic arts of home and hearth," this first Institute may have closed its doors in 1966, but it continues to inspire and inform the current iteration of the IDT.

A number of recipes feature the Institute's famous FlavorBar, a list of suggestions for adding or replacing ingredients to change the recipe's flavor profile in subtle or dramatic ways. Notice that there are few to no measurements listed here, as these ideas are intended as a starting point for your own experimentation once you've nailed down and aced the master recipe. Always start with small amounts of each new ingredient, tasting as you proceed. Remember, more of each new item can always be added, but it's next to impossible to remove it.

In order to get the big picture, I suggest you approach the projects and recipes in this book by first reading the complete instructions and sidebars on the item you are going to make. Reading the instructions first will spell out the time you'll need to set aside to complete the project. Some take only a few minutes (coffee roasting), while others may take weeks or months (many fermented items). A complete reading of each chapter will also tell you if there are any special pieces of equipment or ingredients you'll need to source ahead of time (see Resources, page 340).

A note about ingredients: many recipes call for ingredients (such as crème fraîche, garlic powder, vanilla extract, and others) that we show you how to make elsewhere in the book. While our recipes will refer you to these pages, for the intrepid souls who wish to make every last component from scratch, we will certainly not judge you if you choose to use store-bought ricotta when making Ricotta Spelt Ravioli (page 138), or purchased miso when making Brown Butter Miso Tarts (page 294). Any time a recipe calls for an ingredient that can be made at home using instructions in the book, feel free to substitute with the store-bought equivalent. Don't miss out on a recipe because you think you have to spend weeks in the kitchen just preparing the components to make it! We use substitutions all the time and we promise, the recipes won't suffer for it.

That said, most chapters include a few selected recipes that showcase the ingredients you just learned how to make. We encourage you to challenge yourself to make as many ingredients as you can! These dishes are meant to inspire you, as well as illustrate unique ways that home-made ingredients can be used.

A few more words to the wise: Wherever temperatures are indicated, pay close attention. (An instant-read digital thermometer would be a good investment.) You'll notice that in some sections, such as Grains and Caffeine, where accuracy of measurement is essential, we've ditched unreliable volume measurements altogether in favor of metric weights (so you might consider throwing in a digital kitchen scale, too). Measuring out ingredients in grams will reduce your need to trouble-shoot from the start.

Despite all the measuring, temperature taking, and recipe-following, things may still occasionally go awry. Fluctuations in temperature, humidity, altitude, and freshness of ingredients can all affect your outcomes. To learn from your mistakes (as well as your successes), I highly recommend that you begin your foodcrafting journey by keeping a journal to record exactly what you did, and under what conditions, so that if something goes wrong, you can go back and discover why it may have happened, and if it went well, how to re-create it.

No matter what, we encourage the spirit of experimentation! Some improvisations might fall flat, but failure is the best teacher and leaves us with even more ideas for what—and what not—to try next time. Either way, if you keep at it, you'll ultimately end up with new and valuable skills—ones that have the potential to bring you immense satisfaction throughout your lifetime, and which will begin to redefine your cooking, your kitchen, and most of all, you.

THE INSTITUTE IS BORN

I would have loved to attend the Institute's grand opening in Los Angeles, as chronicled by an anonymous (and effusive) reporter back in 1911.

The Los Angeles Herald, August 26, 1911 — Regarded with the kind of enthusiasm usually reserved for a reigning queen, the noted author, teacher, and cook Mrs. Eliza Taylor Reynolds offered the public their first peek inside her newly founded Institute of Domestic Technology yesterday afternoon in the fair city of Los Angeles. Mrs. Taylor Reynolds is best known for her many pamphlets, including *The Perfect Art of Canning and Preserving: A Useful Household Guide*. Standing before the Institute's gaily beribboned entrance on South Main Street, the handsomely dressed proprietress and director made welcome to the overflowing throng, officially opening her new Institute in a stentorian voice worthy of the occasion: "Welcome ladies, to this house of knowledge, a house which is, and will ever remain, open to all who wish to learn and sustain the domestic arts of home and hearth."

Noting with distaste the growing prevalence of "food in boxes" increasingly making its way into our pantries, Mrs. Taylor Reynolds told those assembled that she has made it her mission "to assure that our grandmothers' 'kitchen wisdom' will not fade away completely by 1920." When asked by an admirer to deliver herself of her opinion on the packaged gelatin dessert "Jell-O," Mrs. Taylor Reynolds averred, "Convenience of preparation is certainly important to the Modern Woman and Jell-O most certainly has a place in her household, but it—and other such dishes made in factories—should not be allowed to crowd out those we make ourselves from our own freshly prepared ingredients. That would be like the telephone completely displacing paper, pen, and envelope!" These words were received with much amusement by the crowd, whose merry laughter, nodding, and whispered encomiums signaled their approval and delight.

KANUSKA / AKA NIGELLA Chipotle BLACK MUSTARD ...ardamom

SEMOLINA

Chamomile
Matricaria recutita

FLOR de JAMAICA 6-24 Berbere

HAWAI... CHONA-BARK

BROWN MUSTARD SEED

Licorice
Glycyrrhiza glabra

...anise
Illicum verum

HOMEGROWN THYME ROSE PETALS FENUGREEK 6-17 Juniper

...mint
...piperita

POPPY SEEDS ORANGE PEEL ...stick ...ger CUMIN SEED

...bark
Betula pubescens

Sassafras
Sassafras albidum

Pantry Department | CH .01

THE PANTRY DEPARTMENT

There are a number of important factors that contribute to a well-functioning kitchen, including the cook who occupies it, of course, and the fresh ingredients brought into it. In addition, we believe that the pantry is the backbone of any great kitchen. All those jars of spices, condiments, and sauces quietly sitting in our cupboards and refrigerator doors are the unsung heroes, silently waiting for us to use them.

Whether your pantry shelves are overflowing with bottles and jars, or you are pantry-challenged, this chapter will show you how to deconstruct common pantry items, then reconstruct them yourself with better ingredients. No matter how many pantry items you end up with in your kitchen, we want you to think of these as a little something-something you can add to any recipe to make it your own.

Sourcing, organizing, and replenishing your arsenal of pantry items is also important. We include our sources at the end of the book, but we encourage you to seek out your own local ethnic markets as well. If you think about where spices, nuts, or seeds come from, you'll realize the Silk Road is now global and it's called the internet. Because most chain supermarkets purchase in bulk, many items are held in distribution centers that act as regional hubs. They may sit there for months, depending on sales, which is why we try to source from smaller stores known for their selection and high turnover of their products. These tend to be stores with bulk bins, which also allow you to purchase in any quantity you want, or ethnic markets, especially Indian and Middle Eastern ones whose customers rely on a large spice selection.

We are all guilty of owning a few mystery jars, so certain we'd always remember what was in them. Keeping your stash organized can be as simple as making sure everything is labeled. Going one step further, noting the date you created or purchased an item will help when you get around to next year's purging. We have multiple old-school drafting-tape dispensers around the Institute kitchen with permanent markers nearby. If you'd like to get super-crafty, you'll want to get groovy printed labels that project an air of confidence and style. They can be purchased, made by hand, or downloaded online, and should allow enough room for the name, date, ingredients, and even a message to your future self. Think about upcyling jars and containers you find pleasing, or, if you prefer uniformity, purchase them by the case, which may help with tight storage space if they fit nicely together. With a few exceptions, we prefer glass or glazed ceramic, which do not absorb flavors. David Asher, the Institute's Dean of Dairy, points out that if some types of plastic containers can *absorb* odors, they can also *leach themselves* into their contents. Play it safe by using only food-safe plastic, or opt for nonporous containers.

Many of us suffer from having jars that we carry around for years. I'm not proud to admit that in the past I have been known to pack up my entire refrigerator and schlep it with me when moving to a new home. Spices and condiments *do* have a shelf life. Their "use by" date on the label may be subjective, but they will lose their potency if kept for a ridiculously long time. We advocate the same method professional closet organizers employ: If you haven't used something in a year, out it goes. We also strongly believe in zero waste, so we suggest you make or purchase items in small quantities and replenish often. Another option is to earmark a portion of your freshly made creations to give away as gifts. Watch heads explode when your friends receive homemade spice blends or deconstructed condiments as a housewarming or hosting gift. It may even encourage them to clean out their own fossilized pantry items and start fresh.

In the Institute kitchen, we always try to have the basic condiment essentials on hand: Mayonnaise (page 35), a few types of mustards (page 28), Fermented Ketchup (page 32), Sweet Pickle Relish (page 36), Sriracha (page 33), and one or two salad dressings. We also keep a few unusual items around for special occasions. These include Harissa (page 32), Domestershire Sauce (our version of Worcestershire sauce, page 34), and a jar of Preserved Lemons (page 36). You'll find all of these recipes in this chapter, plus some extras to round out your own pantry.

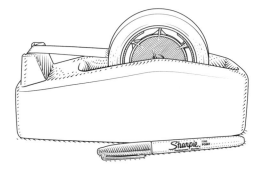

DRAFTING TAPE DISPENSER

While attending a fermentation residency at Sandor Katz's Foundation for Fermentation Fervor in Walnut Ridge, Tennessee, I was struck by how simple it was to have a drafting tape dispenser and marker handy on the kitchen counter for labeling, well, everything. The Institute produces a myriad of fancy-schmancy printable labels for take-home swag and food gifts, but sometimes you just want to get a good brain-dump onto your jar or bucket quickly. Drafting tape, masking tape, and painter's tape all work, plus you can pick from different colors.

MORTAR AND PESTLE

Different than a spice grinder or food processor, a mortar and pestle mashes ingredients entrusted to it. Some say that grinding in a mortar and pestle preserves the natural flavors of ingredients

since it produces a completely different texture than the cutting action of a whirling, high-speed metal blade. Without the use of electricity, you gain total domination over how rough or smooth, coarse or fine your ingredients become. They are excellent for making pesto, sauces, and salsas, and perfect for crushing nuts, making a garlic paste, or grinding whole spices into powders. When shopping for a mortar and pestle, stone, such as marble, is the most common material as well as the easiest to wash. Opt for one with enough room to keep things from flying out, and avoid wood and rough stone models since ingredients tend to get ground into the pores, making them difficult to clean.

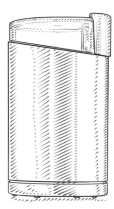

SPICE GRINDER
(AKA NON-COFFEE GRINDER)

Those of us who bought an electric spice grinder to grind whole coffee beans before the third wave of the coffee movement thought we were on the cutting edge. At the time, we were, but now we know the difference between a spice grinder's blade and a coffee grinder's burr (see Department of Caffeine, page 51). Many of us have relegated our blade grinders to their best-practice use: grinding spices. They are inexpensive, easy to clean, and take up very little storage space. (See Spices: Ground vs. Whole, page 26, for more about spice grinders.)

ZACH NEGIN
Dean of the Pantry

Professor Zach Negin crashed an early mustard-making demo I was giving at a food festival in Los Angeles years ago. He was there offering samples from SoNo, the San Diego, California–based artisanal mustard company he co-owned, and thought to himself, *Who is this pipsqueak, and what does he know about mustard?* Actually, he was correct. I was using mustard as a gateway into my rant about food and creativity, and was advocating that individuality is not measured by what you consume but rather by what you create. When Zach eventually moved to Los Angeles, I quickly realized that not only did I need to be around his creative mind, but also that I had to hire him to head up All Things Pantry for the Institute.

TIPS FROM THE PROFESSOR
Don't feel daunted by ingredients and unusual flavor profiles. Experimentation is key with condiments, spice mixes, and sauces. Start off using a tried-and-true base recipe, then start exploring by adding other flavor ideas. A good rule of thumb is to add spices pinch by pinch, tasting as you go along. Our mantra in class is, "You can always add more, but you can't take away when you've added too much." Keep good records of what you added so that when you hit on a winning combination, you can easily re-create it.

HARISSA (PAGE 32)

PRESERVED LEMONS (PAGE 36)

DOMESTIC SEASONS ITALIAN DRESSING MIX (PAGE 39)

SPICES: GROUND VS. WHOLE

While we don't want anyone to lie awake at night thinking about their spice jars, we do want to point out that we take all flavor-delivery devices seriously. It's hard to disagree about the importance of cooking with the freshest fruits, vegetables, dairy, or meat; the same principle applies to seasonings, too. Therefore, let's consider how we purchase, use, and store spices in particular.

Specialty spice stores are ground zero for the most variety and the freshest selection. If you're lucky enough to have one close by, hallelujah! If not, ethnic markets and online sources are now your new best friends.

Our guidelines are as follows:

- Grow fresh herbs in your garden or in your kitchen.

- Buy dried spices in small quantities and replenish often.

- Purchase whole spices whenever possible. Their shelf life is longer than ground because their volatile oils have not been exposed to air yet. After one year, discard and replenish.

- Invest in a spice grinder and grind small quantities at a time—only what you'll use up in a day or two.

- Store ground spices in airtight containers away from heat, light, and fluctuating temperatures. After six to eight months, discard and replenish.

- Label your jars, including the date of purchase.

A spice grinder is your new favorite kitchen tool. Specialty spice shops know this already and may even have multiple grinders so as not to cross-contaminate strongly flavored spices. We don't feel that's necessary at home, but we do have some suggestions on how to clean yours in between grinds. Using a soft-bristle or pastry brush, it's easy to sweep out the grinder bowl. Wipe with a damp cloth or grind a few tablespoons of uncooked rice into a powder to absorb lingering oils and flavors from particularly pungent spices, such as cloves, cinnamon, or cardamom. Discard the rice powder and wipe with a cloth again.

HANDCRAFTED MUSTARD

Handmade mustard is the perfect vehicle to explore your creative powers and invent your own unique flavor profiles since the simplicity of the technique lends itself to unusual combinations of spices, vinegars, and sweeteners. For classes at the Institute, we bring out our Mustard FlavorBar, an apothecary cabinet brimming with jars of flavoring ingredients to choose from. Our intention is to use the practice of personalizing condiments as an opportunity to counter the commercial food industry's mind-numbing standardization and to demonstrate a core Institute tenet: that our individuality is expressed not by what we consume, but by what we create.

Whether you're acting as a mustard provocateur or just like to eat the stuff, we've provided master recipes for three basic styles of prepared mustard: Coarse Ground, Whole Grain, and Spicy Brown. When you're ready to channel your inner mustard maker, follow the master recipe for the mustard style you'd like to make. Our recipes are designed with flexibility and experimentation in mind. Consult the Mustard FlavorBar chart to create your own personalized flavor profile. Think of this as a set of training wheels to give you an idea of which spices and flavorings work well with the sharp taste and sinus-clearing heat of mustard seed.

Note that when making a fresh batch of mustard, the flavor will continue to develop over the first two to three days and the initial heat of the mustard will also mellow as it ages.

Mustard Seeds: Mustard seeds are available in three different varieties. Yellow mustard seed (*Sinapis alba*), the most common in America, is our go-to for its relative mildness. It's also ground into powder for classic ballpark-style mustard. Brown mustard seed (*Brassica juncea*) is a bit hotter and used for Spicy Brown and Dijon mustard, or whenever a bit more heat is desired. Black mustard seed (*Brassica nigra*) can be harder to source, but is commonly found in Indian spice shops and supermarkets. These seeds have a heat that is similar to the brown *Brassica juncea* seeds.

RECISES

MUSTARD MASTER RECIPES: Use the proportions in the recipes below to customize the mustard to your own personal taste using specific ingredient suggestions from the Invent-a-Mustard FlavorBar (page 30).

Coarse Ground Mustard Master Recipe

Coarse ground mustard is exactly what its name implies: mustard that's been ground just enough to roughly come together, with some of the mustard seeds left whole. Perfect on a soft pretzel. **YIELD: 1¾ CUPS [420 G]**

¾ cup [125 g] mustard seeds
1 cup [250 ml] wine or other booze
½ cup [125 ml] vinegar
1½ tsp salt
1 tsp mixed spices
½ to 1 tsp sweetener (optional)
½ tsp freshly ground black pepper

SPECIAL EQUIPMENT
1 qt [1 L] mason jar (optional)
Food processor or blender

In a 1 qt [1 L] mason jar or a medium bowl, combine all of the ingredients. Cover and soak at room temperature for 3 days.

Transfer the mixture to a food processor or blender and process until emulsified, 1 to 2 minutes, scraping down the bowl as needed and adding 1 Tbsp of water at a time, if necessary, until your desired consistency is achieved.

Use immediately or transfer the mustard to an airtight container and store in the refrigerator for up to 6 months. The flavor will continue to develop over the first 2 to 3 days and the initial heat of the mustard will mellow as it ages.

Whole Grain Mustard Master Recipe

Whole grain mustard is not ground or cracked, leaving all of the mustard seeds whole. It makes a nice addition to a cheese plate and goes well with sausages. **YIELD: 1½ CUPS [375 G]**

¾ cup [125 g] mustard seeds
½ cup [125 ml] wine or other booze
½ cup [125 ml] vinegar
1½ tsp salt
1 tsp mixed spices
½ to 1 tsp sweetener (optional)
½ tsp freshly ground black pepper

SPECIAL EQUIPMENT
1 qt [1 L] mason jar (optional)

In a 1 qt [1 L] mason jar or a medium bowl, combine all of the ingredients. Cover and soak at room temperature for 3 days.

If desired, drain off some of the excess liquid. Use immediately or transfer to an airtight container and store in the refrigerator for up to 6 months. The flavor will continue to develop over the first 2 to 3 days and the initial heat of the mustard will mellow as it ages.

Spicy Brown Mustard Master Recipe

Brown mustard seeds are hotter than yellow ones, producing a sinus-clearing level of heat. This is Jewish deli mustard, best used on pastrami and corned beef sandwiches. **YIELD: 1½ CUPS [375 G]**

¾ cup [125 g] brown mustard seeds

1 cup [250 ml] vinegar

1½ tsp salt

1 tsp mixed spices

½ tsp freshly ground black pepper

SPECIAL EQUIPMENT

1 qt [1 L] mason jar (optional)

Food processor or blender

In a 1 qt [1 L] mason jar or a medium bowl, combine all of the ingredients. Cover and soak at room temperature for 3 days.

Transfer the mixture to a food processor or blender and process until thick and emulsified, about 3 minutes, scraping down the bowl as needed and adding 1 Tbsp of water at a time, if necessary, until your desired consistency is achieved.

Use immediately or transfer the mustard to an airtight container and store in the refrigerator for up to 6 months. The flavor will continue to develop over the first 2 to 3 days and the initial heat of the mustard will mellow as it ages.

INVENT-A-MUSTARD

Choose from these ingredient ideas to create an infinite number of unique mustard flavors. Begin with the Mustard Master Recipes (pages 28–29) as a base, then improvise with one or more ingredients from each category. Think outside the box by interpreting flavors from other products or cuisines such as Indian curry, baked goods, or salad dressings. Start with our recommended ratios, then adjust as needed for desired taste and consistency.

**¾ CUP [125 G]
MUSTARD SEEDS**

With just three types to choose from, think yellow = mild and easy to source; brown and black = hotter.

Whole black
Whole brown
Whole yellow

**½ CUP [125 ML]
VINEGAR**

Choose a type of vinegar to match the spice profile you're after. Think of the vinegar as the base note of your mustard's overall flavor.

Apple cider
Balsamic
Champagne
Fig
Raspberry
Red wine
Sherry
White wine

Dijon Style
Champagne
Rice
Verjus

**½ CUP [125 ML]
BOOZE**

Alcohol pairs well with mustard, both as a drink, but also as part of the recipe. Light flavors = wine; stronger flavors = stout/spirits.

Beer
IPA
Lager
Stout

Hard Apple Cider (page 298)

Dry Red Wine
Cabernet Sauvignon
Pinot Noir
Syrah

Dry White Wine
Albariño
Pinot Grigio
Sauvignon Blanc

Liqueur
Limoncello
Luxardo
Nocino

Spirit
Cognac/brandy
Gin
Rum
Tequila/mezcal
Whiskey/bourbon

1 TSP TOTAL
SPICES & FLAVORINGS

Here's where your creativity shines. Experimentation is key. Go easy on the quantities and taste as you go; you can always add more, but not the opposite. Use one or a combination of spices.

Traditional
Allspice (ground)
Cinnamon (ground)
Clove (ground)
Garlic powder
Nutmeg (ground)
Onion powder

Unusual
Cardamom (ground)
Chai tea mix
Curry powder
Dried apricots
Earl Grey tea leaves
Finely ground coffee beans, or Cold Brew Coffee Concentrate (page 66)
Red pepper flakes
Smoked paprika

Dijon Style
Bay leaves (crushed)
Black peppercorns (ground)
Dried thyme
Juniper berries (ground)
Minced shallots

½ TSP
SALT

Salt not only acts as a preservative but can carry its own weight when flavored varieties are used. Start with ½ tsp and adjust to taste.

Flavored salt
Fleur de sel
Himalayan
Kosher
Sea salt
Smoked salt

½ TO 1 TSP
SWEETENER

A spoonful of sugar makes the mustard go . . . well, you know.

Brown sugar
Coconut sugar
Date sugar
Honey
Maple syrup
Molasses
Palm sugar
Piloncillo

FLAVORBAR

COMBINATION IDEAS:

yellow mustard seeds + champagne vinegar + cognac + clove + cinnamon + honey

brown mustard seeds + red wine vinegar + stout + finely ground coffee beans or coffee concentrate + cardamom + cinnamon + nutmeg

brown mustard seeds + balsamic vinegar + cinnamon + date sugar

yellow mustard seeds + apple cider vinegar + bourbon + dried apricots + brown sugar

Fermented Ketchup

The store-bought ketchup we grew up with is tasty enough in a nostalgic way, but it loses some of its appeal when you read the ingredient label. In this homemade version, tomato paste and spices are fermented with active whey or brine, infusing this ketchup with deeper flavors and more complexity than the bottled, commercial condiment of your childhood. It's also probiotic and preservative-free, the perfect ketchup for grown-ups. You can make it three ways: with whey, which has the most neutral taste; with kimchi brine, which adds an extra-spicy kick; or our favorite: with sauerkraut brine, with its salty, slightly funky flavor. **YIELD: 2 CUPS [500 ML]**

12 oz [340 g] tomato paste

6 Tbsp [90 ml] strained active whey from yogurt (page 168), active brine from sauerkraut (page 278), or kimchi brine (page 282), plus more for thinning, if desired

¼ cup [60 ml] raw, unfiltered apple cider vinegar

¼ cup [45 g] packed brown sugar

1 tsp kosher salt

½ tsp Mushroom Powder (page 327)

½ tsp Onion Powder (page 327)

¼ tsp Garlic Powder (page 326)

¼ tsp mustard powder

¼ tsp ground cloves

¼ tsp ground allspice

¼ tsp ground cayenne pepper

SPECIAL EQUIPMENT

1 pt [500 ml] mason jar with lid

In a medium bowl, combine all the ingredients, mixing well.

Transfer the mixture to a 1 pt [500 ml] mason jar and cover loosely with a lid. Allow to sit for 3 to 5 days at room temperature, tasting and stirring once each day, until you are happy with the degree of fermented flavor.

Once fermentation is complete, the ketchup can be thinned, if desired, with a bit more whey or brine. Use immediately or seal the jar tightly and store in the refrigerator for up to 6 weeks.

Harissa

Many countries have a spicy red pepper sauce they call their own. Tunisia's harissa is one of them. Ubiquitous all over North Africa, this red pepper sauce goes well on meat, vegetables, couscous, roasted potatoes, roasted vegetables, or even scrambled eggs. **YIELD: 2 CUPS [500 ML]**

4 oz [110 g] dried chiles (see Notes), stems and seeds discarded

1 tsp caraway seeds

1 tsp coriander seeds

1 tsp cumin seeds

1 Tbsp smoked paprika

1 tsp kosher salt

1 tsp freshly ground black pepper

5 garlic cloves, peeled

2 Tbsp fresh lemon juice

1 Tbsp chopped fresh mint

¼ cup [60 ml] olive oil, plus more for storing

SPECIAL EQUIPMENT

Spice grinder or mortar and pestle

Food processor

1 pt [500 ml] mason jar with lid

Place the chiles in a heatproof bowl. Cover them with boiling water and let stand, uncovered, for 30 minutes.

Meanwhile, in a dry, heavy skillet over medium heat, toast the caraway, coriander, and cumin seeds until fragrant, about 2 minutes. Transfer to a plate to cool briefly.

Grind the cooled spices in a spice grinder or mortar and pestle. Add the paprika, salt, and black pepper, stirring or pulsing to combine.

Drain the chiles, reserving the liquid, and transfer them to the bowl of a food processor. Add the spices, garlic, lemon juice, and mint and pulse until the mixture is coarsely chopped.

With the food processor running, slowly drizzle the olive oil through the feed tube. Scrape down the sides of the bowl, adding some of the reserved chile soaking liquid as needed, 1 Tbsp at a time, processing after each addition until the mixture has formed a smooth, thick, and spreadable paste.

Use immediately or transfer the harissa to a 1 pt [500 ml] mason jar and cover the surface with a thin layer of olive oil. Seal the jar tightly and store in the refrigerator for up to 1 month.

NOTE ON CHILE VARIETIES: Choose a single variety or make your own combination.

Very Mild: Roasted red bell peppers

Mild: Guajillo or New Mexico

Spicy: Arbol or puya

Smoky: Chipotle or morita

Rich: Ancho, mulato, or pasilla

NOTE ON HANDLING CHILES: When handling chiles, you may want to use disposable gloves. Otherwise, wash your hands thoroughly after handling and remember not to touch your eyes.

Sriracha

When this Thai hot sauce burst onto the Western palate, it became so ubiquitous that even fast-food chains and junk food brands felt the need to jump on the flavor bandwagon. While its origin has been traced to Si Racha, Thailand, its popularity exploded when it began being produced in Southern California. The Institute's version contains only natural ingredients and is naturally fermented. The only thing missing is the iconic green-tipped "red rooster" bottle. **YIELD: ABOUT 2 CUPS [500 ML]**

1½ lb [680 g] red Fresno chiles, stems trimmed (See Note on Handling Chiles, above, and Note on Chile Varieties, following)
5 to 8 garlic cloves, peeled
¼ cup [45 g] packed brown sugar
1 Tbsp sea salt
½ cup [125 ml] vinegar (cane vinegar, distilled white vinegar, palm vinegar, or any other neutral, clear vinegar)

SPECIAL EQUIPMENT
Food processor
1 qt [1 L] mason jar
Blender (optional)

In a food processor, process the chiles, garlic, sugar, and salt, pulsing until coarsely puréed.

Transfer the mixture to a 1 qt [1 L] mason jar and cover loosely. Allow it to sit for 5 to 7 days at room temperature, stirring once each day. By the second or third day you should begin to see the mixture bubble and rise in the jar as fermentation begins. Continue stirring down and tasting the mixture each day until you are happy with the degree of fermented flavor.

Once fermentation is complete, add the vinegar, stirring to combine, then transfer to a blender or food processor and blend until smooth.

Strain the mixture through a fine-mesh sieve placed over a medium saucepan, using a rubber spatula to push as much of the mixture through as possible and discarding any remaining solids.

Over medium-low heat, cook, stirring occasionally, until the mixture thickens, 5 to 10 minutes or longer if you desire a thicker consistency.

Use immediately or transfer the sriracha to a jar or bottle and store, tightly sealed, in the refrigerator for up to 6 months.

NOTE ON CHILE VARIETIES: Mature, red Fresno chile peppers are often mislabeled "red jalapeño" at supermarkets. Though they are about the same size as jalapeños, if you look and sample closely, you'll see it typically has wider shoulders and a hotter flavor. You can replace the Fresno chiles with red jalapeños or another red chile if you want to adjust the spiciness.

Domestershire Sauce

We have John Weeley Lea and William Henry Perrins to thank for that omnipresent bottle of steak sauce on many of our dining room tables growing up. Lea and Perrins were British chemists from Worcester county who developed the original recipe in 1838. While their exact recipe is still a secret, the Institute's own "Domester" county version is just as delicious. Most of the ingredients can be found online or in a good gourmet supermarket or Asian market. It's a workhorse on steak and burgers, but it's also great on a Caesar salad or in a Bloody Mary. **YIELD: ABOUT 2 CUPS [500 ML]**

2 cups [500 ml] white wine vinegar

½ cup [160 g] molasses

½ cup [125 ml] soy sauce

¼ cup [75 g] tamarind concentrate

3 Tbsp yellow or brown mustard seeds

2 garlic cloves, peeled and crushed

2 dried shiitake mushrooms, chopped

One 1 in [2.5 cm] piece fresh ginger, peeled and finely chopped

1 anchovy, chopped

4 by 4 in [10 by 10 cm, or 10 g] piece kombu (dried kelp)

5 cardamom pods, roughly crushed

1 tsp coriander seeds, roughly crushed

One ½ in [12 mm] piece cinnamon stick

3 Tbsp kosher salt

2 tsp red pepper flakes

1 tsp black peppercorns

1 tsp cloves

½ cup [100 g] granulated sugar

SPECIAL EQUIPMENT

2 qt [2 L] mason jar

16 oz [500 ml] glass bale-top bottle

In a medium saucepan over medium-high heat, combine all of the ingredients except the sugar. Bring to a boil, then lower the heat to medium-low and simmer for 10 minutes.

While the mixture is simmering, prepare the caramel: In a small saucepan over medium-high heat, add the sugar. Swirl the pan gently without stirring until the sugar melts and turns a syrupy, dark amber color, about 5 minutes.

Add the caramel to the simmering vinegar mixture, stirring to combine (use caution, as the caramelized sugar will splatter when hitting the mixture).

Continue to simmer for an additional 5 minutes, then remove from the heat and allow to cool to room temperature.

Transfer the mixture, including the solids, to a 2 qt [2 L] mason jar, seal tightly, and allow to steep in the refrigerator for 3 weeks.

Strain the steeped Domestershire sauce through a fine-mesh sieve, discarding the solids. Decant the sauce into a 16 oz [500 ml] glass bale-top bottle. Use immediately or seal tightly and store in the refrigerator for up to 1 year.

NOTE: For a vegan variation, omit the anchovy and add an additional ½ tsp of salt and 2 additional shiitake mushrooms, or 1 Tbsp Umami Cocaine (page 328).

Prepared Horseradish

In my home growing up, horseradish was basically eaten once a year at Passover, spread on matzo as a symbolic reminder of the bitterness of slavery endured by the ancient Hebrews in Egypt. While I may always associate horseradish with ancestral suffering on some level, I've since discovered how amazing it is in Bloody Marys, on poached salmon, with lamb, in a seafood cocktail sauce, and, of course, on raw oysters. We've included a number of vinegar options to choose from, such as white wine (mild flavored) as well as cane, coconut, and palm vinegars (strong and sweet flavored). If you've never made fresh horseradish before, brace yourself, as it can be eye-wateringly strong when freshly made. As horseradish ages and is exposed to oxygen, it will mellow. If you prefer a milder taste, allow it to mature for 1 to 2 weeks in the refrigerator before using. **YIELD: ABOUT 1 CUP [250 ML]**

1 cup [225 g] peeled and grated fresh horseradish root

½ cup [125 ml] vinegar (white wine vinegar, cane vinegar, coconut vinegar, or palm vinegar)

½ tsp kosher salt

¼ tsp granulated sugar

SPECIAL EQUIPMENT

Food processor

In a food processor, combine all of the ingredients and pulse until they come together in a thick, creamy, slightly coarse paste. If the mixture seems dry, add water 1 Tbsp at a time to help blend and thin the mixture. Taste, adjusting the seasoning if desired, but keep in mind that horseradish will be shockingly pungent immediately after making it.

Use immediately (if you dare) or transfer the horseradish to an airtight container and allow it to mellow in the refrigerator for 1 to 2 weeks, or up to 3 months.

VARIATION: RED BEET HORSERADISH

Place ½ lb [225 g] whole, scrubbed, and unpeeled red beets in a large saucepan and add water to cover. Bring to a boil and cook until tender, 30 to 45 minutes. Drain the beets and rinse them under cold water until they're cool enough to handle. Using your fingertips, slip off the skins and discard. Coarsely grate the beets, then prepare the recipe as written, adding the grated beets to the rest of the ingredients when processing.

Mayonnaise

Most people have never tasted homemade mayonnaise and once they do they're ruined. Homemade is almost like another substance, impossible to even compare with store-bought. Making it by hand involves a bit of alchemy to emulsify the ingredients into a smooth, silky cloud, but starting with room-temperature ingredients will help ensure success. If the sauce breaks, we've included a quick fix to rescue it. **YIELD: 1 CUP [250 ML]**

1 egg yolk, at room temperature

½ tsp fine sea salt

1 Tbsp fresh lemon juice

2 tsp Dijon mustard, at room temperature

¾ cup [180 ml] vegetable oil, such as sunflower, at room temperature

SPECIAL EQUIPMENT

Hand mixer or immersion blender (optional)

Set a medium bowl on top of a folded, damp kitchen towel to prevent it from slipping.

Add the egg yolk and salt to the bowl and beat with a whisk, hand mixer, or an immersion blender fitted with a whisk attachment until foamy and pale yellow in color. Add the lemon juice and mustard, whisking to combine.

Begin adding oil a few drops at a time, whisking steadily until the mixture begins to form an emulsion. Continue whisking, slowly adding the remaining oil in a thin, steady stream until incorporated and the mayonnaise is thick and spreadable.

Use immediately or transfer the mayonnaise to an airtight container and store in the refrigerator for up to 1 week.

NOTE: If the mayonnaise breaks, separates, or refuses to thicken, it can still be saved. In a clean bowl set over a pan of warm water, add a fresh egg yolk and 1 Tbsp of the broken mayonnaise, and whisk until the emulsion is restored. Continue whisking and slowly adding the broken mayonnaise until it's reincorporated.

Sweet Pickle Relish

A must for making Thousand Island Dressing, pickle relish also plays well on a hot dog bun. We bet you didn't know this, but it cleans up real good on a cheese and charcuterie plate as well. **YIELD: 1 CUP [250 ML]**

1 lb [450 g] cucumbers (see Note), finely diced
½ cup [70 g] finely chopped onion
1¼ tsp kosher salt
½ cup [125 ml] white wine vinegar
2 Tbsp sugar
1 tsp yellow mustard seeds
1 tsp dill seeds
½ tsp ground turmeric

In a medium bowl, toss the cucumber and onion with 1 tsp of the salt and allow it to sit at room temperature for 1 to 2 hours. Transfer the cucumber and onion to a clean kitchen towel set over a bowl and twist the towel to squeeze out as much moisture as possible. Discard the liquid.

In a small saucepan over medium heat, combine the drained cucumber and onion with the remaining ingredients, including the remaining ¼ tsp salt. Bring the mixture to a boil, then simmer over medium-low heat for 5 minutes to reduce slightly, then remove from the heat.

Allow the relish to cool to room temperature in the pan, then transfer it to an airtight container and chill it overnight in the refrigerator before using. Store sweet pickle relish in the refrigerator for up to 1 month.

NOTE ON CUCUMBERS: English hothouse, pickling, Kirby, Persian, and Japanese varieties are all good here and do not need to be peeled or seeded. If using the common American "slicing cucumber," start with 1½ lb [675 g]. Remove the seeds and peel the skin (if waxed) before proceeding with the recipe.

Preserved Lemons

A common flavoring ingredient in South Asia as well as North Africa, preserved lemons provide a salty-sour flavor to savory dishes. The pulp is usually discarded since it becomes exceedingly salty, and it's the peels that are the main attraction. We try to use organic fruit to avoid waxes or pesticide residue, though scrubbing nonorganic fruit with a vegetable brush and diluted vinegar solution can also do the trick. Use these lemons in vinaigrettes (see page 37), sauerkraut, braised chicken, or simply as a condiment on a sandwich. **YIELD: 2 PT [1 L]**

Kosher salt
2 tsp fennel seeds
2 tsp black peppercorns
4 dried bay leaves
8 large or 10 small Meyer lemons, preferably organic, or more as needed

SPECIAL EQUIPMENT
Two 1 pt [500 ml] mason jars with lids

Add 2 Tbsp of salt, 1 tsp of the fennel seeds, 1 tsp of the peppercorns, and 2 of the bay leaves to the bottom of each of two 1 pt [500 ml] mason jars and set aside.

Juice 2 of the lemons and set the juice aside in a separate bowl.

Cut the remaining lemons into quarters lengthwise, stopping short of the base by ½ in [12 mm] so that each lemon remains intact at the base.

Take a lemon in the palm of your hand, gently spread the cut quarters open, and rub a heaping tablespoon of salt into the exposed flesh. Close up the lemon and repeat with the remaining lemons.

Place half of the salted lemons into each prepared jar, pressing down firmly with the back of a wooden spoon or a cocktail muddler to fit them into the jar and release their juices. Top off each jar with the reserved lemon juice, being sure to leave ½ in [12 mm] of headspace.

Seal the jars tightly and allow the lemons to ferment at room temperature for 3 to 4 weeks. Invert the jar once a day for the first week, and every few days after that. If the lemons do not stay submerged below the brine after the first few days, press them down and add more lemon juice to cover.

When the lemons are soft and glossy and the brine is thick and syrupy, they are ready to use immediately or can be transferred to the refrigerator for long-term storage. Preserved lemons will keep in the refrigerator, stored whole in their brine, for at least 1 year.

To use, take a piece of lemon from the brine, rinse it, and remove and discard the pulp, which will be inedibly salty. Chop and use the rind only.

VARIATION: PRESERVED LIMES
Omit the spices and substitute limes for Meyer lemons. A 1 pt [500 ml] jar will fit 6 to 8 limes.

Vinaigrette Master Recipe

If you memorize only one recipe by heart, this should be the one. It's easy to remember: 3 parts oil to 1 part acid. Any oil (such as olive, canola, or sunflower) and any acid (vinegar, lemon juice, lime juice, or even pickle brine) will do. The same goes for the mustard—use store-bought or make your own Coarse Ground (page 28) or Spicy Brown (page 29). **YIELD: 1 CUP [250 ML]**

¼ cup [60 ml] red wine vinegar

1 garlic clove, minced

1 tsp mustard (see recipes, pages 28–29)

½ tsp kosher salt

¼ tsp freshly ground black pepper

¾ cup [180 ml] olive oil

In a medium bowl, add the vinegar, garlic, mustard, salt, and pepper, whisking to combine. Slowly add the olive oil while whisking constantly until the dressing has emulsified. Alternatively, place all of the ingredients into a jar with a tight-fitting lid and shake vigorously until combined.

Use immediately or transfer to an airtight container and store in the refrigerator for up to 2 weeks. Bring to room temperature and mix thoroughly before using.

FLAVORBAR

VINAIGRETTE IDEAS:

Armed with the Vinaigrette Master Recipe, you can let your inner *chef garde manger* loose. Using the basic method to the left and the 3 parts oil to 1 part acid ratio, try adapting the recipe with one of the following combinations.

Greek: olive oil + red wine vinegar + oregano + minced preserved lemon rind (facing page)

Miso: sunflower oil + rice wine vinegar + Miso (page 291) + grated fresh ginger + mirin

Fermented Brine: olive oil + fermented sauerkraut or kimchi brine + chopped Sauerkraut (page 278) or Kimchi (page 282)

Kōji: sesame oil + rice wine vinegar + Shio Kōji (page 295)

DOMESTIC SEASONS VINAIGRETTE

"Fresh lettuce . . . Fresh tomato . . . Bottled dressing? Not on MY fresh salad! I want my dressing as fresh as my salad. So I use 'Good Seasons.' It's easy! Just pour in vinegar and dressing mix. Then, add oil and shake. If you want your dressing as fresh as your salad, you want Good Seasons. Pour it on a tossed green salad, fresh and sassy! Fresh, because you make it yourself!"

Believe it or not, that's the script of a 1965 television commercial for Good Seasons salad dressing mix. Still to be found in supermarkets today, these little foil packets of herbs and spices even come with their own equipment: a small glass cruet (essentially a glass carafe with a narrow neck and a plastic top). Once you've added oil, water, and vinegar to the handy fill-lines on the cruet, you pour in the contents of the packet, shake, and—Alakazam!—you've got yourself some fresh and sassy salad dressing.

The unintended joke of the old 1960s TV commercial, of course, is that vinaigrette is ridiculously easy to make and doesn't require special, premeasured packets of "secret" ingredients or fancy equipment. Yet the underlying message of the spot is this: Making your own salad dressing is difficult and unreasonably inconvenient; and now that we've sold you on our blah-tasting, industrial, bottled dressing for decades, we're coming to the rescue with our shiny packets—and get this!—a free cruet! The sad truth is that by 1965, the knowledge of how to make a simple vinaigrette had been virtually lost. This product took advantage of the mysterious alchemy of oil and vinegar to, in effect, market a once commonplace kitchen technique as a miracle of modern science. ("Ooh, look, Mom! It turned into salad dressing! All by itself!")

The ultimate point of this rhetorical shell game—a trick played over and over again in the modern era—is that, yes, we'll admit that something you make yourself from scratch is inherently better than something premade, but, come on: You still need us—and our packaged products.

Kvetching aside, I actually like the idea of premeasuring ingredients, but with ingredients you really do "make yourself." (Anything to silence that cranky little voice inside that says, "You've had a rough day. You're too tired to measure out the vinegar and oil. And don't even think about oregano.") Once you've mixed up a few batches of your own herb and spice mix, make your own upcycled, DIY cruet, and you've got the Institute's version of an "instant" salad dressing we call "Domestic Seasons."

It's easy!

Domestic Seasons
Italian Dressing Mix

YIELD: ¼ CUP [55 G]

2 Tbsp dried parsley (page 331)
2 Tbsp dried basil (page 331)
2 Tbsp dried oregano (page 331)
2 Tbsp Lemon Peel Powder (page 326)
2 Tbsp Garlic Powder (page 326)
2 Tbsp Onion Powder (page 327)
1 Tbsp Tomato Powder (page 327, optional)
1 Tbsp fine sea salt
1½ tsp red pepper flakes
1½ tsp freshly ground black pepper

In a small bowl, add all of the ingredients, whisking to combine. Use immediately or transfer to an airtight container away from light and heat and store for up to 3 months. Alternatively, divide the dressing mix into ¼ cup [18 g] portions and store in foil or plastic packets, in an airtight container, premeasured and ready to use.

TO MAKE A DOMESTIC SEASONS CRUET

SPECIAL EQUIPMENT

1 pt [500 ml] clear glass jar with tight-fitting lid, all labels removed
Oil-based paint marker

Set the jar on a level surface and pour in ¼ cup [60 ml] of water. With a paint marker, mark the level on the outside of the glass and write the word "vinegar" below the line.

Add an additional ¾ cup [180 ml] of water to the jar and mark its level on the outside of the glass with the word "oil" below the line.

Empty the water, then follow the paint marker manufacturer's directions, allowing the ink to dry before using the cruet.

USING THE DOMESTIC SEASONS CRUET

In your clean, dry Domestic Seasons cruet, pour in vinegar to the first fill-line. Add olive oil to the second fill-line, then sprinkle in ¼ cup [18 g] of the dressing mix.

Affix the lid tightly to the cruet and shake vigorously until the dressing is emulsified. The dressing can be used immediately or stored tightly covered in the refrigerator for up to 2 weeks. Bring to room temperature and mix thoroughly before using.

Nut Butter

Sourcing different types of nuts, then grinding them into fresh butters at home, is something special. There are so many ways of personalizing the texture, flavor, and saltiness that are not possible with store-bought nut butters. Experiment with roasted vs. raw nuts, salted vs. unsalted, nut combinations like peanuts and cashews, and sweeteners to come up with a blend to suit your own ideal taste profile. See the FlavorBar (facing page) for ideas. **YIELD: 1 CUP [250 G]**

2 cups [280 g] peanuts, almonds, pistachios, or cashews, raw or roasted
Sunflower oil, as needed
Kosher or sea salt (optional)

SPECIAL EQUIPMENT

Food processor or blender

In a food processor or blender, add the nuts and process until the desired consistency is achieved, about 5 minutes for a chunky style, or 10 minutes for a smoother consistency. Stop the motor and scrape down the sides occasionally to keep the nuts from clumping up around the blade. If using roasted nuts, you may need to add 1 to 2 Tbsp (or more) of oil to achieve a smooth texture.

Add salt to taste, if using, and pulse until thoroughly combined.

Use immediately or transfer the nut butter to an airtight container and store in the refrigerator for up to 3 months.

Domestella (Chocolate-Hazelnut Spread)

Europeans have known about the symbiotic combination of hazelnuts and chocolate for years, specifically as a spread enjoyed on toast. Though late to the game, we not only enjoy this morning ritual, but also make it ourselves. **YIELD: 1½ CUPS [420 G]**

2 cups [240 g] raw hazelnuts
1 cup [120 g] powdered sugar
⅓ cup [25 g] unsweetened cocoa powder
⅓ cup [80 ml] hazelnut oil, plus more as needed
1 tsp Vanilla Extract (facing page)
⅛ tsp fine sea salt

SPECIAL EQUIPMENT

Food processor

Preheat the oven to 350°F [180°C]. Spread the hazelnuts on a rimmed baking sheet and bake in the oven until dark brown but not burnt, about 12 minutes, shaking the baking sheet once or twice during baking. Remove from the oven and, while still hot, rub the nuts vigorously in a clean kitchen towel to remove most of the skins. Don't worry if some skins are still attached.

In a food processor or blender, add the skinned nuts and process until mostly smooth, about 10 minutes. Stop the motor and scrape down the sides occasionally to keep the nuts from clumping up around the blade.

Add the sugar, cocoa powder, ⅓ cup [80 ml] of hazelnut oil, the vanilla, and salt to the food processor and process until fully incorporated and the mixture becomes glossy and spreadable, about 2 minutes. If needed, add more hazelnut oil, 1 Tbsp at a time.

Press the mixture through a fine-mesh sieve if a smoother texture is desired. Use immediately or transfer the Domestella to an airtight container and store in the refrigerator for up to 3 months.

Vanilla Extract

One of the easiest and most rewarding projects taught at the Institute is making real, homemade vanilla extract. The next best thing to using an actual vanilla bean in a recipe is to always have a bottle of vanilla extract at the ready. Stashed in your pantry, it will last for years and can be replenished over and over. It also makes a great no-brainer gift when decanted into a small, attractive bottle. The lucky recipient will be amazed!

YIELD: 1 CUP [250 ML]

2 vanilla beans
1 cup [250 ml] unflavored vodka

SPECIAL EQUIPMENT
1 pt [500 ml] mason jar

Use a sharp paring knife to split the vanilla beans lengthwise, then cut them in half.

Place the vanilla beans in a 1 pt [500 ml] mason jar, pour the vodka over the top, and seal the jar tightly.

Leave in a cool, dark place for 3 to 5 months, shaking the jar occasionally.

Strain out the vanilla beans and reserve them for your next batch of extract, or dry them completely and add to granulated sugar for vanilla-flavored sugar. Decant the extract into a clean bottle with an airtight lid. Use immediately or store the vanilla at room temperature, away from light, for at least 1 year.

NOTE: To start a new batch, keep the vanilla beans in the pint jar after decanting the extract and replenish with a fresh cup of vodka. The vanilla beans can be reused up to four times, depending on the quality and variety of beans. Additional fresh beans can be added to boost flavor as needed.

VARIATION
For a different flavor, substitute bourbon or rum for the vodka.

FLAVORBAR

NUT BUTTER IDEAS:

Experiment with the flavor combinations below, using 2 cups [280 g] of nuts and starting with small amounts of each flavoring (¼ tsp for spices, 1 tsp for sweeteners), then tasting and adding more if desired.

peanuts + sea salt + smoked paprika

walnuts + maple syrup + cinnamon

cashews + dates + smoked sea salt

pistachios + honey + cardamom

almonds + vanilla extract + orange zest

We have an aberrant fascination with deconstructing ingredients at the Institute. Usually it's sparked by something compli-cated or mysterious, but it also applies to simple things that we normally take for granted. Going through the sugars in our pantry in preparation for this chapter, we realized how curious we were about how they were processed. Making them yourself is fun and can also save you a trip to the market if you run out of one of them during a spontaneous urge to bake.

Brown Sugar

Unfortunately, commercial sugar is a bit of an engineered affair. During processing, raw sugar has its molasses stripped out, then it's refined even further to produce what we recognize as white sugar. Brown sugar is essentially white, refined sugar that has had the molasses added back in. We figured we could do that ourselves, and it's a great trick to have up your sleeve when you run out of store-bought brown sugar during a baking emergency.

YIELD: 1 CUP [240 G]

1 cup [200 g] granulated sugar
1 to 4 Tbsp molasses

SPECIAL EQUIPMENT

Food processor

In the bowl of a food processor, combine the granulated sugar and 1 to 2 Tbsp of the molasses (for light brown sugar), or 2 to 4 Tbsp of the molasses (for dark brown sugar) and pulse until combined.

Use immediately or transfer to an airtight container and store at room temperature for up to 1 year.

INSTITUTE TIP:
Softening Brown Sugar
Brown sugar tends to solidify into one rock-hard mass after a while in storage. To soften, place a few wet cotton balls on a small saucer on top of the sugar and seal the container tightly. Check after a day or two; the sugar should have softened as though it were fresh. If it hasn't, replace the cotton balls with fresh ones and repeat as needed.

Powdered Sugar

We use powdered sugar in a number of recipes throughout the book. It dissolves quickly when mixed with other ingredients (see Shrikhand, page 170) but also looks pretty when dusted on top of cookies and pastries. **YIELD: ABOUT 2 CUPS [230 G]**

1 cup [200 g] granulated sugar
3 Tbsp cornstarch or arrowroot powder

SPECIAL EQUIPMENT

Blender

Place the ingredients in a blender and process until fine and powdery, 10 to 15 minutes, resting the blender every few minutes so as not to burn out the motor.

Use immediately or transfer to an airtight container and store at room temperature for up to 1 year.

Sugar Cubes

Don't judge us. We think this is ridiculously fun. These beautifully rustic versions of store-bought cubes provoke questions when brought out for company and also make great presents. **YIELD: ABOUT SIXTY ½ IN [12 MM] CUBES**

2 cups [400 g] pure cane sugar or granulated sugar

SPECIAL EQUIPMENT

9 by 5 in [23 by 13 cm] loaf pan

Preheat the oven to 250°F [120°C]. Line the bottom and sides of the loaf pan with parchment paper, leaving a 5 in [13 cm] overhang on the two longer sides. Set aside.

In a medium bowl, combine the sugar and 2 Tbsp of water, mixing vigorously with your fingers or a fork until the water is evenly distributed and the sugar has a consistency similar to damp sand.

Firmly pack the damp sugar into the loaf pan. Drape the extra parchment paper over the top and use a flat-bottomed glass or jar to tamp down the sugar until the surface is smooth, compact, and flat.

Fold up the parchment paper flaps and use a sharp knife to gently cut the sugar block into ½ in [12 mm] squares, disturbing the surface as little as possible and without removing or separating the cubes from the pan.

Transfer the pan to the oven and bake for 1 hour. Remove from the oven and allow to cool completely, undisturbed.

Use the parchment paper flaps to carefully lift the sugar from the pan. Use your fingers to gently break the cubes apart. Discard the parchment paper.

Use immediately or transfer to an airtight container and store at room temperature for up to 1 year.

THE INSTITUTE'S HEADQUARTERS

For some reason, no definitive photograph of the original Institute headquarters' exterior has survived, but you can make it out, somewhat obliquely, in these two views from 1917 and 1920, respectively. The Institute occupied the basement, second, and third floors of the Colyear's Furniture Building at 511 South Main Street in downtown Los Angeles, next to the still-standing Rosslyn Hotel. Sadly, the rest of the block was demolished to make way for a parking structure in the late 1980s, so we'll never be able to actually walk in the footsteps of our illustrious predecessors. There is, however, an "IDT Organizational Plan" from 1918 in the archives that gives us a glimpse of what was clearly a state-of-the-art facility for its time. (Note Institute founder Eliza Taylor Reynolds's initials under the word "Approved" in the bottom right-hand corner.) An entire Fermentation Laboratory?

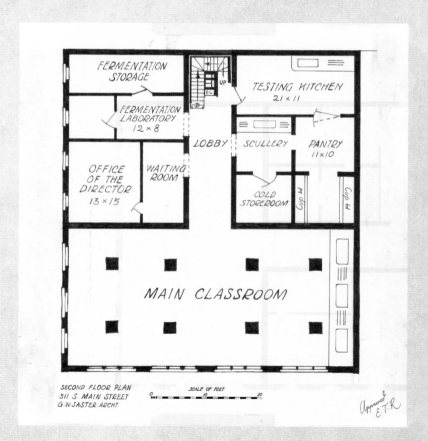

Institute Headquarters
511 S. Main Street

Institute Headquarters
511 S. Main Street

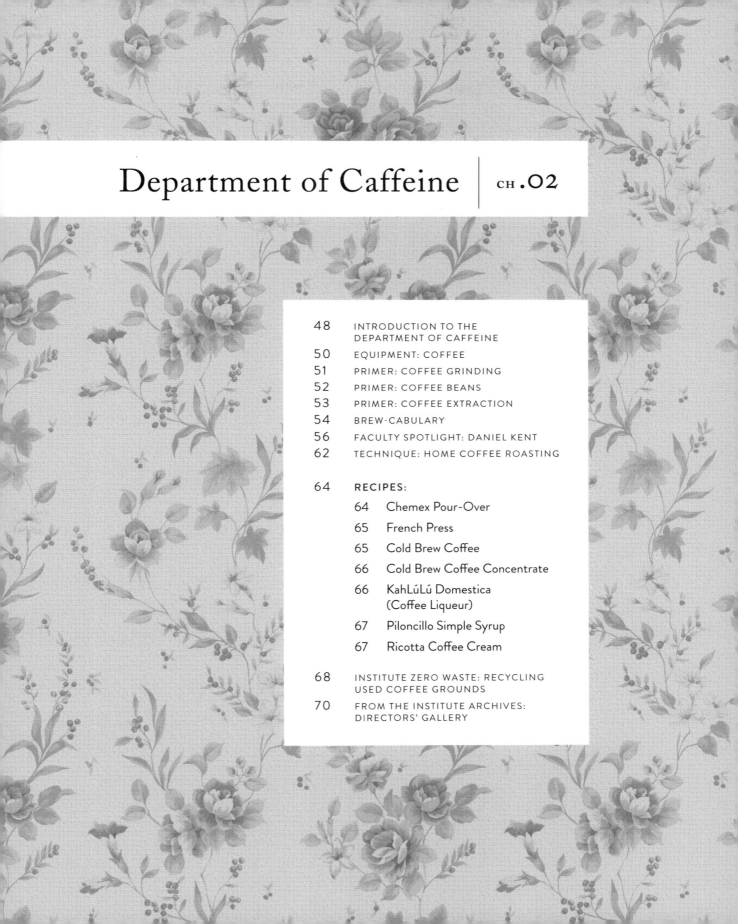

Department of Caffeine | CH.O2

THE DEPARTMENT OF CAFFEINE

Home Coffee Roasting was one of the Institute's very first classes. Before he joined the Institute, Daniel Kent, who would go on to become our Dean of Caffeine, was starting up a small coffee-roasting business out of his mountain cabin with a college friend. The problem was, they didn't have the money they needed to buy a commercial coffee roaster. Hearing this, I thought about Ross Merrick, a coffee bean vendor I'd met at the Altadena Urban Farmers' Market. According to Ross, he was roasting his coffee beans with a stovetop Whirley Pop popcorn popper on his tiny apartment's kitchen stove, one bag at a time! Right before he moved out of state, I convinced him to show me how he did it. I wondered, would Daniel consider giving it a try? Even though the Whirley Pop could roast only a small number of beans at a time, I thought he could at least test it out until he could afford that commercial roaster and see how his customers would react. Well, it worked beautifully and Daniel ended up teaching the technique at the Institute. The rest is history.

Speaking of history, coffee has been consumed since the thirteenth century, but in the last fifty years we've seen a quantum shift in how we approach its preparation. The invention of freeze-dried coffee after World War II changed coffee drinking for decades. Coffee aficionados refer to this occurrence as the "first wave." While

convenient, freeze-dried coffee is devoid of subtlety and flavor and is processed from the lowest grade of beans.

Then, in the late twentieth century there was a proliferation of large chains offering higher-end coffee and espresso drinks. By using better-quality beans, but incinerating them beyond a French Roast, these chains could offer uniform-tasting beverages no matter where in the world their beans were being roasted or consumed. This marked the second wave of the modern coffee movement.

Contemporary coffee aficionados say that we are now in the third wave, a reaction to the homogenization of the previous eras' substandard products. Coffee roasters today obsess over the origin and quality of their beans. Third wave coffees are generally medium to lighter roasts, which bring out the inherent nature of the beans' flavor.

Third wave coffee drinkers have been turning to the Institute's Coffee Roasting and Brewing Program to learn how to source, prepare, and drink a better cup of coffee at home. Roasting coffee beans yourself is a great way to control the process and experiment with varying levels of light, medium, and dark roast flavors. Due to growing demand by home roasters, it's now easier to source high-quality green (unroasted) beans previously only available to commercial coffee roasters. Not only can you find fresher green beans to roast yourself, but also purveyors now offer a much greater variety of single origin (from a single farm and/or single estate) beans from around the world.

The Institute's method of DIY coffee roasting requires just a few pieces of simple equipment commonly found in a home kitchen. The main player is that same, inexpensive Whirley Pop you can purchase online or at a big-box store (and you can still use it to make popcorn between coffee roasting!). While very similar to large-batch professional roasting, the stovetop method allows you to roast ½ lb [225 g] of green coffee beans at a time. This is really the perfect amount for an average week of coffee drinking, so you can add small-batch roasting to cold brew,

pour-over coffee, and all the rest of your caffeine-centered rituals.

Another essential piece of equipment you'll need for all aspects of making a great cup of coffee is a digital scale. This inexpensive addition to your kitchen arsenal will allow you to measure both beans and water with precision. In addition, we provide measurements in this chapter only in grams. Why? One gram is about the weight of a single paper clip, which means that measurements in grams will be extremely exact. Plus, try weighing one measuring cup of coffee beans—it will be different every time. With a digital scale, 50 grams is always exactly 50 grams. End of discussion.

COFFEE

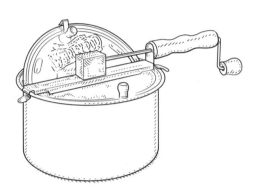

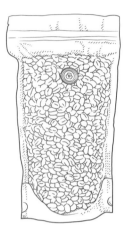

WHIRLEY POP STOVETOP POPCORN POPPER

Yes, it can still be used as a popcorn maker; and no, your popcorn will not taste like coffee. (Too bad, that would be an amazing flavor profile!) While you could try this in a heavy cast-iron skillet, the benefit of using the Whirley Pop as a coffee roaster is its patented stirring mechanism, which keeps the beans evenly moving over the hot surface while keeping a tight lid on top throughout the roasting process. It's also nice to be able to peek inside while the beans are roasting and determine your roast level.

VALVE STORAGE BAGS

These are essentially resealable plastic storage bags with valves that preserve freshness and flavor aromatics in roasted coffee. Carbon dioxide from freshly roasted coffee flushes the oxygen out of the one-way degassing valve, but won't let oxygen in. Once you open the bag, squeeze it while resealing to help force the oxygen out again.

BAKING SHEET PANS

Select heavy-gauge, sturdy sheet pans (approximately 13 by 18 in [33 by 46 cm]) with a rolled edge. You'll need two pans per every ½ lb [225 g] of green beans roasted in order to give them breathing room to cool properly.

COFFEE GRINDING

The most important step in showcasing the flavor of roasted coffee beans is to properly grind them. Rather than the brewing, it is the grind that will determine how well the flavor is extracted.

Grinding coffee just prior to brewing is one of the keys to great flavor, but it isn't the only factor. For the best taste, the beans should be uniformly ground so that the flavors will extract evenly.

The grind size and uniformity, especially in the pour-over method of preparation, will affect the ultimate strength of the brew. This has to do with the total surface area of the ground coffee, which governs both access to the soluble solids in the coffee beans and the speed at which hot water will filter through the coffee particles. The finer the grind, the greater the surface area; the soluble solids will extract more quickly from the coffee, and it will take longer

for the water to pass through the coffee bed. The longer the water is in contact with those particles, the stronger the brew.

Spinning-blade grinders produce particles of wildly different sizes within the grind, from fine powder to large, broken pieces. This will lead to both over- and under-extraction in the same brew. Over-extraction (fine powder) results in coffee with a bitter taste. Under-extraction (large pieces) produces coffee that is thin, watery, and sour. In our opinion, spinning-blade grinders should be used only for grinding spices, period.

Burr grinders, on the other hand, have two spinning, sharply serrated plates facing one another through which coffee beans pass. The space between the two plates can be finely adjusted, ensuring that the size of the particles is consistent.

TROUBLESHOOTING

If your coffee tastes muddled or lacks depth, grind more finely.

If the coffee has a harsh finish or is bitter, grind more coarsely.

THE BEAN BELT

While there are 125 species of coffee plants, we use only 2 species for consumption as a beverage; Arabica (*Coffea arabica*) and Robusta (*Coffea canephora*).

Originating in Ethiopia, Arabica is said to produce the finest coffee beans. Robusta has a less delicate flavor than Arabica, has more caffeine, and is mostly used to make instant coffee products.

From its origins in Africa, the cultivation of coffee spread both east and west, eventually occupying a geographic belt roughly bounded by the Tropics of Cancer and Capricorn. This warm, equatorial region provides some of the best growing conditions for the coffee plant—moderate sunshine and rain, steady temperatures around 70°F [21°C], and rich, porous soil.

THE COFFEE PLANT

The coffee plant is a shrub that produces fruit called cherries. When they're ripe, they look like cranberries, both in shape and color.

ANATOMY OF A BEAN

Each cherry contains two coffee beans, which are technically seeds surrounded by an outer layer of pulp and skin. This outer husk is called cáscara and can be brewed as a tea, producing a caffeinated beverage with notes of hibiscus and maple.

PROCESSING

Because the coffee cherries cling to the shrub's branches in a tight formation and ripen at different rates, they are gathered manually most of the time. One *Coffea arabica* plant will produce about four thousand beans annually—that's 1 lb [450 g] of roasted beans, or roughly twenty-two cups of coffee per plant. After harvesting and being separated from the cherries, the best method of processing the beans is "wet processing." This involves soaking the beans in water and allowing them to ferment for two days. This process dissolves any pulp or sticky residue that may still be attached to the beans. Next, they are dried, after which they are ready to be roasted.

COFFEE EXTRACTION

In order to brew coffee properly, four variables must be tightly controlled:

BREW STRENGTH
WATER TEMPERATURE
GRIND
INFUSION TIME

Roasted coffee is about 30 percent extractable solids by mass. However, if you were to extract every drop of water-soluble material from the beans, the resulting cup would be horribly bitter.

Fortunately, the tastier elements of coffee (sugars, acids, aromatics) extract faster than the less tasty elements. If the brew is stopped at some point before absolutely everything is extracted, a smooth cup of coffee—without the lingering bitterness—can be achieved.

Various eminent coffee researchers (i.e., baristas) have determined that optimal extraction is achieved when 19 to 21 percent of the coffee mass has been extracted. Achieving a 20 percent extraction consistently does take some practice, but once you've absorbed the methods in this chapter, your brew technique will provide reliably exceptional cups day after day.

BREW-CABULARY

SOLUBLE SOLIDS: The chemical compounds in roasted coffee that can be washed out with hot water.

EXTRACTION: The period during which hot water and ground coffee are in contact, aka "brewing." During extraction, hot water acts as a solvent, washing the soluble solids out of the coffee grounds and into the brewed coffee, which is a suspension of coffee particles, carbon dioxide, and water.

INFUSION TIME: The length of time during which extraction takes place.

FILTER: A permeable medium, such as a paper filter, cloth, or metal screen, through which water and soluble coffee solids may pass.

FRACTIONAL EXTRACTION: Roasted coffee contains 30 percent soluble solids, but not all of that tastes good. What we are after is only the first 20 percent, or the fractional extraction. This percentage was originally computed by the Coffee Brewing Institute, under the direction of Professor E. E. Lockhart at MIT in the 1950s. It has also been subjectively confirmed by coffee drinkers everywhere.

CHAFF: The thin layer of skin that remains on the coffee bean until it is roasted. Usually discarded afterward, chaff is biodegradable and great for gardens.

FIRST CRACK: Roasters use a combination of bean temperature, smell, color, and sound to monitor the roasting process. The first audible sound that indicates bean temperature during roasting is a hollow, popping sound, similar to that of popcorn popping. This is called First Crack, and marks the beginning of light roasts. It should have a temperature between 392°F and 396°F [200°C and 202°C].

SECOND CRACK: The second sound beans make when they reach 435°F to 439°F [224°C to 226°C]. Pressure inside the bean has increased to the point where the structure of the bean fractures, rapidly releasing gases and creating an audible sound. Second Crack is characterized by a higher, snappier cracking sound, much like the sound of Rice Krispies in milk, and marks the beginning of medium roasts.

DANIEL KENT
Dean of Caffeine

Professor Daniel Kent heads the Institute's Department of Coffee. In addition to developing course curriculum and writing recipes for the Institute, he was the proprietor of Plow & Gun, a small-batch coffee-roasting company located in Southern California. Kent is also known for his encyclopedic knowledge of his subjects and his theatrical sense of humor. (He's been known to don a lab coat while wheeling out a soon-to-be deconstructed Mr. Coffee coffee maker on a gurney.)

He began his love affair/addiction with brewed beverages at a young age when his father gave him a small cup of coffee on a family camping trip. Fortunately for the Institute, he discovered that when he liked something, he wanted to take it apart and learn how to make it. This led him to gathering as much information as he could find on brewing coffee beverages.

The Institute has spawned a sizable community of home coffee roasters based on Daniel's straightforward method utilizing a Whirley Pop stovetop popcorn popper. Inspired by Daniel's class, some students have not only added coffee roasting to their home foodcrafting routine, but also gone on to start their own coffee businesses.

Professor Kent's teaching skills also bleed over into other Institute departments. His theory that one foodcrafting technique builds upon another explains his holistic approach.

"When you learn about beer brewing, you're going to learn about distillation," he points out. "When you learn about distillation, you'll learn about spirits and cocktails. The world of cocktails leads to infusions and liqueurs, which then leads back to coffee through KahLúLú Domestica (page 66). Beer making also leads to fermenting, which brings us to vegetable ferments. It's all the same connection."

TIPS FROM THE PROFESSOR

STORAGE: Once roasted, coffee beans contain a fair amount of carbon dioxide. During the first two weeks after roasting, the beans will be giving off the majority of this CO_2, which means they shouldn't be stored in an airtight container. That said, coffee beans left in the open will quickly become stale through contact with oxygen. The best way to store roasted coffee beans is to use airtight bags or tins with one-way valves that let CO_2 out, but no oxygen in. Medium-roasted coffee will stay fresh for two weeks after roasting, while French-roasted coffee will stay fresh for one week.

TEMPERATURE: Proper brewing temperature means that the water is neither too hot, nor too cool to extract the desirable 20 percent of soluble solids. Use only filtered, good-tasting water between 195°F and 205°F [91°C and 96°C].

MEASURING: When measuring coffee, always use a digital scale, preferably in grams. Since the coffee bean expands during roasting, darker roasts take up more volume than lighter roasts.

BLOOMING: Letting the coffee bloom for 15 seconds during the initial pour will allow CO_2 to "fluff up" the coffee bed and promote even, thorough infusion and flow.

SPEED: Avoid pouring in all the water at once. Doing so will bring the level to the top of the filter. As it drains, the grounds will be left high and dry, remaining un-infused on the sides of the filter. Instead, pour to keep pace with the rate of flow from the bottom of the filter.

GRIND: It should take 5 minutes for 520 g of water to drip through 40 g of ground coffee. If it takes longer, the grind is too fine. If it finishes dripping sooner than 5 minutes, the grind is too coarse. Adjust your grind setting accordingly, one increment at a time, while timing the brewing process until the correct grind setting and timing is achieved.

57

COFFEE BEANS (PAGE 52)

ROASTED COFFEE BEANS (PAGE 62)

RICOTTA COFFEE CREAM (PAGE 67)

Disable smoke alarms, fling open windows, and prepare for smoke—there's going to be lots of it!
YIELD: 8 OZ [225 G]

8 oz [225 g] green coffee beans

SPECIAL EQUIPMENT

Digital scale

Whirley Pop stovetop popcorn popper

Weigh out the green coffee beans and set them close to the stove, along with two baking sheets. Place the Whirley Pop roaster on the stove and preheat over medium-low heat for 2 minutes. When the roaster is hot, turn the heat up to medium and add the green coffee beans. Close the lid and start turning the hand crank to move the agitator. Pace yourself, turning the handle with a slow, steady motion—you'll be turning that crank for 10 minutes.

Lift the roaster lid occasionally, checking the beans for color changes. By minute 3, the beans should start to turn a lighter shade of green at the edges. This stage is called Yellow. If the beans have not changed color at this point, turn up the heat slightly. If they have turned yellow prior to minute 3, turn down the flame.

By minute 6, the beans should be uniformly golden. If the beans haven't turned color by the sixth minute, turn up the flame slightly. If they are darker than golden, turn down the flame.

At about minute 9 you will reach First Crack, which sounds like hollow popping, similar to the sound of popcorn popping. First Crack will often last for 1 to 2 minutes before it dies down.

Once First Crack is over, the coffee is now considered a City Roast. If you prefer this light roast, stop here. It is up to you to decide how much you want to develop the roast flavor (see chart, facing page).

For a darker roast, keep the Whirley Pop on the flame and continue cranking the handle until you reach Second Crack, characterized by a higher, snappier cracking sound, like the sound of Rice Krispies in milk. The roast will progress very quickly from the beginning of Second Crack, so keep a close eye on the beans.

About 45 seconds into Second Crack, the beans will smooth out very quickly and turn a deep umber color. They'll also begin taking on a sheen, which is caused by the oils migrating out of the bean. This is considered a Vienna Roast. If you prefer this medium roast, stop here.

If you would like to continue roasting even darker, small beads of oil will begin to form on the outside of the beans as Second Crack starts to fade. The beans will become carbonized, effectively *burning* the coffee. This is considered French Roast.

When you have reached your preferred roast level, quickly dump the beans, dividing them between the two baking sheets. Be careful—everything is very hot. Shake the baking sheets gently to spread out the beans as evenly as possible, then place in a well-ventilated area to cool completely, preferably outside.

STORAGE: Once roasted and cooled, store the whole beans in a cool, dry place, preferably in an airtight bag or tin with a built-in gas valve. Allow beans to rest for 1 day before grinding, brewing, and serving. Consume within 1 week before roasting a new batch.

	TASTING NOTES	TIMING
City (Light)	Light bodied, bright, more distinct regional flavors	At the end of First Crack
Vienna (Medium)	Sweet, thick, syrupy body	45 seconds into Second Crack
French (Dark)	Strongly roasted flavors	At the end of Second Crack

Bring the water to a boil over high heat, then remove from the heat, allowing it to cool to between 195°F and 205°F [91°C and 96°C] while you prepare the coffee grounds and brewer.

Using a burr coffee grinder, grind the coffee beans to a medium coarseness, about the size of kosher salt granules, and set aside.

Open a Chemex filter into a cone. One side should have three layers. Place the cone in the top of the brewer with the triple-layered side toward the pouring spout.

Preheat the Chemex brewer: When the water has cooled to between 195°F and 205°F [91°C and 96°C], pour 300 g of hot water through the filter, wetting it thoroughly. Leaving the filter in place, pour out and discard the water.

Brew the coffee: Place the ground coffee in the paper filter and pour 50 g of the hot water over the coffee grounds, just enough to wet them thoroughly without floating. Allow them to "bloom" for about 15 seconds.

Continue pouring the remaining 470 g of hot water slowly over the coffee grounds in gentle circles, keeping pace with the rate of flow out of the bottom of the filter.

Once all the water has drained through, discard the filter and grounds. Serve the coffee immediately.

NOTE: The entire brewing process should take no more than 5 minutes. If it takes significantly longer, the coffee beans should be ground more coarsely. If the brewing time is much shorter, the beans should be ground more finely.

Chemex Pour-Over

Dr. Peter Schlumbohm, a German chemist inspired by the precision and beauty of his lab equipment, designed the Chemex coffee brewer in 1941 to prepare coffee with chemistry in mind. Glass doesn't corrode; that's why it's good for lab equipment as well as home coffee preparation.

The Chemex brewer is a one-piece vessel designed to extract, hold, and serve coffee. According to Chemex, "There is no such thing as 'good, fast coffee.'" Infusion time should be 4 to 5 minutes for a 6-cup [1.5 L] brewer. It is also important to use the Chemex filter, because the shape is designed to promote an even flow of water through the bed of coffee grounds. **YIELD: 2 CUPS [500 ML]**

820 g filtered water
40 g roasted coffee beans

SPECIAL EQUIPMENT

Digital scale

Instant-read thermometer

Burr coffee grinder

Chemex pre-folded square paper filter

Chemex 6-cup brewer (Makes six 5 oz [150 ml] cups)

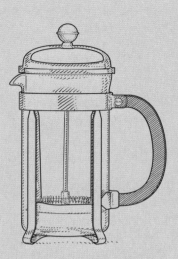

French Press

With a French press, both grounds and hot water go into the carafe together. When ready, the coffee is strained with a built-in plunger. It's a classic favorite among coffee drinkers, probably because its all-in-one operation makes it easy to use and produces such consistent results. **YIELD: 2 CUPS [500 ML]**

980 g filtered water
40 g roasted coffee beans

SPECIAL EQUIPMENT
Digital scale
Burr coffee grinder
French press

Bring the water to a boil over high heat, then remove from the heat and set aside.

Using a burr coffee ginder, grind the coffee beans to a medium coarseness, about the size of kosher salt granules, and set aside.

Pour 300 g of the hot water into the beaker of the French press. Swirl the water around for a few seconds to warm the brewer, then pour out and discard the water.

Place the ground coffee into the French press, then add the remaining 680 g of hot water, making sure to wet all the coffee grounds. Let the grounds

bloom for 1 minute, then gently stir the crust that has formed on top of the slurry until it is replaced by a cream-colored foam.

Place the lid and plunger on top of the beaker, but do not plunge. Allow the coffee to brew for 3 minutes more.

Using the weight of your hand, gently depress the plunger completely and serve immediately.

Cold Brew Coffee

Brewing with cool water extracts less of the bean's acidity, producing a sweeter beverage that is perfect for making iced coffee. It's also a convenient way to make ready-to-drink coffee with no fuss. **YIELD: 2 CUPS [500 ML]**

50 g roasted coffee beans
450 g filtered water, at room temperature

SPECIAL EQUIPMENT
Digital scale
Burr coffee grinder
1 qt [1 L] mason jar
Butter muslin (see Note) or paper coffee filter

Using a burr coffee grinder, grind the coffee beans to a medium coarseness, about the size of kosher salt granules, and place in a 1 qt [1 L] mason jar. Add the filtered water, seal the jar, and let stand at room temperature for 12 hours.

Strain the coffee through a fine-mesh sieve lined with clean, damp butter muslin or a paper coffee filter, discarding the grounds.

Coffee can be served immediately over ice or stored in an airtight container in the refrigerator for up to 2 weeks.

NOTE ON BUTTER MUSLIN: Dedicate a fresh piece of butter muslin to this preparation. When cleaning, avoid using any dish soaps with fragrance, as coffee picks up odorants very easily. Instead, rinse the butter muslin thoroughly with hot water. If laundering by machine, avoid using bleach or dryer sheets.

Cold Brew Coffee Concentrate

Using concentrated, cold-brewed coffee instead of espresso or freeze-dried espresso powder is a simple way of infusing many recipes with a rich coffee flavor with less bitterness than hot-brewing techniques. This coffee is prepared using the cold-brew method (page 65) but, like espresso, the coffee-to-water proportions are greatly increased. **YIELD: ¾ CUP [180 ML]**

50 g roasted coffee beans
250 g filtered water, at room temperature

SPECIAL EQUIPMENT
Digital scale
Burr coffee grinder
1 qt [1 L] mason jar
Butter muslin or paper coffee filter

Using a burr coffee grinder, grind the coffee beans to a medium coarseness, about the size of kosher salt granules, and place in a 1 qt [1 L] mason jar. Add the filtered water, seal the jar, and let stand at room temperature for 12 hours.

Strain the coffee through a fine-mesh sieve lined with clean, damp butter muslin (see Note from preceding recipe) or a paper coffee filter, discarding the grounds.

The concentrate can be used immediately or stored in an airtight container in the refrigerator for up to 2 weeks.

KahLúLú Domestica (Coffee Liqueur)

Coffee's flavorful soluble solids are most commonly extracted with water, but they also lend themselves nicely to being extracted by alcohol. For this coffee liqueur we use an overproof rum, which extracts the coffee's flavor most efficiently. Adding vanilla, orange zest, and cacao nibs along with the deep notes of molasses from the piloncillo simple syrup make this one of our most versatile homemade spirits. Use in the White Russian cocktail (page 254), on top of ice cream, in a boozy milkshake, or, for some daytime drinking, add to your cup of coffee. **YIELD: 4 CUPS [1 L]**

100 g roasted coffee beans
½ vanilla bean
2 or 3 cacao nibs (optional)
One 1 by 3 in [2.5 by 7.5 cm] strip orange zest
2 cups [500 ml] rum, preferably 100 to 151 overproof (see Note)
2 cups [500 ml] Piloncillo Simple Syrup (see recipe following)

SPECIAL EQUIPMENT
Digital scale
Burr coffee grinder
1 qt [1 L] mason jar
Butter muslin or paper coffee filter

Using a burr coffee grinder, grind the coffee beans to a medium coarseness, about the size of kosher salt granules, then set aside.

Use a sharp paring knife to split the vanilla bean lengthwise, then use the tip of the knife to scrape out the seeds into a 1 qt [1 L] mason jar and add the pod.

Add the coffee, cacao nibs, if using, orange zest, and rum to the jar and seal with the lid.

Allow the mixture to infuse at cool room temperature for 2 weeks, keeping it away from direct sunlight. Give the jar a shake once a day, or whenever you pass by it and want to say hello.

After 2 weeks, strain the mixture through a fine-mesh sieve lined with clean, damp butter muslin or a paper coffee filter, discarding the solids. Transfer the strained mixture to a clean, dry 1 qt [1 L] mason jar and add the piloncillo simple syrup, stirring to combine.

KahLúLú can be used immediately or sealed tightly and stored in a cool, dark place, where it will continue to improve with age.

NOTE ON RUM: There are several options regarding what type of rum to use. Depending on your taste, tolerance for high-proof alcohol, or simply what's knocking around in your liquor cabinet, here are a few choices to consider: Using an 80-proof rum will work just fine, but since high-proof spirits extract aromatic flavors better than low-proof spirits, we prefer to use an overproof rum. These are available in proofs ranging between 100 and 151. White rums are clear, and will have a mild taste. Gold or dark rums are aged longer in wooden barrels and will have a stronger flavor.

Piloncillo Simple Syrup

Use this thick, dark syrup with molasses undertones to make KahLúLú Domestica (left), or try in place of maple syrup on pancakes or waffles. For cocktails, use it instead of regular simple syrup; it pairs beautifully with spirits like rum and tequila.

YIELD: 2 CUPS [500 ML]

360 g grated or chopped piloncillo (see Note)

SPECIAL EQUIPMENT
Digital scale
2 cup [500 ml] measuring pitcher

In a small saucepan, combine the piloncillo with 1 cup [250 ml] of water.

Bring to a boil over medium-high heat, then reduce to a simmer, stirring gently until the piloncillo has dissolved.

Remove from the heat and transfer the syrup to a heatproof 2 cup [500 ml] measuring pitcher. Top with water, for a total of 2 cups [500 ml] liquid, stirring to combine. Allow the syrup to cool completely before using.

Piloncillo simple syrup can be used immediately or transferred to an airtight container and stored in the refrigerator for up to 1 month.

NOTE ON PILONCILLO: Piloncillo is an unrefined whole-cane sugar from Mexico. It is made by boiling and evaporating pure sugarcane juice, then pouring it into small, cone-shaped molds. In order to soften the piloncillo for grating, place the cones in a microwave-safe container and heat in the microwave on high power in 30-second intervals until soft enough to grate or chop. Brown sugar or unrefined cane sugar can be substituted.

Ricotta Coffee Cream

Fresh ricotta can be used in so many ways, both savory and sweet. One of our favorite ways to serve it is this easy dessert. Rich homemade ricotta, cream, and an added jolt of strong coffee—both brewed (Cold Brew Coffee Concentrate) and extracted with alcohol (KahLúLú Domestica)—make this "Pudding 2.0." **SERVES 6**

1 batch Ricotta (page 164), about 1 lb [450 g]
½ cup [100 g] granulated sugar
⅓ cup plus 1 Tbsp [95 ml] Cold Brew Coffee Concentrate (facing page)
1 Tbsp KahLúLú Domestica coffee liqueur (facing page) or store-bought Kahlúa
¼ cup [60 ml] heavy cream
Chocolate-covered coffee beans or chocolate shavings, for garnish

SPECIAL EQUIPMENT
Food processor
Six 5 oz [150 ml] ramekins or custard cups

Place the ricotta and sugar in a food processor and process to a smooth purée. With the machine running, add the coffee concentrate in a steady stream, followed by the KahLúLú.

Scrape down the sides of the bowl, then turn the machine on again and add the cream. Process for 10 seconds more.

Divide the mixture between six ramekins or custard cups. Wrap each ramekin tightly in plastic wrap and chill for several hours or overnight before serving.

Garnish with chocolate-covered coffee beans and/or chocolate shavings and serve immediately.

RECYCLING USED COFFEE GROUNDS

One of our many mantras at the Institute is that nothing goes to waste. At the very least we will compost everything, including junk mail, but if we can squeeze one more use out of something before-hand, we get excited. We generate a fair amount of spent coffee grounds after we've roasted and brewed our weekly stash of beans, but we're not done with them just yet. Here are ten ways we like to extend their contribution to our lives.

#1: Scouring Paste for Cleaning Pots and Pans
While you can also use kosher salt for scrub-bing messy cast-iron pans, coffee grounds essentially accomplish the same task. They are abrasive but won't scratch like a stainless steel scrubby sponge would. Use a rag to scrub the grounds on grimy cast-iron, stainless steel, or copper pans.

#2: Add to a Compost Pile
A healthy compost pile needs a balance of carbon-rich and nitrogen-rich material. Carbon-rich materials include dried leaves and twigs, while nitrogen-rich materials include food scraps, green leaves, lawn clippings, and, lucky for us, spent coffee grounds. A good compost pile ratio to aim for is two parts carbon-rich materials to one part nitrogen-rich materials. A note to Chemex lovers: Those paper coffee filters are in the carbon-rich family.

#3: Add to a Worm Bin
If you're keeping a composting worm bin, you're in luck, as worms are coffee junkies. To prove our point, try putting potato skins or eggshells on one side of your bin and coffee grounds on the other. You'll see them go straight to the grounds before anything else. After coffee grounds, our worms love banana peels and strawberry tops next. Go figure!

#4: Eliminate Garlic and Onion Smells
You may have noticed that we use a lot of fresh garlic in our recipes. We do, however, have an Institute rule: If there is a large garlic-chopping task, everyone must chip in so no one gets singled out as "the smelly one." If we do have some used coffee grounds handy, we use them afterward as a hand scrub to neutralize garlic's sulfur compounds that cause the familiar smell. Works on onions as well.

#5: Eliminate Refrigerator Odors
Similar to baking soda, coffee grounds can serve as a deodorizer as well. Place a bowl of grounds in the refrigerator to neutralize odors. Remember to change out often, composting the previous batch.

#6: **Hide Counter and Furniture Scratches**
We are partial to natural, dark wood at the Institute and are klutzes when it comes to scratching their surfaces. While a coffee stain on your clothing may be traumatic, the same pigment can come in handy masking a scratch on your wood surfaces. Mix equal amounts leftover coffee grounds, warm water, and distilled white vinegar in a jar. Give the jar a good shake, then let it steep for at least an hour before using. Test on an inconspicuous area first before proceeding. For lighter wood scratches, apply the stain, then wipe off and repeat in 10-minute intervals until the scratch is diminished. On darker wood scratches, let the coffee stain sit for up to an hour before wiping away.

#7: **Make Bourbon-Maple-Coffee Bacon**
Even though they've already been used to make coffee, used coffee grounds actually still have a lot of flavor. We love our cured bacon recipe with bourbon and maple syrup (page 208) as is, but adding ¼ cup [30 g] of used coffee grounds adds yet another flavor note to the curing mixture.

#8: **Use as a Meat or Vegetable Rub**
Coffee grounds impart a distinct color and flavor to a braised brisket, as a barbecue rub for ribs, or when mixed with equal parts softened butter and brown sugar and rubbed on chicken before roasting. We like to share the love with our vegetables as well. Robust vegetables such as cauliflower, Brussels sprouts, and winter squash get a coat of olive oil, then we rub-n-roast them with a mixture of used coffee grounds, salt, pepper, smoked paprika, onion powder, garlic powder, and other spices such as oregano, chili powder, coriander, and cinnamon in a hot oven.

#9: **Give Yourself a Spa Treatment**
Pots and pans aren't the only things that benefit from a good scrubbing with used coffee grounds. Your skin deserves the same attention and you should know that the grounds also make a good exfoliating body scrub that removes dead skin cells. Mix equal parts sea salt, coffee grounds, and coconut oil and test first on your feet and elbows before using on sensitive areas.

#10: **Garbage Disposal Cleaner**
Garbage disposals need some love, too. With the water running, run used coffee grounds through your disposal to give your kitchen sink drain an aromatherapy treatment.

DIRECTORS' GALLERY

According to my immediate predecessor, Institute Director Theodore J. Hoover III, his portrait, along with those of past directors, was displayed in the Institute's long, hallway-like lobby. As you can see, they were all, shall we say, "colorful."

Eliza Taylor Reynolds
1911–1933

Confronted with what she saw as the decline of the domestic arts of her Victorian childhood, the visionary Taylor Reynolds single-handedly founded the Institute of Domestic Technology and was its imperious yet beloved director for twenty-two years. "We called her 'the iron hand in the velvet glove,'" recalled her successor, Melinda McCracken, when she was interviewed in 1971. "Behind her back, of course." (For a more in-depth biography, see Taylor Reynolds's obituary on page 300.)

Melinda "Cricket" McCracken
1934–1941

"Cricket," as she was affectionately known, is best remembered for her efforts to expand the Institute's overall curriculum, most notably by establishing the new "Department of Freezing," as refrigerators were replacing iceboxes in the late 1930s. She sparred regularly with the supposedly retired Taylor Reynolds (who continued to "offer" her advice) over the most unimaginably petty details. When Taylor Reynolds died in 1952, McCracken infamously insinuated that she had succumbed to her own contaminated pickled carrots, which, it turned out, was not the case. (See page 300.)

Eudora Cunningham
1942

Eudora Cunningham's tenure as director lasted less than one year, as she was forced to resign when it was discovered that she was "skimming" more than milk at the Institute. (She was caught with her hand in the cookie jar, shall we say.) Cunningham was sentenced to five years in prison for embezzlement at the California Institution for Women in Chino and served three. A short article about her conviction appeared in *Domestica*, the Institute's quarterly journal. The headline? "Eudora Cunningham: From Institute to Institution"!

Maria Wojciechowski
1942–1948

In the Institute's own version of Cinderella, the ambitious Maria Wojciechowski (pronounced Voi-chih-KAHF-skee) rose from the ranks of the Institute's student body, her many Los Angeles County Fair first-prize ribbons paving the way (see From the Institute Archives, page 225). She is said to have coined the slogan, "Grow Your Own, Can Your Own" during the height of the "Victory Garden" movement of the Second World War.

Theodore J. Hoover III
1954–1966

The Institute's first male director, Hoover worked tirelessly to keep IDT afloat into the mod, "instant everything" early 1960s. His despairing letter to Nellie Archer, the founder's daughter and president of the board of directors, bears witness to the difficulty of the Institute's final years (see From the Institute Archives, page 188). In a curious footnote, after presiding over the closing of the Institute, Hoover and his "longtime companion," Alton Baker, moved to New York City, where they were among those arrested at the Stonewall Riots in 1969.

Olive Mae Elliott
1949–1953

Considered a bit too demure for a leadership position when she first took over the Institute's directorship in 1949, Olive Elliott proved to be tougher than she looked. In 1952, she was hauled before the House Committee on Un-American Activities, accused of harboring communists among the Institute's staff. Steadfastly refusing to name names, Elliott famously replied, "Senator McCarthy, if you're looking for something 'red' at my institute, the only thing you're going to find are maraschino cherries."

Department of Pickles & Preserves

CH .03

THE DEPARTMENT OF PICKLES & PRESERVES

For many of us, making our own jam turns out to be the "gateway drug" that gets us hooked on home preserving and foodcrafting. Fruit preserves are beautiful, sweet, fun to prepare, and so much better than store-bought jam. As if that weren't enough, they make great gifts that come with a truly personal touch.

Like jam making before it, pickling now seems to have entered the made-at-home zeitgeist in a big way. Once the de facto food preservation method of home-steaders, pickling lost steam for a few generations (due to the industrialization of our food supply) but has recently seen a resurgence, with a new crop of pickle makers taking up the torch of the domestic arts revival, inventing new recipes with unusual flavors and ingredients as they go. Taking it one step further, many of these neo-pickle makers have made a commitment to sourcing their products exclusively from small, local farmers or growing ingredients in their own backyards to supply their all-consuming pickling habit.

To understand how the Great Pickle Renaissance of the aughts came about, look no further than the growth of farmers' markets and the rising demand for organic produce. Add to that a new, restless generation of eaters who started asking themselves, "Why are there only two or three types of the same, old [insert ingredient

or product here] available at my grocery store?"

In fact, the recent explosion of food makers hasn't escaped the notice—or lacerating wit—of the blogosphere's pop culture commentators, who've given pickling the same satiric treatment they've given exercise crazes like yoga, Pilates, and Zumba. On television, IFC's *Portlandia*, a comedy series poking fun at Portland, Oregon, zeroed in on its growing population of pickle makers. In a sketch that went viral, two hipsters brag to the camera, "We can pickle that" when presented with literally anything, including (in no particular order): eggs, an ice cream cone fallen on to the sidewalk, a used bandage, discarded plastic CD jewel cases, a City of Portland parking violation ticket, and a broken high-heeled shoe. As far as the Institute is concerned, being the butt of satire like this only makes us more excited about what we're doing: When the new food makers have become big enough to be made fun of, you know they've arrived.

For almost a decade, we've been teaching scores of students how to "put up" their first batches of jam and pickles. A big part of what we do involves schooling these beginners on safe water bath canning and allaying their fears of contracting botulism. We've also lectured them on the difference between homemade jam versus commercial products. (Hint: Homemade jam is mostly fruit, whereas commercial jam is mostly sugar, since sugar is cheaper than fruit.) And, we've discussed the mysteries of pectin, answering one of the most frequently asked questions: "Can you make jam without adding sugar?" (See page 107 for more on this endlessly fascinating discussion.) In the end, it all boils down to this simple equation:

FRUIT + SUGAR + HEAT = JAM.

We've also made lots of pickles with our students. A lot. We usually put our first-timers through their paces with our Pickled Chipotle Fennel Carrots (page 96), which are steeped in spices and vinegar. They're super easy to make and give you an idea of how the pickling process and a few spices can transform a simple carrot into something absolutely amazing. It's a rite of passage, too; making your first jar of pickles can be liberating.

On the culinary front, more and more restaurant chefs are now making their own in-house jams and pickles, realizing their increasingly sophisticated customers have come to expect it. These savvy chefs know that a restaurant without its own handmade "pickle program" or "jam plan" will inevitably fall behind the competition. A perhaps unexpected benefit of having more good pickles on the menu is the balance and acidic counterpoint that pickles provide to perennial favorites such as rich, fatty meats, fried chicken, or grilled cheese. Given that charcuterie and cheese plates are also on the rise at bars and restaurants, house-made pickles make the perfect acidic pairing with foods like aged salumi and strong blue cheeses.

Once you've tackled canning on your own, we encourage you to share your homemade pickles and preserves with your friends and family. After they get a taste of the real thing, you may find complete strangers wanting to be your best friend. But why stop there? Get the whole world pickling! Here in Los Angeles, we created "Pickle Party," a public community event with celebrated fermentation author Sandor Katz, in which five hundred people came together to make 1,000 lb [454 kg] of sauerkraut in one day. Okay, five hundred people may be too many to start with on your own, but why not meet up with ten of your best friends and throw your own pickle party? You can pickle that!

PICKLES & PRESERVES

CANNING ESSENTIALS

PRESERVING PAN

Preserving pans are designed to cook down jam ingredients as quickly and efficiently as possible to preserve flavor and color. The ideal pan is wide and shallow to maximize surface area, speeding evaporation. Many preserving pans have tapered sides to facilitate this, but a large chef's rondo pan is also fine. Heavy-gauge copper is the best, albeit most expensive, material for the pan due to the way it conducts heat. In a pinch, a wide stockpot can be used, but the shape of the pan means that jam ingredients will need to cook longer to achieve gel set than in a preserving pan.

WATER BATH CANNING POT & RACK

Water bath canners can be purchased in the form of specifically made pots that come with their own removable wire racks and fitted lids. They are available in either aluminum or porcelain-covered steel. Though having a dedicated commercial canner is certainly nice, you probably have enough common equipment in your own kitchen to supply everything you need. You can cobble together your own water bath canner with a large enough stockpot and a wire cake or cooling rack. Just make sure your pot is deep enough to be able to cover the tops of the jars with 1 in [2.5 cm] of boiling water during processing, while also accommodating a 1 in [2.5 cm] rack below. If you're using an electric range to process the water bath, make sure the bottom of the pot is flat in order to maintain a consistent temperature.

CANNING RACK HACK: If you don't have a rack that fits the bottom of your pot, you can make one by attaching mason jar screw bands together with twist-ties, to form a makeshift rack.

JAR LIFTER

Jars of jam ready to be submerged into the canning pot can literally be too hot to handle. The same goes for removing them after processing in the boiling water. Make sure to use a jar lifter—hinged tongs with a secure grip and nonslip coating—to hold each jar securely as you place it in or take it out of the hot water bath.

MASON JARS
WITH LIDS & SCREW BANDS

Regular and widemouthed mason jars with self-sealing lids and threaded metal screw bands are the best choice for water bath canning. They are inexpensive and available in ½ pt [250 ml], 1 pt [500 ml], 1½ pt [750 ml], and 1 qt [1 L] sizes (we also use the 2 qt [2 L] size throughout the book for non-canned preparations), and, except for the lids, may be reused many times, requiring just a good washing with warm soapy water and a thorough rinse before use. The rim of each metal lid features a rubbery gasket around its circumference that softens during processing in the hot water bath. This allows the gasket to mold itself to the lip of the glass jar while simultaneously allowing air to escape. Note that the metal lid cannot be used again after its first and only water bath voyage since its gasket cannot remold itself to another jar. Do save the used lids, however, since they are handy for storing dry goods in the pantry. Rust-free metal screw bands may be reused for canning. At the Institute, we use widemouthed jars whenever possible for everything except pickles, which benefit from the "shoulder" on a regular-mouthed jar, which helps keep the pickles submerged.

CONT'D

THINGS THAT ARE FUN TO HAVE
BUT NOT EXACTLY NECESSARY

CANNING FUNNEL

These funnels are either plastic or metal and have widemouthed openings to provide plenty of space for ladling in ingredients and narrow mouths at the bottom that fit nicely into the opening of any size mason jar. Wouldn't a large tablespoon and a steady hand do just as well, you may say? Maybe so, but we Virgos have "issues."

EXTRA-LONG SPOON

A hot pan of boiling jam is a third-degree burn waiting to happen. Give yourself some distance when stirring the pot by using an extra-long wooden spoon (long sleeves and/or an elbow-length oven mitt also help).

HEADSPACE MEASURER

The unfilled gap above the food and below the lid in a jar of preserves is called the headspace. This gap is needed to allow for expansion of the food when jars are processed and for creating a vacuum as the jars are cooling. Directions for measuring the headspace should be included in any well-tested recipe, but in general, it is usually ¼ in [6 mm] for jams and jellies and ½ in [12 mm] for most pickles and tomatoes. A headspace measurer is a nifty plastic gizmo that helps measure the jar's headspace. It features ziggurat-like "tiers" on one end that indicate a series of headspace widths in ¼ in [6 mm] increments for your preserving pleasure. Could you simply use a school ruler? Yes. Would that be as fun? No. (Anger Management Alert: The USDA, with its strict rules, doesn't want anyone using metal tools to measure the headspace when using mason jars, which are glass and might chip, resulting in a bad jar seal. While this makes sense on a certain level, we also think that, unless you're taking out some kind of extreme frustration on your jar with your metal ruler, there's little risk of chipping.)

WATER BATH CANNING

SPECIAL EQUIPMENT

Mason jars with lids and screw bands

Canning pot and rack

Distilled white vinegar

Headspace measurer or ruler

Jar lifter

PREPARE THE CANNING EQUIPMENT

Check the jars and lids for chips or hairline fractures and discard any damaged pieces. Wash the jars, lids, and screw bands in hot, soapy water, or run through a dishwasher. Keep the jars warm in a low (200°F [95°C]) oven until ready to use. Dry the lids and screw bands, setting aside until ready to fill the jars.

Select a canning pot designed for home preserving, or a deep stockpot large enough to fully immerse the jars by several inches. Place a canning rack or wire cooling rack in the bottom of the pot or use twist-ties to link extra jar screw bands together to form a flat trivet wide enough to cover the bottom of the pot.

Fill the canning pot three-quarters full of water and add a splash of white vinegar to prevent mineral deposit spotting on the outside of the jars. Cover with a lid and bring the water to a boil, then maintain a strong simmer until ready to can.

PREPARE THE PRODUCT

Fill the jars with the prepared product.

Use a headspace measuring tool or a ruler to measure headspace (the space between the top of the product and the lip of the jar) according to the recipe instructions. If there is not enough product to fill a jar completely, store it in the refrigerator instead. Do not process a half-filled jar.

Release air bubbles by running a wooden skewer or chopstick around the inside edges of the jars.

Wipe the rim and outside threads of the jars with a clean, damp kitchen towel to remove any particles that may interfere with a clean seal and prevent sugar left in the threads from becoming moldy when stored.

Place the lids on top of the jars, then screw on the metal bands, but do not over-tighten. The metal screw band's only job is to keep the lid in place while the jar is processing in the water bath. To ensure a proper seal, first tighten the band firmly, then slightly loosen the band by about ¼ in [6 mm].

Use a jar lifter to lower the jars into the canning bath, adding more boiling water if needed to cover the jars by 1 in [2.5 cm]. Replace the lid and bring the canning bath back to a full, rolling boil before beginning to track processing time according to the recipe. Note that safe processing times can vary depending on the size of the jar used. Jar sizes are not interchangeable unless specified in the recipe.

CONT'D

After processing, turn off the heat. Wait for 5 minutes before removing the jars from the bath.

Use a jar lifter to transfer the jars to a towel-lined surface (to prevent the hot glass jars from cracking upon contact with a cold countertop) and allow to rest undisturbed for 8 to 12 hours, without tilting or inverting the jars.

Test each jar's seal by pressing down on the center of the lid. The button should be concave and not pop up and down with an audible click. You can also remove the screw band and gently lift the jar up by holding only the lid, which should not lift away.

If some jars are not properly sealed, reprocess following the same instructions within 24 hours. Improperly sealed jars may also simply be stored in the refrigerator and consumed within 1 month.

Label jars and store without their rings to prevent possible mold growth on jar threads or rusting of metal screw bands. They will keep for up to 1 year when stored in a cool, dry, dark place.

HIGH-ALTITUDE ADJUSTMENT: Water boils at different temperatures depending on altitude, boiling at a lower temperature as altitude increases and atmospheric pressure decreases. Safe canning practices depend on temperature and timing (in addition to acidity) to help control the growth of bacteria. The Institute Laboratory is located at sea level and the processing times given in this book are for altitudes at or below 1,000 ft [305 m] (where water boils at 212°F [100°C]). For altitudes above 1,000 ft [305 m], see the following chart and adjust processing time accordingly.

ALTITUDE (IN FEET)	INCREASE PROCESSING TIME BY
1,001 [305 m] to 3,000 [914 m]	5 minutes
3,001 [914 m] to 6,000 [1,829 m]	10 minutes
6,001 [1,829 m] to 8,000 [2,438 m]	15 minutes
8,001 [2,438 m] to 10,000 [3,048 m]	20 minutes

BOTULISM THWARTED

Growing up, my mother warned us that eating anything from a dented can could give you botulism. I didn't really know what botulism was at the time, but she made it sound so scary, I assumed it would instantly kill me. While botulism is a potentially serious issue when it comes to canned food, the connection between dented cans and the disease is a myth. (The "dent" would have to be an open gash for there to be a threat.) This whole dented can = botulism thing is still a concern of at least a handful of students in every Institute class. We tell them that the only way you would be likely to endanger yourself from using a dented can would be to bang it over your head.

Here's a quick high school science class refresher. Botulism forms when the bacterium *Clostridium botulinum*, which is present in the soil and water, finds just the right environment—namely, low-acid ingredients and no oxygen. Given these conditions, the anaerobic *C. botulinum* (its nickname for short) will grow and reproduce. The bacterium can also survive in a hostile (oxygen-rich) environment by forming protective spores. These spores have a hard, protective coating that encases the bacterium, allowing it to survive for years, during which time it remains dormant. While dormant, it can easily become airborne as well, landing on your food and skin until it reactivates in a more hospitable environment.

The saving grace that keeps us from regularly contracting botulism from food preserved in cans or jars is that *C. botulinum* cannot grow when it is in contact with ingredients that have a pH of 4.6 or lower (i.e., are more acidic). If the ingredients have a higher pH (i.e., are less acidic), it creates an environment where the bacteria can multiply and, what's more, it will not be killed by the boiling water in a water bath canner (212°F [100°C] at sea level). It will be killed, however, in a higher temperature environment (250°F [120°C] for 5 to 10 minutes), such as in a pressure canner.

Ultimately, the best way to control *C. botulinum*, which is invisible to the naked eye, is by using high-acid ingredients, such as 5 percent vinegar or stronger, when canning vegetables; canning high-acid fruits (or adding extra acid, like lemon juice, to lower-acid fruits); and using enough sugar in jams and high enough salt concentrations in pickles to inhibit bacterial growth. Always follow recipes you trust, such as the ones in this book, and you will never have to worry about contracting botulism—just watch your head around those dented cans.

KEVIN WEST

Dean of Pickles & Preserves

As I've mentioned before, pickling and preserving can be the "gateway drugs" that start you down the road to making your own homemade ingredients. They certainly were for me. Early on (when the Institute was still in its infancy), I was looking for a good pickling and preserves instructor. During my search, I came across *Saving the Season*, a blog written by preserver Kevin West. In his blog, Kevin gave readers a view inside his world of making jams, pickles, spirits, and cordials. His posts also conveyed his passionate interest in and deep understanding of fruits and vegetables, as well as the farmers who grow them.

In fact, Kevin would drive for hours just to visit a specific plum orchard. Poking around his website, I learned that he was also a journalist and magazine editor, something familiar to me through my own career trajectory. I felt I simply had to meet this guy in person and convince him to help me build the Institute's Department of Pickles & Preserves. Hell, I'd stalk him if necessary.

Fast-forward to today. Kevin West did indeed end up becoming the Dean of Pickles and Preserves. He developed a long list of workshops for us inspired by his website and, ultimately, by the book he wrote based on (and named after) his blog. Each summer, we'd look forward to stone fruit, cherry, and tomato recipes, and citrus fruit in winter. Given our location in Los Angeles, we even held a "Taco Truck" workshop, featuring Pickled Carrots, Taquería Style; Horchata; and Guajillo and Chile de Árbol Salsa.

Occasionally when Professor West was out of town, I would substitute for him, leading his workshops while unapologetically channeling his teachings, which included many of his great preserving stories. Once, while staying in a remote, rented cabin, he had a sudden urge to make jam—what he refers to as a "canning emergency." Although the cabin's kitchen was poorly stocked, Kevin cobbled something together by MacGyvering a set of canning equipment and was able to make jam that day. The "teaching moment" of the story? As long as one is armed with the basic principles of safe canning, no specialized equipment is necessary—except the fruit!

TIPS FROM THE PROFESSOR

Beginning preservers should start by making small amounts of jam or pickles, say only 3 to 4 pints [1.4 to 2 L]. Although it's tempting to make a huge batch in one sitting (thinking that you'll make a whole day of it and then store the fruits of your labor for later in the year), resist the urge if you can. Unfortunately, we see newbies make this mistake time and again, especially when they've stumbled upon an overabundance of fruit from a neighbor's tree or a rock-bottom price on a full fruit crate at the farmers' market. If you overextend yourself, you may realize too late that your preserving pan is too small, making it necessary to cook up several separate batches. Bummer! You may also find yourself staying up all night (and into the next morning) cutting, pitting, and processing a mountain of fruit or vegetables. If you play it safe with a small batch, you can easily make a few jars from start to finish in about an hour or two. Gather some friends to help you and you'll even be done by cocktail time!

PICKLED CHIPOTLE FENNEL CARROTS (PAGE 96)

ROSE WATER PICKLED ONIONS (PAGE 96)

AMAZUZUKE (CUCUMBER SWEET VINEGAR PICKLES) (PAGE 97)

MIXED VEGETABLE QUICK PICKLES (PAGE 93)

SWEET TOMATO CONSERVE (PAGE 102)

APRICOT MISO CARAMEL SAUCE (PAGE 104)

CANDIED CITRUS PEELS (PAGE 105)

WHAT MAKES A PICKLE?

You may notice that the recipe for Kosher Dill Pickles (page 281) can be found in the Department of Fermentation, whereas pickled carrots, onions, and others can be found right here in the Department of Pickles & Preserves. This is not a filing error! What gives? The simple explanation is that there are *two* main types of pickles: vinegar pickles and fermented pickles.

VINEGAR PICKLES

Vinegar pickles are preserved in an acidic solution, such as vinegar, which is usually heated while adding salt, sugar, and spices and then poured over whatever ingredients are to be pickled. Some vinegar pickles, known as "quick pickles," aren't heated in a water bath canner, which means they need to be stored in the refrigerator. Because they aren't exposed to heat for a long time, these pickles are usually crunchy and fresh tasting, with a subtle flavor. They can generally be eaten within a few hours of being made, and they will keep for several weeks. Vinegar pickles can also be water bath canned, which will allow them to be stored at room temperature for at least one year after being sealed.

FERMENTED PICKLES

Fermented pickles are preserved in brine, made by adding salt or salt water. The brine prevents the growth of harmful bacteria and promotes lactic acid fermentation. The resulting pickles have uniquely delicious flavors and varying textures, depending on factors like the amount of time the pickles are allowed to ferment and the temperature of the pickling environment. These pickles are less predictable and often take days or weeks to ferment, but they have the added benefit of containing live probiotic cultures.

Although cucumbers are usually considered the quintessential pickle choice, almost any vegetable (or fruit) can be pickled. ("We can pickle that!") Some of our favorite recipes for pickles include: fermented Kosher Dill Pickles (page 281) and Pickled Chipotle Fennel Carrots (page 96).

Quick Pickles Master Recipe

Vinegar quick pickles are easy to make and the perfect way to begin exploring your inner creative pickling impulses. Use the proportions in the recipe below to create your own custom pickle, using ingredient suggestions from the Invent-a-Pickle FlavorBar (page 94). Remember that quick pickles will become even more delicious as they sit in the refrigerator for a few days, allowing the flavors of the spices to develop and meld with whatever it is you're pickling. Go wild! **YIELD: TWO 1 PT [500 ML] MASON JARS**

Mixed vegetables (enough to fill two
1 pt [500 ml] jars)
Mixed spices and flavorings, to taste
1 cup [250 ml] vinegar
1 to 2 tsp salt
1 to 3 tsp sweetener (optional)

SPECIAL EQUIPMENT
Two 1 pt [500 ml] mason jars

Wash and scrub the vegetables, peeling if desired, then cut into spears, slices, or 1 to 1½ in [2.5 to 4 cm] chunks. Divide vegetables and any spices or flavorings evenly between two prepared 1 pt [500 ml] mason jars, wedging the vegetables in as closely as possible to prevent them from floating once submerged in the pickling solution.

To make the pickling solution, in a small saucepan over medium-high heat, combine the vinegar, salt, sweetener, if using, and 1 cup [250 ml] of water. Bring to a boil, stirring until the salt and any sweeteners are dissolved, about 1 minute. Remove from the heat and carefully pour the solution over the vegetables, dividing it evenly between the jars and leaving ½ in [12 mm] of headspace.

Allow the liquid to cool completely before sealing the jars and storing in the refrigerator overnight, or up to 3 weeks before serving.

FLAVORBAR

PICKLE IDEAS:

Pimm's Cup:
cucumber + lemon peel + ginger, thinly sliced + splash of Pimm's No. 1

The Heart of a Cauliflower:
cauliflower hearts + celery + carrots + crushed cardamom pods + turmeric

Dilly Beans:
green beans + fresh dill + garlic + red pepper flakes + dill seed

Baby Zucchini:
baby zucchini + mustard seed + coriander seed + saffron + garlic

INVENT-A-PICKLE

Choose from these ingredient ideas to create your own signature pickle combination. Begin with the Quick Pickles Master Recipe (page 93) as a base, then swap in one or more ingredients from each category. We encourage you to experiment with our Invent-a-Pickle FlavorBar by selecting a mix of vegetables and flavors that sound appealing to you.

94

VEGETABLES

**Enough to fill
two 1 pt [500 ml] jars**

Asparagus
Beets*
Bell peppers
Burdock
Cabbage
Carrots
Cauliflower florets
Cauliflower hearts
Celery
Cucumbers
Daikon radishes
Eggplants
Fennel
Green beans
Green onions
Green peas
Jalapeños
Okra
Onions, red
Onions, white
Onions, yellow
Pepperoncinis
Radishes
Turnips
Zucchinis

*Steam or boil beets until just tender before quick pickling.

VINEGAR

Use 1 cup [250 ml] of one or a combination of the following:

Apple cider vinegar
Champagne vinegar
Distilled white vinegar
Red wine vinegar
Rice vinegar
White wine vinegar

NOTE: While canned pickles require the use of vinegar with 5 percent or higher acidity, quick pickles can be made with lower acidity vinegars, such as rice vinegar.

SALT

1 to 2 tsp

Kosher salt
Pink Himalayan salt
Sea salt
Smoked salt

SWEETENER

1 to 3 tsp (optional)

Agave
Brown sugar
Granulated sugar
Honey
Piloncillo
Raw sugar

SPICES & FLAVORINGS

Use whole rather than powdered spices, and start with ½ tsp of each per 1 pt [500 ml] jar of pickles. Choose three or four spices and flavorings to start.

Allspice
Bay leaves
Black peppercorns
Cardamom pods
Chiles (whole, dried)
Cilantro (fresh)
Cinnamon sticks
Cloves
Coriander seeds
Cumin seeds
Dill (fresh or dried)
Dill seeds
Fennel seeds
Garlic (fresh)
Ginger (fresh)
Herbes de Provence
Juniper berries
Lemon peels
Marjoram (fresh or dried)
Mustard seeds
Oregano (fresh or dried)
Pink peppercorns
Red pepper flakes
Rosemary (fresh or dried)
Saffron threads
Sichuan peppercorns
Star anise
Thyme (fresh or dried)
Turmeric (fresh)

FLAVORBAR

BASIC PICKLING SPICE MIX

If you'd like to start with our Basic Pickling Spice Mix (instead of building your own), it uses eight classic ingredients and yields about 1 cup [120 g]. It can be stored long term in your pantry and used for multiple batches of pickles. Use 1 to 2 tsp per 1 pt [500 ml] jar of pickles.

6 Tbsp [60 g] mustard seeds

3 Tbsp allspice

2 Tbsp dill seeds

2 Tbsp coriander seeds

1 Tbsp red pepper flakes

6 cloves

3 bay leaves, crushed

3 cinnamon sticks, broken up into small pieces

In a small bowl, combine all of the ingredients and mix well. Transfer to an airtight container and store in a cool, dark place for up to 1 year.

Pickled Chipotle Fennel Carrots

This is our go-to pickle recipe at the Institute. Carrots are great, and we mean no disrespect, but when they are infused with smoky chipotle peppers and fennel seeds (for starters), they really come into their own. In the Institute kitchen we were going through so many jars of these pickles that we started to feel guilty tossing the leftover pickling liquid out. So one day, we dumped it into a blender with some olive oil and voilà!—a new, incredibly delicious (and zero waste) salad dressing was born.

YIELD: FOUR 1 PT [500 ML] MASON JARS

PICKLING SOLUTION

5½ cups [1.4 L] white wine vinegar (5 percent acidity) or apple cider vinegar

1½ cups [300 g] granulated sugar

2 tsp kosher salt

PICKLES

2¾ lb [1.3 kg] carrots, trimmed and peeled

8 tsp mustard seeds

4 tsp celery seeds

4 tsp coriander seeds

4 tsp fennel seeds

24 black peppercorns

4 garlic cloves, peeled

4 dried chipotle peppers

SPECIAL EQUIPMENT

Four 1 pt [500 ml] mason jars, prepared according to the instructions on page 79

Canning equipment (see page 76)

Prepare the jars and canning equipment, fill the water bath canner with water, and begin heating (see Water Bath Canning, page 79).

To make the pickling solution, in a medium saucepan over medium-high heat, combine the vinegar, sugar, salt, and 1 cup [250 ml] water and bring to a boil. Turn the heat to medium-low and simmer gently for 3 minutes, then cover and turn off the heat, keeping the solution warm until ready to pack the jars.

To assemble the pickles, slice the carrots crosswise into 3½ in [9 cm] lengths in order to fit standing up in the jars, then slice lengthwise into uniform ½ in [12 mm] thick sticks.

Divide the spices, garlic cloves, and peppers evenly between the prepared jars, leaning one chipotle pepper upright against the side of each jar.

Pack the carrot sticks into the jars, tightly wedging in as many as possible to prevent them from floating once submerged in the pickling solution.

Using a ladle or heatproof measuring pitcher, carefully fill each jar with the hot pickling solution, covering the tops of the carrot sticks and leaving ½ in [12 mm] of headspace.

Release any air bubbles by running a skewer or chopstick around the inside of each jar. Wipe the rims, seal the jars, and process in a hot water bath (see page 79) for 15 minutes.

Store unopened jars of pickles in a cool, dark place for up to 1 year.

Rose Water Pickled Onions

Pickling onions in rose water transfigures them, lending their usual savory quality an appealing floral note. Juniper berries and star anise add to the exotic atmosphere, and the acidity of this quick pickle makes it the perfect foil to rich or unctuous dishes like pot roast, or a brightener for your favorite grain bowl. **YIELD: 1 PT [500 ML]**

1 medium red onion, halved and thinly sliced

½ cup [125 ml] rice or white wine vinegar

2 tsp granulated sugar

1 tsp kosher salt

6 juniper berries

6 black or pink peppercorns

1 star anise pod

1½ tsp rose water

1 pt [500 ml] mason jar

Pack the onion slices into a 1 pt [500 ml] mason jar and set aside.

In a small saucepan over medium heat, combine the vinegar, sugar, salt, spices, and ½ cup [125 ml] of water. Bring to a boil, stirring until the sugar and salt dissolve, then immediately remove from the heat and pour the mixture over the onions.

Add the rose water, then set aside for at least 30 minutes, allowing the liquid to come to room temperature. Pickled onions may be used immediately but will become pinker with additional time. They taste best within the first week but may be stored in an airtight container in the refrigerator for up to 1 month.

Amazuzuke (Cucumber Sweet Vinegar Pickles)

Given that they can be found in nearly every Japanese home kitchen, Dean of Fermentation Yoko Maeda Lamn urged us to include at least one *sunomono* (Japanese vinegar pickle) recipe in this book. (In Japan, *tsukemono* vs. *sunomono* is the analogue of fermented vs. vinegar pickles in the West.) Ready in just a few hours, this Japanese quick pickle can be made right before you start dinner, or, for that matter, whenever the impulse strikes. Eat them right away or wait awhile; the longer you pickle them, the tastier they become. *Oishii, ne!* ("Mmmm!") **SERVES 4**

Fine sea salt
4 Japanese or 6 Persian cucumbers, ends trimmed
¼ cup [60 ml] rice vinegar
¼ cup [50 g] raw cane sugar
1 Tbsp toasted sesame oil
½ tsp red pepper flakes

Rub a pinch of salt on the cut ends of the cucumbers and massage gently. The salt will draw out the bitter compounds and should create a bit of froth.

Sprinkle another healthy pinch of salt over each cucumber and rub vigorously with your hands to massage the salt into the skin.

Slice the cucumbers diagonally crosswise into ¾ in [2 cm] thick pieces and set aside.

In a medium bowl, combine the vinegar, sugar, sesame oil, and pepper flakes. Add the cucumbers to the bowl and toss to coat the pieces well. Cover and refrigerate for 1 to 2 hours.

Serve immediately or transfer to an airtight container and store in the refrigerator for up to 3 days.

Canned Tomatoes

While tomatoes are available year-round in the supermarket, they do not taste the same as they do when in season—late spring through early fall. If you grow tomatoes in a home garden or support a local farmers' market, you'll have access to an abundance of varieties and an abundance of tomatoes. You may grow weary of finding ways to consume all of them while in season, but admit it, you'll be sad come winter when your only choices are watery, tasteless supermarket tomatoes. Yes, there are those cans of tomatoes in the pantry, but honestly, they pale in comparison with ones you've canned yourself.

First, we suggest you read our water bath canning instructions on page 79 because you'll need to refer to it in the directions below. You'll also need to get cozy with the science of acidity levels and canning safety and avoid angering the *Clostridium botulinum* spores.

Only foods with an acidity of pH 4.6 and lower (that is, lower on the pH scale but higher in acidity) can be safely water bath canned. Tomatoes are generally acidic, but with the increase in heirloom and other varieties now available in markets and seed catalogs, their acidity can vary widely, often landing right on the edge of the pH 4.6 safety zone. Some are more acidic, but others are more alkaline. To be safe, we recommend adding a splash of acidity, rather than playing chicken with botulism. Fresh lemon juice won't cut it since the acidity of lemons can also vary depending on variety. One safe method is to use commercial bottled lemon juice, the acidity of which is standardized by the FDA. Many brands add chemical preservatives, but they do come in cute little lemon-shaped plastic bottles. An alternative to bottled lemon juice is food-grade citric acid, which comes in powdered form and, unlike lemon juice, is tasteless.

YIELD: TWO 1 PT [500 ML] OR ONE 1 QT [1 L] MASON JAR

Whole or Halved Tomatoes

2 Tbsp bottled lemon juice or ½ tsp citric acid

1 tsp kosher salt (optional)

3 to 3½ lb [1.4 to 1.6 kg] firm, ripe tomatoes

SPECIAL EQUIPMENT

Two 1 pt [500 ml] or one 1 qt [1 L] mason jars, prepared according to instructions on page 79

Canning equipment (see page 76)

STEP 1 Prepare the jars and canning equipment, fill the water bath canner with water, and begin heating (see Water Bath Canning, page 79). Fill an additional large saucepan with water and bring to a boil, for blanching the tomatoes in Step 3. In a large bowl, prepare an ice bath by filling it with roughly equal parts ice and water.

STEP 2 To each prepared 1 pt [500 ml] jar, add 1 Tbsp of the lemon juice (or ¼ tsp citric acid) and ½ tsp of the salt, if using. For a 1 qt [1 L] jar, add 2 Tbsp of the lemon juice (or ½ tsp citric acid) and 1 tsp of the salt, if using.

STEP 3 With a sharp paring knife, cut a 1 in [2.5 cm] long slit anywhere through the skin of each tomato, which will help facilitate skin removal. Working in batches, blanch the tomatoes in boiling water for 30 to 60 seconds, then immediately use a slotted spoon to remove and transfer them to the prepared ice bath. Gently slip off the skins and use a paring knife to trim out the core where the stem attaches and remove any blemishes. Cut the tomatoes into halves or leave whole.

STEP 4 Fill the jars with the tomatoes, packing them down until the space between the tomatoes fills with juice, leaving ½ in [12 mm] of headspace.

STEP 5 Release any air bubbles by running a skewer or chopstick around the inside of each jar. Wipe the rims and seal the jars.

STEP 6 Process in a hot water bath (see page 79) for 85 minutes. Store unopened jars of tomatoes in a cool, dark place for up to 1 year.

VARIATION: CRUSHED TOMATOES

2 Tbsp bottled lemon juice or ½ tsp citric acid

1 tsp kosher salt (optional)

2¾ to 3¼ lb [1.2 to 1.5 kg] firm, ripe tomatoes

Follow steps 1 through 3 of the whole or halved tomato recipe, preceding, cutting the tomatoes into quarters instead.

In a large, nonreactive saucepan over medium-high heat, add half of the tomatoes and bring to a boil. Crush the tomatoes with a potato masher to release their juices and stir with a wooden spoon to prevent scorching. When the first batch of tomatoes comes to a boil, add the remainder, crushing and allowing them to soften as they heat. Return to a gentle boil, stirring occasionally, and cook for an additional 5 minutes.

Follow steps 4 through 6 of the whole or halved tomato recipe, preceding, leaving ½ in [12 mm] of headspace. Process 35 minutes for pint [500 ml] jars or 45 minutes for quarts [1 L].

Tomato Juice

2 Tbsp bottled lemon juice or ½ tsp citric acid

1 tsp kosher salt (optional)

3¼ to 3¾ lb [1.5 to 1.7 kg] firm, ripe tomatoes

SPECIAL EQUIPMENT

Two 1 pt [500 ml] or one 1 qt [1 L] mason jars, prepared according to instructions on page 79

Canning equipment (see page 76)

Food mill fitted with the fine disk

STEP 1 Prepare the jars and canning equipment, fill the water bath canner with water, and begin heating (see Water Bath Canning, page 79).

STEP 2 To each prepared 1 pt [500 ml] jar, add 1 Tbsp of the lemon juice (or ¼ tsp citric acid) and ½ tsp of the salt, if using. For a 1 qt [1 L] jar, add 2 Tbsp of lemon juice (or ½ tsp citric acid) and 1 tsp of salt, if using.

STEP 3 Use a sharp knife to remove any blemishes from the tomatoes and cut them into quarters, then place in a large, nonreactive saucepan over high heat, crushing the tomatoes with a potato masher to release their juices, and bring to a boil. Stir with a wooden spoon to prevent scorching. When the tomatoes come to a boil, reduce the heat to medium-low and simmer gently for 5 minutes to soften.

STEP 4 Transfer the mixture to a food mill set over a large bowl and run it through the mill until only the peels and seeds remain. Discard the solids.

STEP 5 Return the tomato juice to the saucepan and bring to a boil before packing the jars.

STEP 6 Fill the jars with the tomato juice, leaving ½ in [12 mm] of headspace.

STEP 7 Release any air bubbles by running a skewer or chopstick around the inside of each jar. Wipe the rims and seal the jars.

STEP 8 Process in a hot water bath (see page 79), 35 minutes for pint [500 ml] jars or 40 minutes for quarts [1 L]. Store unopened jars of tomatoes in a cool, dark place for up to 1 year.

STEP 9 Tomato juice may separate during storage but can be reconstituted by stirring, or by giving the jar a shake.

VARIATION: TOMATO SAUCE

2 Tbsp bottled lemon juice or ½ tsp citric acid

1 tsp kosher salt (optional)

6½ to 7 lb [3 to 3.2 kg] firm, ripe tomatoes

Follow steps 1 through 4 of the tomato juice recipe, preceding.

Return the tomato juice to the saucepan and bring to a boil, then lower the heat and simmer until the sauce is very thick, and the volume has reduced by half. Stir frequently to prevent scorching.

When the volume is reduced by half, pack the jars. Follow steps 6 through 8 of the tomato juice recipe, preceding, leaving ¼ in [6 mm] of headspace. Process 35 minutes for pint [500 ml] jars or 40 minutes for quarts [1 L].

Universal Jam

The Universal Jam recipe is a simple, three-part ratio used to measure fruit, sugar, and acid for almost any prepped fruit, making it the perfect blank slate for all of your creative flavor ideas.

When weighing fruit, "prepped" refers to the weight of the fruit after all pits and stems have been removed. The lemon juice here provides an extra boost of acid, which is helpful when working with low-acid fruits, and helps brighten and balance flavor. This universal recipe yields five ½ pt [250 ml] jars of jam. While it can be scaled up to make more, Professor Kevin West advocates small-batch preserving and recommends starting out with 3 lb [1.4 kg] batches. **YIELD: FIVE ½ PT [250 ML] MASON JARS**

3 lb [1.4 kg] prepped fruit
3 cups [600 g] granulated sugar
2 Tbsp fresh lemon juice

SPECIAL EQUIPMENT
Five ½ pt [250 ml] mason jars, prepared according to the instructions on page 79
Canning equipment (see page 76)

Place a small ceramic saucer in the freezer to test for gel set later on. Prepare the jars and canning equipment, fill the water bath canner with water, and begin heating (see Water Bath Canning, page 79).

In a preserving pan, heavy-bottomed stockpot, or Dutch oven, add the fruit, sugar, and lemon juice and stir to combine. Set aside to macerate for 30 minutes. This is Stage I.

Bring the mixture to a boil over high heat, stirring frequently. In Stage II, the jam should reach a full rolling boil, a boil that you can't stir down. Stir continuously until the jam is thick, reduced, and beginning to pull away from the sides of the pan, signaling Stage III. This should take 8 to 10 minutes from the time the jam reaches a boil, depending on the size of your pan and the strength of the heat source. When it reaches Stage III, remove from the heat and test for gel set using the chilled-saucer technique (see facing page).

Once gel set has been reached (Stage IV), ladle the hot jam into the prepared jars, leaving ¼ in [6 mm] of headspace. Release any air bubbles by running a skewer or chopstick around the inside of each jar. Wipe the rims, seal the jars, and process in a hot water bath (see page 79) for 10 minutes.

Store unopened jars of jam in a cool, dark place for up to 1 year.

NOTE ON TIMING: If you are interrupted during the cooking phase, simply turn off the heat to temporarily stop the process. (Do not walk away while the heat is still on, as the jam can burn without constant stirring.) Jam can be set aside off the heat for up to 5 hours; cover the pan if more than a few minutes. Return to a full rolling boil and proceed where you left off.

NOTE ON CONSISTENCY: If a smoother consistency is desired, you can use an immersion blender to blend the preserves in the pan or run them through a food mill before ladling into jars.

OPTIONAL FLAVORINGS: Try adding other flavorings, such as a vanilla bean or a sprig of fresh herbs, stirred in at the end of cooking. Start with a small amount and work your way up, as a little can go a long way. A splash of liqueur, wine, or bitters can also be a nice addition, just be sure to add it at the very end so as to maintain the alcohol's delicate flavor.

FLAVORBAR

JAM IDEAS:

plums + star anise + vanilla bean

blackberries + tarragon + gin + black pepper

figs + lemon zest + bay leaves + ouzo

TESTING JAM FOR GEL SET

"Gel set" is reached when enough water has evaporated from the cooked fruit, and its inherent pectin has been sufficiently activated by heat, sugar, and acidity to form a thick, gelatinous web that holds the fruit juices and fiber together (see What Is Pectin?, following). While you can test for gel set with a thermometer (220°F [104°C]), we routinely fall back on the frozen saucer test, which is a more visual and tactile method. There's also less chance of getting scalded by molten jam as you attempt to take its temperature.

Place a small ceramic saucer in the freezer to chill before you begin preparing the preserves.

Follow instructions for macerating and cooking jam ingredients (facing page). When the jam is thick and reduced and begins to pull away from the sides of the pan, turn off the heat and test for gel set.

Remove the saucer from the freezer and place 1 tsp of hot jam on top, then return the saucer to the freezer. After 1 minute, remove and check to see if the jam has formed a glossy skin. Gently push your finger through the dollop; it should wrinkle like the skin of a Shar-Pei dog. If it does, congratulations, you have reached gel set and can proceed to packing the jam into jars. If not, return the saucer to the freezer and resume cooking the jam over high heat, stirring constantly, for another minute or two before testing again.

— PRIMER —

WHAT IS PECTIN?

Pectin is a complex carbohydrate that naturally occurs in fruit's cell walls. Some fruits, including apples, citrus, plums, cranberries, and quince, have a super abundance of pectin that can be used to achieve the characteristic "gel" of jams and jellies.

Pectin is activated by sugar and heat, and requires a suitably acidic environment to thicken or reach "gel set."

Regardless of variety, all fruit has the most pectin when it is slightly unripe. As fruit ripens, enzymes start to break the pectin down.

The Dean's Marmalade

This easy-to-make marmalade is another recipe from Kevin West. We love citrus, and it helps that we are based in sunny Southern California, where it seems to be some type of citrus season all year long, allowing us to use this recipe for many of our preserve-making classes. If a marmalade was asked to introduce herself during an interview, she would say, "I'm a sweet preserve made from whole citrus, peels and all." The trouble is that the white albedo layer just below the colorful outer peel contains phenols, which are extremely bitter. Traditionally, this meant soaking the peels overnight, then blanching them in boiling water, draining, and repeating multiple times with fresh water until the bitterness was removed. Unfortunately, during this laborious process, esters, the flavorful citrus oils in the zest, are also diminished. The genius of this recipe is that it involves a simple step that separates the bitter albedo from the zest right from the start, eliminating the countless hours of work and making it possible to make marmalade, from start to finish, in a little over an hour. Once you've mastered the Dean's standard recipe, try some of the FlavorBar variations (facing page) for even more deliciousness. **YIELD: FOUR ½ PT [250 ML] JARS**

1 lb [450 g] oranges
1 lb [450 g] grapefruits
1 lb [450 g] lemons or limes
4½ cups [900 g] granulated sugar

SPECIAL EQUIPMENT

Four ½ pt [250 ml] mason jars, prepared according to the instructions on page 79

Canning equipment (page 76)

Place a small ceramic saucer in the freezer to test for gel set later on. Prepare the canning equipment and fill the water bath canner with water and begin heating (see Water Bath Canning, page 79).

Using a vegetable peeler, remove the zest from the citrus in wide strips, leaving behind as much albedo (white pith) as possible.

Slice the peels into ¼ in [6 mm] wide strips, or in wider confetti-like pieces for a more textured marmalade. Set aside.

With a sharp paring knife, trim the remaining albedo away from the citrus flesh and discard. Chop the pulp into a ½ in [12 mm] dice, discarding any seeds.

Combine the sliced peel, diced pulp, and 3 cups [750 ml] of water in a preserving pan, heavy-bottomed stockpot, or Dutch oven and bring to a boil over high heat, then turn the heat to low and simmer gently for 20 minutes, until the peel is soft but still has some give when you bite into it.

Add the sugar, stirring to dissolve, then return to a boil over high heat and reduce the mixture while stirring constantly. After about 15 minutes, remove from the heat and test for gel set using the chilled-saucer technique (see page 101). If the marmalade is ready, proceed to the next step. If not, resume cooking over high heat, stirring constantly, for another minute or two before testing again.

Ladle the marmalade into the prepared jars, leaving ¼ in [6 mm] of headspace. Release any air bubbles by running a skewer or chopstick around the inside of each jar. Wipe the rims, seal the jars, and process in a hot water bath (see page 79) for 10 minutes.

Store unopened jars of marmalade in a cool, dark place for up to 1 year.

Sweet Tomato Conserve

Though technically a fruit (haven't we settled this one already?), the humble tomato is often overlooked where other fruits shine, especially when it comes to making jam. No more! In this sophisticated sweet preserve, it is the main attraction, and like the versatile fruit, it can go sweet on toast in the morning, or hold its own as a savory spread, not unlike its cousin ketchup. Try it as a layer cake filling or spread it on a sandwich of bacon, lettuce, and (why not?) a slice of fresh tomato. Don't skip the swig of gin—it blends the flavors into something more than the sum of its parts. **YIELD: TWO OR THREE ½ PT [250 ML] JARS**

5 lb [2.3 kg] Roma tomatoes

1½ cups [300 g] granulated sugar

2 Tbsp fresh lemon juice

One 1 in [2.5 cm] piece fresh ginger, peeled and sliced into thin rounds

2 star anise pods

1 tsp kosher salt

½ vanilla bean

1½ tsp gin (preferably a floral variety, such as The Botanist)

SPECIAL EQUIPMENT

Two or three ½ pt [250 ml] mason jars, prepared according to the instructions on page 79

Food mill fitted with the fine disk

Canning equipment (page 76, optional)

Place a small ceramic saucer in the freezer to test for gel set later on. Prepare the canning equipment and fill the water bath canner with water and begin heating (see Water Bath Canning, page 79).

Cut the tomatoes into 1 in [2.5 cm] chunks and place in a colander set over a medium bowl to drain.

Combine the tomatoes, sugar, lemon juice, ginger, star anise, and salt in a preserving pan, heavy-bottomed stockpot, or Dutch oven. Use a sharp paring knife to split the vanilla bean lengthwise, then use the tip of the knife to scrape out the seeds into the tomato mixture. Add the bean pod, stir, and set aside to macerate for 30 minutes.

Bring the mixture to a boil over high heat and continue to boil, stirring constantly, for 25 to 30 minutes or until mixture has reduced to a thick paste and no excess liquid is pooling on the sides of the pan. Remove from the heat and test for gel set using the chilled-saucer technique (see page 101). If the conserve is ready, proceed to the next step. If not, resume cooking over high heat, stirring constantly, for another 1 or 2 minutes before testing again.

CONT'D

FLAVORBAR

———

MARMALADE IDEAS:

Once you've gotten to know the recipe and its unique process, take a look at Kevin's suggestions, mixing and matching as your creativity strikes you. The only constant is that the combined fruit must add up to a total of 3 lb [1.3 kg] and the sugar must remain at 4½ cups [900 g]. Flavorings should be stirred in just before ladling into jars, except for tea bags, which can be added toward the end of the initial simmering stage and then removed.

oranges + grapefruit + lemons + 2 Tbsp Scotch or 4 teabags Earl Grey tea

oranges + grapefruit + limes + 2 Tbsp gin

blood oranges + grapefruit + lemons + 2 Tbsp limoncello

oranges + lemons + ¼ tsp orange flower water

Cara Cara oranges + Meyer lemons + 2 Tbsp Aperol

In batches if necessary, transfer the mixture to a food mill set over a large bowl and run it through the mill until only the peels and seeds remain. Discard the solids.

Stir the gin into the remaining tomato conserve and ladle into the prepared jars, leaving ¼ in [6 mm] of headspace. If desired, follow instructions for Water Bath Canning (see page 79) and process for 10 minutes. Or, allow to cool completely before using immediately or sealing the jars tightly and storing in the refrigerator for up to 2 weeks.

Apricot Miso Caramel Sauce

Inspired by Professor Kevin West's jam recipe, this version adds another layer of salty, umami caramel to the sweet apricots. It's delicious on vanilla ice cream, pound cake, or eaten right out of the jar with a spoon. **YIELD: TWO 1 PT [500 ML] MASON JARS**

2½ lb [1.1 kg] pitted apricots
2 Tbsp fresh lemon juice
1¾ cups [350 g] granulated sugar
½ cup [160 g] maple syrup
1 vanilla bean
2 Tbsp bourbon, scotch, or brandy
2 Tbsp sesame seeds
½ cup [125 ml] heavy cream
2 Tbsp smooth Miso (page 291)

SPECIAL EQUIPMENT
Food mill fitted with the coarse disk,
food processor, or immersion blender
Spice grinder or mortar and pestle
Two 1 pt [500 ml] mason jars

Slice the apricots into quarters and place in a preserving pan, heavy-bottomed stockpot, or Dutch oven, along with the lemon juice, 1 cup [200 g] of the sugar, and the maple syrup. Use a sharp paring knife to split the vanilla bean lengthwise, then use the tip of the knife to scrape the seeds into the pan. Add the pod, then stir to combine and set aside to macerate for 30 minutes.

Bring the mixture to a boil over high heat, stirring constantly, until thick and reduced, 8 to 10 minutes.

Remove the vanilla bean pod and coarsely purée the mixture with a food mill, food processor, or immersion blender, then return it to the pot and bring to a boil again, stirring constantly and continuing to reduce until the mixture is thick, but still spreadable, 5 to 10 minutes. Add the bourbon, stirring to combine, then turn off the heat. Keep the pan warm while you prepare the caramel.

In a small, dry, heavy skillet over medium heat, toast the sesame seeds until fragrant and lightly browned, about 3 minutes. Transfer to a plate to cool briefly, then finely grind in a spice grinder or with a mortar and pestle. Set aside.

In a medium, heavy saucepan over medium-high heat, combine the remaining ¾ cup [150 g] of sugar and ¼ cup [60 ml] water, stirring carefully just until the sugar is dissolved, then bring the mixture to a boil, without stirring, until the mixture turns a deep golden brown, 5 to 10 minutes.

While the sugar mixture is cooking, place the cream in a small, heavy saucepan over medium-low heat and bring to a gentle simmer. When the caramel is ready, immediately whisk the cream into the hot sugar, which will cause it to bubble vigorously. Continue to cook over medium-low heat for 2 to 3 minutes, stirring constantly, then remove from the heat and whisk in the miso and sesame seeds.

Add the caramel mixture to the apricots, stirring well to combine. Cool completely before using or transferring to two 1 pt [500 ml] jars. The sauce can be stored, tightly sealed, in the refrigerator for up to 3 weeks.

Prunes in French Armagnac

This classic French dessert is made by steeping prunes in Armagnac, France's regional brandy, transforming the humble dried fruit into a soft, boozy dessert in thick syrup. Both fruit and syrup are delicious served with vanilla ice cream, spooned over a slice of unfrosted cake, or even drizzled on top of a warm chocolate soufflé. **YIELD: ABOUT 3 CUPS [750 ML]**

2 Tbsp granulated sugar

½ vanilla bean

12 oz [340 g] large, pitted prunes

¾ cup [180 ml] Armagnac

SPECIAL EQUIPMENT

1 qt [1 L] mason jar

In a small, nonreactive saucepan, combine the sugar and 1½ cups [375 ml] water. Use a sharp paring knife to split the vanilla bean lengthwise, then use the tip of the knife to scrape the seeds into the pan, and add the pod. Bring the mixture to a boil over medium-high heat, stirring until the sugar dissolves. Once the mixture comes to a boil, remove the syrup from the heat and set aside.

Place the prunes in a clean, dry 1 qt [1 L] mason jar and pour the still-hot syrup over them. Allow to cool completely, then stir in the Armagnac. Seal tightly and refrigerate for at least 1 week to allow the prunes to infuse before serving.

Store the prunes, tightly sealed, in the refrigerator for at least 1 year.

Candied Citrus Peels

Made using techniques that are literally hundreds of years old, sugared citrus peels continue to be an important part of many European and Middle Eastern recipes. Served as a dessert item or as a counterpoint to meat dishes, candied citrus peels allow the fruit to do double duty, providing a use for the peels that are so often discarded. We use them to decorate cakes, tarts, and cookies, and as garnishes in cocktails. Wrap them up in tissue paper and place in a decorative box for a seasonally appropriate holiday gift or to score big with your host or hostess.

YIELD: ABOUT 2 CUPS [230 G]

6 to 8 citrus fruits, such as lemons, oranges, or grapefruits

3 cups [600 g] granulated sugar, plus more for coating

With a sharp paring knife, score 4 to 6 straight lines along the sides of each citrus fruit from the stem to the bottom, cutting only through the peel and leaving the flesh inside intact. With your fingers or using a paring knife, gently pull the peel away, reserving the flesh for another use.

Slice each peel segment lengthwise into ¼ in [6 mm] strips. Leave the white pith on lemon and orange peels, but if using grapefruit, trim away and discard any spongy, excess white pith with a paring knife.

Place the peels in a medium saucepan with cold water to cover by 1 in [2.5 cm]. Bring to a rolling boil over medium-high heat, then remove from the heat and drain. Repeat this process two more times with fresh water to remove the bitterness from the pith, then set the strips aside.

In the same saucepan over medium-high heat, bring the sugar and 3 cups [750 ml] of water to a boil, stirring occasionally just until the sugar dissolves. Add the citrus strips to the boiling syrup, lower the heat to medium-low, and simmer gently without stirring until the strips are translucent, about 1 hour. Remove from the heat and allow the strips to cool completely in the syrup.

Using a slotted spoon, transfer the strips to a wire cooling rack placed over a rimmed baking sheet. Spread the strips out in a single layer and allow them to drain and dry for 12 to 24 hours, until slightly sticky but no longer dripping with syrup.

Fill a small bowl with sugar and roll the strips around to coat. Spread the sugar-coated strips in a single layer on a wire cooling rack or on a baking sheet lined with parchment paper and allow them to dry for at least 1 hour or overnight. Transfer to an airtight container and store at room temperature for up to 2 months.

ZERO-WASTE ALERT! Save the leftover simple syrup from boiling the citrus strips and use it for citrus-infused cocktails. Allow to cool completely, then transfer to a clean glass jar and store, tightly sealed, in the refrigerator for up to 1 month.

SUGAR CONTENT IN JAM

Whether for health reasons or for personal taste, Institute students frequently ask if the amount of sugar in a given jam recipe may be reduced, substituted with another sweetener, or omitted entirely. The answer is: maybe. Sugar plays three important roles in jam making: Along with heat and acid, it helps activate pectin in the fruit (see What Is Pectin?, page 101), producing the thick "gel set" that most people think of when they imagine a thick, spreadable jam for their morning toast. Sugar also plays an important role as a preservative, keeping harmful bacteria at bay and creating a shelf-stable product when properly canned. Finally, it also provides and enhances flavor.

DECREASING OR OMITTING SUGAR

If you want to decrease the amount of sugar in a jam recipe, be aware that it may compromise the keeping qualities of a preserve and may also require a longer time to thicken the fruit. It may also interfere with the fruit's ability to form gel set.

Even high-pectin fruit such as crabapples or quince require some added sugar to form gel set. Specially formulated, commercial pectin can be used to offset this problem. (Make sure it's made for low- or no-sugar jams.) You can also omit the sugar entirely, but you will not be making jam— you'll be making fruit butter, which is pure fruit that's been cooked for an extended period to concentrate its liquids and thicken the final product.

SUBSTITUTING SUGAR

Sweeteners such as brown sugar, molasses, or honey can be used as a substitute for white, granulated sugar, but remember that they will impart their own (stronger) flavors into the final jam. We recommend using them sparingly and replacing only part of them for the white sugar called for in a recipe. We do not recommend using sugar-free chemical substitutes, which can produce off-flavors when heated. They will also not produce gel set, nor act as a preservative.

FINAL THOUGHTS

Though we generally like the idea of using unrefined or minimally processed ingredients whenever possible, when it comes to preserves, our preference is for white, granulated sugar. Not only is it the most budget-friendly of sweeteners, but it also imparts the cleanest taste and allows the flavor of the fruit to shine through. Anyone concerned about the amount of sugar in a jam recipe should consider the serving size: When enjoying the jam you've made, you'll rarely consume more than 1 to 2 tsp at a time. What's more, if you're accustomed to the cloyingly sweet taste of store-bought, commercial jam, keep in mind that it's mostly sugar, with the fruit playing second fiddle. The corporate metric is simple: Sugar is cheaper than fruit. Homemade jams, however, including the recipes in this cookbook, typically contain far less sugar and far more flavor.

A USEFUL HOUSEHOLD WORK

A 1912 advertisement for one of the Institute of Domestic Technology's most popular publications, a sixteen-page pamphlet entitled The Perfect Art of Canning and Preserving, a "useful household work," written by Eliza Taylor Reynolds, the Institute's founder and original director. It is my fervent hope that the "important subject" of my own modern compendium is as "intelligently handled" as Reynolds's was.

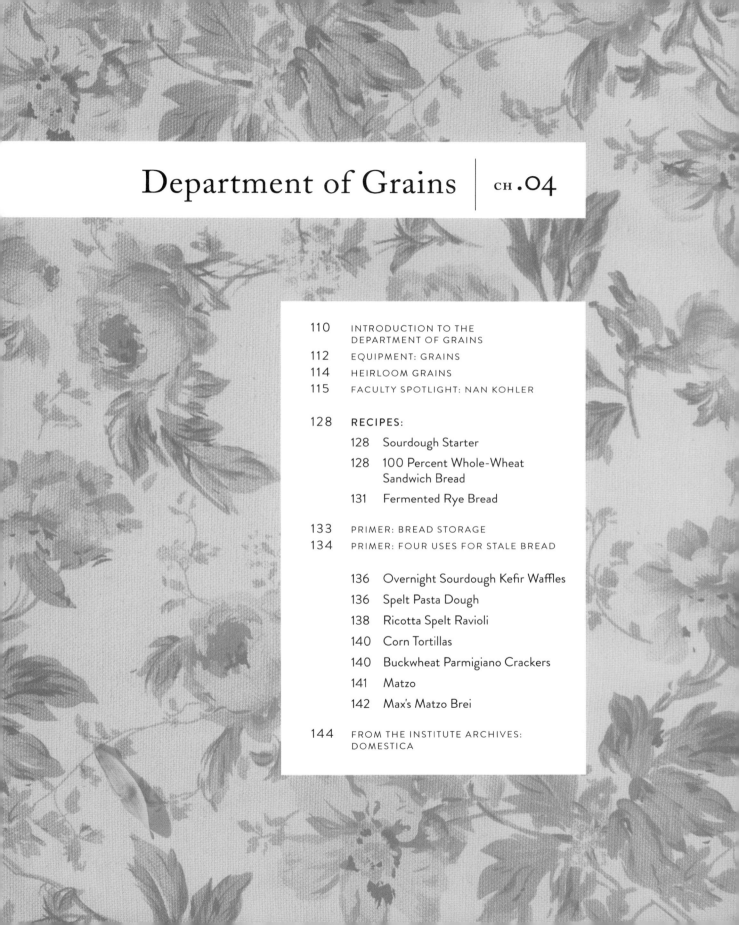

Department of Grains | CH.04

THE DEPARTMENT OF GRAINS

My mother was an early devotee of "health food" author Adelle Davis, whose *Let's Eat Right to Keep Fit*, published in 1954, was her bible. As a young boy growing up in Los Angeles, I often accompanied my mother on her local errands in search of unrefined food ingredients that, in the dark days of the Wonder Bread era, were almost impossible to find. One place she regularly frequented that fascinated me as a child was El Molino Mills, originally opened in 1926. It was the last of its kind, and though technically the mill wasn't open to the public, you could slip through the side door and feel like you entered a time warp. There my mom could purchase freshly stone-ground, whole-wheat flour, which was sold in old-fashioned, cotton flour sacks. Needless to say, you couldn't get that at our local supermarket. They also sold strange, exotic things like "soya" (soy) flour for baking and powder for making soy milk, buckwheat flour, cornmeal, and carob powder.

El Molino and its freshly ground, whole-wheat flour are long gone, a casualty of competition with the cheap, high-volume, commercially processed and refined flour found at supermarkets. Like so many foods, whose flavor and nutrition have been compromised in favor of increasing shelf life, refined flour is made from grain that has been stripped of its germ and bran. The germ (or embryo) of

the grain contains protein, B vitamins, and trace minerals and has a fat content of 10 percent, which, when exposed to air, quickly goes rancid, reducing shelf life.

The result is an aesthetically pleasing product that is easy to use, but basically devoid of nutrients. It's interesting to note that the poor nutritional status of young men enlisting for service during World War II was found to be due to the loss of nutrients that had been stripped out of this processed flour. In fact, in 1941, the FDA recommended that white flour be "enriched" with thiamin, riboflavin, niacin, folic acid, and iron, essentially replacing the nutrients that had naturally been a part of the grain *before* it was refined, a somewhat ironic process that continues to this day.

The beginning of the modern bread-baking movement can be traced to the 1960s, when "back-to-the-land" hippies started growing and making their own food, including sourcing whole grains. This, in turn, led to a gradual but profound cultural change in attitudes toward processed food. By 1970, Edward Espe Brown, Chief Priest of the San Francisco Zen Center, published *The Tassajara Bread Book*, in which he "flipped the bird" to the "Man" and his over processed, commercial, lifeless white bread. Espe Brown introduced a generation raised on bland white bread to an approachable method of making homemade, healthful, whole-wheat bread at home using instant yeast.

Unfortunately, most of these early versions of whole-wheat bread were, in our opinion, extremely heavy and dense, giving whole wheat a bad name that lasted for decades. Gradually, however, new/old techniques began showing up in small, neighborhood bread bakeries, which started working with natural yeasts. Fermentation, no longer stigmatized as something resulting from "harmful" microbes, yielded natural yeast sourdough. This living result of the fermentation of natural yeast and lactic acid bacteria gives sourdough bread its wonderful tanginess. Most recently, these rediscovered techniques have been adopted and perfected by an influential new wave of home bakers–turned–bread entrepreneurs experimenting not only with fermentation and whole grains, but also with alternative grains that offer new flavors and textures, and thanks to the growth of the "Cottage Food" movement, many of their wares can now be sold to the public.

Unlike the heavy, whole-wheat bread of the 1960s, the breads and other grain-rich recipes in this chapter reflect the innovations of this latest bread renaissance: the use of natural yeast and slow-rise dough, alternative grains, and freshly milled flours. It's a whole new world.

NOTE ABOUT BREAD-MAKING MEASUREMENTS

In the interest of accuracy, which is so critical when baking, most of the measurements for the bread recipes in this chapter are provided in grams only. In our baking classes, we always demonstrate how important this is by having our students measure out their flour using measuring cups. Then, one by one, we weigh the results. Needless to say, there are gasps all around when it becomes clear that they're all different—as much as 20 to 50 g too much or too little. An inexpensive digital scale is all you need to avoid this kind of error, which, when it comes to baking bread, can make the difference between success and failure. (Note: Where you do see ingredients measured in tablespoons and teaspoons, they're generally smaller amounts that either won't read on a scale or are flavorings that won't affect the bread's overall chemistry.)

There are so many tools available today for home foodcrafters making breads and bread-adjacent items. Many of them offer bells and whistles that are fun to play with, but in truth, grains have been prepared by hand for centuries with little more than bowls, spoons, and rolling pins (and the help of the local mill). However, we are admittedly suckers for new gadgets at the Institute and do love a good time-saver. Here are the essentials we swear by.

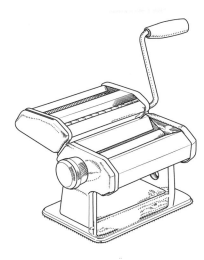

112

PASTA MAKER

Sometimes we like using the old-fashioned, made-by-hand techniques to make pasta, but rolling sheets of dough perfectly thin and cutting strands of pasta by hand takes time, practice, and patience. Do like the Italians do and use a classic countertop pasta maker, which usually comes with a cutter and turns perfectly even sheets of dough into spaghetti or linguine. Beginners may find hand-cranked models work best with two sets of hands, while electric options make it easy to create ribbons of lasagnette (narrow lasagna) while working solo.

TORTILLA PRESS

Living in Los Angeles, one is never too far from a neighborhood taco stand, and there are a couple near the Institute that employ *abuelas* (grand-mothers) to make fresh handmade tortillas, pressing them flat using only the palms of their hands. It's a technique not easily mastered by the uninitiated, and is usually handed down from one generation to another after years of practice and after having made literally hundreds of thousands of tortillas. Thankfully, the invention of the tortilla press makes the process much more approach-able for those of us without a mentor. Presses are typically made from two hinged metal or wooden plates, with a lever that presses them together to flatten small balls of masa (corn dough) into perfectly round, flat tortillas. You can find tortilla presses at Mexican grocery stores or online.

GRAIN MILL

Whole-grain flour is both nutritious and delicious, but because it contains the grain's bran, germ, and volatile oils (components that are stripped away in the refining process), it goes rancid fairly quickly. On the other hand, whole grains, left intact, are more shelf stable than flour and can be stored for up to 1 year under the right conditions—so why not grind your own in small batches as needed? Burr mills grind or crush flour between two plates, made from either stone or metal, and grind grains in a wide range of textures. Impact mills (aka micron-izers) have fast-spinning steel-toothed fins that pulverize grains into tiny pieces. They tend not to heat grains up as much as burr mills and can be a more economical choice, but they can also be quite loud. You also have the option of either a hand-cranked mill or an electric mill. Grinding flour by hand is a lot harder than you might think, so unless you really need the workout or are running "off the grid," we suggest electric if you're going to be milling more than the occasional cup of grain. Some high-end blenders can also grind grain, but this is not our favorite method because the friction of the blades (as opposed to a stone burr) really heats the grain up, potentially destroying nutrients and enzymes.

LAME

The score marks on a loaf of bread are not only decorative; they serve the necessary function of allowing the loaf to expand in the oven. Scoring your bread is also an opportunity to set your bread apart from all the others with your own creative imprint. A sharp, serrated knife will do the trick, but is difficult to control and can make for a wide, haphazard gash. A lame (pronounced LAHM, meaning "blade" in French) is a tool that holds an ordinary, thin, double-edged razor blade that slashes smoothly through sticky dough, allowing you greater control and flexibility in your scoring. We have multiple lames in our baking drawer, from homemade hacks (a double-edged razor blade slipped onto the end of a wooden coffee stirrer) to handmade artisan models with wooden handles.

HEIRLOOM GRAINS

It used to be that only a few, well-known grains were available to the home cook. Unusual heirloom flour was even less available. Now, local farmers are planting crops of formerly rare grains while consumers are rediscovering forgotten varieties of wheat and asking for more flour choices. Supermarkets are heeding the call and stocking new and (to many) exotic options. Here is an Institute-approved list of select grains that you can sneak into that ho-hum, all-purpose flour mix.

BARLEY

As grains go, whole barley is much harder than wheat or rye. It's so hard, in fact, that the most common commercial variety available is mostly made into pearled barley, which has had most of its outer bran and hull layer removed in order to make it easier to cook. Hundreds of years ago, whole barley flour was the main bread flour, well before the rise of wheat's popularity. Barley is also a high-protein/low-gluten flour that is worth a try. You can substitute up to 20 percent for other flours in a blend.

BUCKWHEAT

Even though the word *wheat* appears in its name, buckwheat is actually not a wheat at all, but rather, a seed from *Fagopyrum esculentum*, a flowering plant in the same family as rhubarb. Ubiquitous in Japan, where it is used to produce soba noodles, buckwheat is also popular in Eastern Europe as kasha—a roasted form of the seed used in porridges and pilafs. We like blending a bit of buckwheat flour into our wheat flour to add a hint of earthiness (see Buckwheat Parmigiano Crackers, page 140).

RYE

If you're used to working with wheat flour, you'll find rye flour to be a different beast entirely. Traditionally used in Eastern and Northern European breads and pastries, rye has long been considered the grain of the peasantry—due in part to its ability to thrive in relatively poor soil. Its low-gluten content means that breads made with rye tend to be more dense than those made with all wheat flour. Due to its high soluble-sugar content, rye doughs ferment more quickly and are a great choice for sourdough breads (see Fermented Rye Bread, page 131), adding a delightfully tangy depth of flavor.

SPELT

Spelt, an ancient European grain, is a cousin of wheat. It's sometimes labeled as farro, which is actually hulled wheat. There are three varieties: *Farro Piccolo*, an einkorn wheat; *Farro Medio*, an emmer wheat; and *Farro Grande*, which is spelt (see Spelt Pasta Dough, page 136). When milled, spelt holds its shape and texture like white flour but has a more interesting, nuttier taste.

WHITE SONORA WHEAT

When milled, White Sonora is a whole-wheat grain masquerading as a white flour. It's one of the oldest surviving wheat varieties in North America. It was widely planted by the Jesuits in 1800s California—for flour tortillas as well as communion wafers. Sonora has a lower protein content than traditional all-purpose flour, making it a less-than-ideal choice for baking a loaf of bread all by itself. Since Sonora is a "white" whole wheat, it's best used as a substitute for up to 50 percent of either an all-purpose or even a traditional whole-wheat flour, where its great taste can really shine.

NAN KOHLER
Dean of Grains

Professor Nan Kohler, the founder and sole proprietor of Grist & Toll, "an urban flour mill" in Los Angeles, is a true outlier. In terms of sheer creativity and "thinking outside the box," she has transcended all boundaries. The twenty-first-century maker movement that sparked a resurgence of artisanal mustard, jam, and coffee (not to mention the impetus for the Institute) pretty much overlooked grains and flour, at least initially. When Nan, who had formerly worked in the luxury wine sales business, left to create her own baked goods at a local farmers' market, she began to wonder why there were only two or three types of flour available for pastry chefs such as herself. Around the same time, Nan happened upon an episode of the PBS series *Gourmet's Adventures with Ruth*, in which famed food author Ruth Reichl visits an Italian village still growing and milling its own flour for breads and pizzas. A light bulb suddenly lit up over Nan's head: "How come no one has thought about bringing back traditional grain milling in the new maker movement?"

Inspired, Professor Kohler began researching grains and grain processing, meeting with local small farmers who had started planting heirloom grains in Southern California. These innovators were still experimenting, learning how to grow these different grain varieties while wondering if anyone would want to use them. Nan and other fearless home bread bakers took up the challenge, going where commercial bakeries feared to tread, figuring out how to bake with these grains. They discovered that these new/old flours were quite different from one another and from commercial flours. For instance, because these new grains could be thirstier than typical wheat, Nan and her colleagues had to adapt their recipes to include much more liquid, something that simply had to be puzzled out through trial and error.

Eventually, Professor Kohler took the plunge and opened Grist & Toll, her very own commercial flour mill, purchasing a handmade, 2,500 lb [1,134 kg] wood and stone grain mill from Austria. It was the first commercial flour mill to open in Southern California in over eighty years. Even though Nan opened Grist & Toll some time ago, the California Health Department, unaccustomed to seeing a real stone mill, is still tangling her operation in red tape to this day!

The Institute, of course, was a huge champion of Nan's project,

partnering with her on communal bread bakes with MOMO (Pomona College Professor of Art Michael O'Malley's mobile wood-fired, portable bread oven). Her flours have developed a passionate following among some of the best local bread bakers, and Nan, with her real-life revival of fresh grain milling in Los Angeles, has earned her place in the Institute's pantheon of extraordinary food pioneers.

TIPS FROM THE PROFESSOR

Begin exploring new-to-you grains with recipes you're already accustomed to, replacing small amounts of refined white flour with different varieties and whole grains. Bread recipes that call for typical, all-purpose flour respond well to having a bit of spelt added. You can also try substituting a little White Sonora flour to your favorite shortbread cookie recipe. You can even try baking a pastry crust with a touch of rye flour. See how these new flours perform—if you like the results, try a bit more next time.

SOURDOUGH STARTER "HOTEL" (PAGE 128)

FERMENTED RYE BREAD (PAGE 131)

OVERNIGHT SOURDOUGH KEFIR WAFFLES (PAGE 136)

RICOTTA SPELT RAVIOLI (PAGE 138)

CORN TORTILLAS (PAGE 140)

MATZO (PAGE 141)

MAX'S MATZO BREI (PAGE 142)

Sourdough Starter

Instant yeast is convenient, but it can't beat the delicious, complex flavor of sourdough starter as a leavening agent for bread. If you have a friend who bakes, you might be able to scrounge a ready-made starter from them. Ordering one online is also a possibility. But it's easy—and more fun—to start one yourself at home. Once you have an active sourdough starter, you can use it in recipes without having to remake the starter from scratch every time. Just make sure you feed it regularly. At the Institute, we operate a "hotel" for our staff and students whose sourdough starters need care when they go on vacation.

Whole-wheat flour, as needed

Filtered water, as needed

SPECIAL EQUIPMENT

Digital scale

1 pt [500 ml] mason jar (optional)

DAY 1

Place 100 g of flour in a 1 pt [500 ml] mason jar or other food-safe container with a lid.

Add 100 g of filtered water to the flour, stirring to combine.

Cover loosely with a lid and leave out for 24 hours at room temperature, preferably between 70°F and 80°F [21°C and 26°C].

DAY 2

Discard three-quarters of the previous day's flour and water mixture, then add 100 g of fresh flour along with another 100 g of filtered water to the jar, stirring to combine.

Cover loosely with a lid and leave out for 24 hours at room temperature, preferably between 70°F and 80°F [21°C and 26°C].

DAYS 3 TO 6

Repeat, discarding 75 percent of the previous day's mixture and adding fresh flour and water for the next 4 days. As the starter becomes active, it will establish a pleasant, yeasty smell and should start to rise and fall during the course of the day, forming bubbles of CO_2 on the surface.

Once the starter is active, it is ready to be used. When using in a recipe, be sure to always reserve at least 1 Tbsp of starter to keep it going (see Maintenance, below).

SOURDOUGH STARTER MAINTENANCE

Sourdough starter is a living creature and requires regular feeding. Once you've created your first batch and used a portion to bake with, continue to feed the remainder once a day, building it up for the next time you bake. If you bake bread only once every week or two, or if you begin to feel enslaved by the daily feeding schedule, you can put it to "sleep" in the refrigerator for a few days while you take a vacation from its care. When ready to "wake" it up before baking with it again, remove it from the refrigerator and follow the instructions from Day 2, repeating daily until it is bubbling and active again.

VARIATION: RYE STARTER

Once the starter is active, you can switch to feeding it whole rye flour (or white flour for that matter) instead of whole-wheat flour. Feed it regularly for 2 to 3 days with rye flour before using it in a recipe that calls for rye starter. You can switch flours back and forth in this way indefinitely, or you can maintain multiple starters at one time.

100 Percent Whole-Wheat Sandwich Bread

At the Institute Bread Lab, we've experimented with a wide range of techniques and grains, but somehow, producing a palatable 100 percent whole-wheat loaf always felt out of reach. Home and professional bread bakers alike warned us how difficult such a thing would be to accomplish. Many of us grew up eating only white bread, and it's still what feels familiar. I, however, was raised by a mother who happened to grow up in an early twentieth-century utopian society—didn't everyone's mother?—which predisposed her to the tenets of the 1960s "health food" movement. She sent me to school with sandwiches made on heavy, dense whole-wheat bread, which I called "Commune Bread." (It wasn't meant as a compliment.) Leaden, whole-wheat bread was just a fact of life in my world. In fact, when I first encountered a school classmate's lunchbox sandwich made on Wonder Bread, I squealed incredulously, "Your mother makes you sandwiches on pound cake?"

Knowing where your food comes from, sourcing whole, unprocessed ingredients, and reducing waste by using as many parts of those ingredients as possible is part of the Institute's ethos. Bread made from 100 percent whole-wheat flour, a whole grain with nothing removed, seems to be perfectly consonant with that manifesto. Enter Whole-Wheat Bread 2.0, lighter than my mother's and—while we're at it—in sandwich loaf form. While the recent maker movement has brought rustic boules, batards, and baguettes into vogue again, we thought it was time to give everyday sandwich bread the same treatment. We consulted with Dean of Grains Nan Kohler and think we came up with a winner.

While making this bread involves very little active time, there are a few things that need careful attention. The timing of each step may seem a bit rigorous, but rushing the process will result in an inferior product. With a bit of planning, you'll soon develop a rhythm to baking this bread, making it a nourishing ritual integrated into your life.

It's also worth noting that temperature plays a significant role in the bread's fermentation process. Warmer environments will speed up the process just as cooler conditions will slow it down.

YIELD: 1 LOAF

TOTAL TIME: 24 TO 42 HOURS (SEE SCHEDULING, PAGE 130)

STARTER

25 g active Sourdough Starter (facing page)

75 g whole-wheat flour

75 g filtered water, at room temperature

FINAL DOUGH

100 g active starter

475 g filtered water, at room temperature

500 g whole-wheat flour

10 g fine sea salt

SPECIAL EQUIPMENT

Digital scale

9 by 4 in [23 by 10 cm] Pullman loaf pan

PREPARING THE STARTER

Six to 12 hours before you plan to mix the dough, combine the starter ingredients in a medium bowl, mixing well. Once the starter is bubbly and pleasantly yeasty smelling (the timing depends on ambient temperature and how active your sourdough starter is), you are ready to proceed to the next step.

PREPARING THE FINAL DOUGH

In a large bowl, combine 100 g of the starter with 425 g of the filtered water, stirring with a wooden spoon until incorporated. Reserve the remaining starter for future loaves (see Sourdough Starter Maintenance, page 128).

Add the flour to the bowl and mix thoroughly to ensure it is well integrated and no dry particles remain, kneading the flour in with your hands, if necessary. Cover the bowl with plastic wrap or a clean kitchen towel and rest at room temperature for 1 hour.

Sprinkle the salt and the remaining 50 g of filtered water over the dough. Using a pinching motion with your thumb and index fingers, scissor through the dough to incorporate the water and salt. Rotate the bowl as you work, mixing until all the ingredients are well integrated, about 2 minutes. Cover the bowl and allow the dough to rest at room temperature for 30 minutes.

CONT'D

STRETCHING AND FOLDING

Uncover the bowl. With one hand, grab the far edge of the dough. Lift a portion straight up, stretching it gently, then pull the length of dough toward you, folding it down across the surface of the remaining dough. If the dough is too sticky to handle easily, you may want to lightly wet your hands with water, flicking off any excess. Notice the elasticity of the dough, as it will increase over the next few steps.

Rotate the bowl 90 degrees and repeat, turning the bowl each time, until all four sides of the dough have been stretched and folded. This is considered one "turn." Replace the cover and allow the dough to rest at room temperature for 30 minutes.

Repeat the stretch-and-fold process three more times at 30-minute intervals, replacing the cover and allowing the dough to rest at room temperature each time.

After the last 30-minute rest, stretch and fold the dough again, then allow it to rest, covered, for 1 hour. Repeat one final stretch and fold, then allow dough to rest, covered, for 1 more hour.

SHAPING

After the final 1-hour rest, turn the dough out onto a lightly floured work surface.

Lightly flour your hands and shape the dough into a ball by cupping your hands around the dough and tucking the outside edges underneath as you quickly rotate and drag the ball a few turns on the table. Do not lift the dough from the table; by dragging it, you create surface tension and the ball should begin to form a smooth surface on top. Invert the bowl over the dough ball to cover and allow to rest for 30 minutes.

Lightly oil a Pullman loaf pan and lid and set aside.

Uncover the dough and lightly dust with flour, then flip the dough over. Grab the left and right sides of the dough with the tips of your fingers, lift and stretch them gently, and fold them to meet in the center.

Starting with the side closest to you, begin rolling the dough away from you, forming a tight log. Pinch the seam closed and tuck underneath.

Lift and place the dough into the prepared loaf pan, seam-side down, stretching gently to fill the pan's corners, then slide on the lid. Enclose the pan in a plastic bag and place in the refrigerator for cold proofing overnight, or up to 16 hours.

BAKING

Take the loaf pan out of the refrigerator and remove the plastic bag. Allow it to sit at warm room temperature with the lid on for 2 to 4 hours, or until the dough has risen about 1 in [2.5 cm] below the rim of the Pullman pan or just above the rim of a standard loaf pan (see Loaf Pan Option, page 131).

Forty-five minutes before baking, place an oven rack in the lower third of the oven and preheat the oven to 475°F [240°C].

Place the covered loaf pan in the oven and bake for 25 minutes.

After 25 minutes, remove the loaf pan lid and rotate the pan, then lower the oven temperature to 450°F [230°C]. Continue baking for an additional 15 to 20 minutes, or until the crust is a beautiful chestnut brown.

Remove the bread from the pan and allow to cool completely on a wire cooling rack before slicing, about 1 hour.

SCHEDULING

It might seem like a lot of time, but the majority of the 24-plus hours it takes to make this delicious bread is hands-off, and there is a lot of leeway for adjusting the timing to fit your schedule. If at any time something prevents you from completing a step, just put your dough in the refrigerator, where it will continue to ferment and develop flavor, but at a slower pace. That said, with a little advance planning, it's easy to fit this bread into your regular weekend rotation, or even your weekdays if you have some flexibility. We at the Institute feed our starter in the morning, start mixing our dough by 4 p.m., put the bread and ourselves to bed around 10 p.m., then wake up early the next day to proof and bake before heading to the Lab. Presto!

We find it helpful to use a timing chart to keep track of all the steps. Here's a "cheat sheet" you can follow:

Feed Starter
    Rest 6 to 12 hours
Mix Dough Part I
    Rest 1 hour
Mix Dough Part II
    Rest 30 minutes
Stretch and Fold I
    Rest 30 minutes
Stretch and Fold II
    Rest 30 minutes
Stretch and Fold III
    Rest 30 minutes
Stretch and Fold IV
    Rest 30 minutes
Stretch and Fold V
    Rest 1 hour
Stretch and Fold VI
    Rest 1 hour
Shape Part I
    Rest 30 minutes
Shape Part II
    Rest 8 to 16 hours
Proof (and Preheat)
    2 to 4 hours
Bake
    40 to 45 minutes

LOAF PAN OPTION An alternative to a Pullman pan is a standard 8½ by 4½ in [21.5 by 11.5 cm] loaf pan with handles, with a second, identical pan inverted on top as a lid and secured with an all-metal binder clip on each handle.

VARIATIONS

Add-ins such as olives, dried fruit, and herbs, commonly added to white flour country loaves, will only be overpowered by the strong whole-wheat flavor of this bread. (Plus, it's worth remembering that this is really a sandwich loaf.) However, there's still room for a few tricks. Here are a couple of options to try.

SESAME SEEDS

Add 25 g of toasted sesame seeds right after the salt is added.

SEEDED CRUST

Before your final shape, place a clean, damp kitchen towel on the counter next to a large plate covered with untoasted seeds of your choice (think poppy, fennel, sesame, coriander, celery, sunflower, pepita, or caraway). After you've shaped your loaf and before baking, roll the top (non-seam) side against the wet towel, then into the seed mixture. Place the loaf into the prepared pan, seam-side down, and proceed with the recipe.

Fermented Rye Bread

This recipe comes from Institute faculty member Erik Knutzen. Channeling his Scandinavian roots, Professor Knutzen has developed this loaf with whole grains in mind. Doughs made with rye flour require less fermentation time than those made with wheat flour due to rye's higher acidity and greater percentage of natural sugars and enzymes.

YIELD: 1 LOAF

TOTAL TIME: 12 TO 26 HOURS (SEE SCHEDULING, PAGE 132)

STARTER

100 g rye flour

50 g active Rye Sourdough Starter (page 128)

100 g warm filtered water, preferably 105°F [41°C]

FINAL DOUGH

200 g active starter

500 g rye flour

500 g warm filtered water, preferably 105°F [41°C]

25 g molasses or brown sugar

12 g fine sea salt

1½ tsp caraway seeds

1½ tsp coriander seeds

1½ tsp dill seeds

1½ tsp fennel seeds

CONT'D

SPECIAL EQUIPMENT

Digital scale

Stand mixer (optional)

8½ by 4½ in [21.5 by 11.5 cm] loaf pan

Instant-read thermometer

PREPARING THE STARTER

Six to 12 hours before you plan to mix the final dough, combine the starter ingredients in a medium bowl, mixing well. Once the starter is bubbly and pleasantly yeasty smelling (the timing depends on ambient temperature and how active your sourdough starter is), you are ready to proceed to the next step.

PREPARING THE FINAL DOUGH

In the bowl of a stand mixer fitted with the paddle attachment, or using a large bowl and a wooden spoon, combine 200 g of the starter with the rest of the dough ingredients. Reserve the remaining starter for future loaves (see Sourdough Starter Maintenance, page 128). Mix on the lowest speed until the dough is fully blended and has a thick, batter-like consistency, 7 to 8 minutes. Alternatively, use a wooden spoon to thoroughly mix the ingredients together by hand until well blended.

Oil and flour a standard 8½ by 4½ in [21.5 by 11.5 cm] loaf pan, then spoon in the dough. Smooth the top with the back of a wet spoon or spatula and dust with rye flour.

Cover the dough with plastic wrap and allow to ferment for 2 to 4 hours at room temperature, until the dough has risen slightly. Bake immediately or cover tightly with plastic wrap and refrigerate for 8 to 12 hours before baking.

BAKING THE LOAF

Place an oven rack in the middle of the oven and preheat the oven to 425°F [220°C].

Place the loaf pan in the oven and bake for 45 minutes.

After 45 minutes, rotate the pan and reduce the temperature to 350°F [180°C]. Bake until the internal temperature of the loaf reaches 205°F [96°C], an additional 40 to 45 minutes.

Remove the bread from the pan and allow to cool completely on a wire cooling rack. Wrap it in a clean, dry kitchen towel or place it in a paper bag to rest for 24 to 48 hours before slicing (see Keeping Qualities, following).

KEEPING QUALITIES

Rye flour's tendency to absorb lots of water, along with the use of sourdough starter, keeps this bread fresh for a week to 10 days. The longer the loaf rests before slicing (up to 2 days), the better the taste, honestly! After it has cooled, and before it's been sliced, wrap the loaf and allow it to rest for 1 to 2 days. This allows the crumb to develop and lose the gummy texture it will have when it first comes out of the oven.

SCHEDULING

Since there's no kneading, this loaf comes together quickly. You can start it in the evening and finish it the next morning, or you could start it in the morning and finish it in the evening after work—even baking it the following morning. The fermentation times are flexible since you don't have to worry about the dough keeping its shape. If at any time something prevents you from completing a step, just put your dough in the refrigerator (which is kind of like hitting the pause button), where it will continue to ferment and develop flavor, but at a slower pace.

BREAD STORAGE

You might think we're a bit retentive addressing storing bread, but when you start baking your own, we guarantee you'll be storing more than you're used to.

NO REFRIGERATORS EVER!

First things first: The worst way to store bread is in the refrigerator. The dry environment will dry out your bread. For just a few days, it's better to leave your bread out on the counter, storing it cut side-down on the cutting board.

BREAD BOX OR PAPER BAG

For longer storage periods, do what your grandmother did and use a bread box. They really do help bread stay fresh longer, as they allow the bread to breathe without exposing it to the open air, which dries the bread out. If you don't have space for a bread box, you can simulate one by covering the bread with a clean, dry kitchen towel and then putting it in a paper bag. This method allows the bread to breathe while still protecting it from the elements. Sourdough bread will last up to a week at room temperature when stored this way.

FREEZING BREAD

For even longer-term storage, cut a fresh loaf in half, reserving half to store at room temperature and enjoy over the next week. To freeze the remainder, cut the rest of the loaf into slices and arrange them in a single layer on a baking sheet covered with wax or parchment paper, then transfer to the freezer for at least 1 hour, or until the slices are frozen solid. Once frozen, wrap the slices tightly in plastic wrap and transfer to a resealable plastic freezer bag, removing as much air as possible and sealing tightly to avoid freezer burn. When ready to eat, remove individual slices from the freezer as needed and pop directly into a toaster or defrost on the counter.

FOUR USES FOR STALE BREAD

One of the miraculous properties of sourdough bread is that it is highly resistant to mold growth. Breads made with commercial yeast, whether store-bought or homemade, will mold much more quickly—even when stored in the refrigerator or made with chemical preservatives. Scientists at the University of Alberta, in Edmonton, Canada, discovered that as part of the sourdough fermentation process, bacteria convert linoleic acid found in bread flour to an antifungal compound, essentially safeguarding against mold formation. Sourdough bread will still go stale (see Bread Storage, page 133, for tips on how to slow this down), but before you toss it, try upcycling those hard ends with some of the ideas below.

#1: BREAD CRUMBS

Why on earth purchase store-bought bread crumbs if you have stale end-slices you are thinking of tossing? Even if you have only a few pieces at first, save them in a paper bag or cloth sack until you've collected enough to use them for something. Sourdough bread can sit at room temperature for days, or even weeks, without molding; non-sourdough breads just need to be processed a little sooner. If you have leftovers from different grain loaves, get creative and make a mixed-grain bread crumb blend. Once you have your bag o' stale bread, pick your technique (following), then store in an airtight container at room temperature for up to a month or longer.

• Grate or pulverize dry, stale slices in a food processor using the grating disk or metal blade.

• If you are experiencing a bread crumb–making "emergency" during a power outage, place the stale bread in a strong plastic or canvas bag and pound with a rolling pin, hammer, or cast-iron skillet until the desired coarseness is achieved.

• Only have fresh bread? Make toasted bread crumbs. Place a single layer of bread slices on a baking sheet and bake in a low oven (around 250°F [120°C]) until completely dry, about 20 to 30 minutes depending on the freshness and type of bread, then proceed to one of the methods above.

• For seasoned bread crumbs, place dry crumbs in a skillet over medium-high heat and drizzle in a few drops of olive oil, adding herbs like rosemary or thyme. Toss the crumbs frequently and sauté until crunchy and golden brown, 4 to 6 minutes. Season to taste with kosher salt, then set aside to cool before storing.

#2: "IT'S ALIVE!" REHYDRATING STALE BREAD

Like Dr. Frankenstein's monster, stale bread can be briefly resurrected as a nice piece of toast by reintroducing moisture. This method works best with moderately stale bread—before it goes rock-hard.

Splash fresh water over the top and sides of dry, stale bread slices, until slightly damp.

Toast as usual in a toaster or oven until the bread is toasty and no longer moist. Be careful not to burn it.

Stale bread also makes the best French toast; follow your favorite recipe but allow the stale bread to soak in the custard a bit longer than you would fresh bread before frying.

#3: CROUTONS

If you managed to survive the crouton phase in the 1970s—congratulations. We think it's time for a revival, so we've officially decreed this the New Year of the Crouton. Instead of using tired old white bread for the same bland croutons, try our FlavorBar ideas (facing page) for combining various breads and spices to season them up.

Preheat the oven to 350°F [180°C]. Tear or slice stale bread into ¾ to 1 in [2 to 2.5 cm] cubed pieces.

Transfer to a large bowl, then toss with a splash of olive oil, a sprinkling of kosher salt, freshly ground black pepper to taste, and a few FlavorBar seasonings until the bread cubes are evenly coated.

Transfer the bread cubes to a baking sheet and bake in the oven until crisp and golden brown, 5 to 10 minutes. Use immediately or store in a sealed and covered jar for up to 5 days.

#4: ROASTED CHICKEN WITH INSTANT STALE BREAD DRESSING

Preheat the oven to 425°F [220°C].

Coat the bottom of a roasting pan, Dutch oven, or large cast-iron skillet with a thin layer of olive oil. Tear or cut stale, dry bread into large chunks and line the pan with them, creating a bed to catch the chicken drippings.

Season a whole 3½ to 4 lb [1.5 to 1.8 kg] chicken well with kosher salt, then stuff with onions and lemon slices and place on top of the bread chunks, showering everything with herbs and freshly ground black pepper, and adding chunks

of potato or other vegetables around the bird if desired.

Transfer the pan to the oven and roast until an instant-read thermometer inserted into the thickest part of the thigh registers 165°F [74°C], 50 to 60 minutes.

Remove the chicken from the oven and allow it to rest for 15 minutes before carving and

serving, making sure that each portion includes a piece of the chicken-infused bread dressing.

ANOTHER DRESSING OPTION
In place of plain or store-bought bread cubes, use the FlavorBar crouton ideas from #3 as a base for your favorite turkey dressing recipe and impress your guests on Thanksgiving Day.

FLAVORBAR

—

CROUTON IDEAS:

rye bread + caraway seeds

baguettes + garlic + grated Parmesan

sourdough + smoked paprika

whole wheat + parsley + sautéed shallots

Overnight Sourdough Kefir Waffles

Waffles are basically pancakes, all grown up and living in their first apartment (a waffle iron). Breakfast is one of our favorite meals at the Institute, and coincidentally, our students constantly bemoan the amount of starter and kefir that is discarded as they build their ferments, so this one is for them. Kefir replaces the traditional buttermilk, the acidic makeup of which activates the baking soda. Generic instant yeast is replaced with sourdough starter, which brings its own wild population of lactic acid bacteria and yeast to the party. In addition to being a resourceful way to reduce food waste, these waffles are extremely easy to make since they start the night before and require very little effort to finish off in the morning. **YIELD: 12 WAFFLES**

1 cup [140 g] all-purpose flour
½ cup [70 g] whole-wheat flour
½ cup [70 g] buckwheat flour
2 Tbsp sugar
2 cups [500 ml] Milk Kefir (page 172)
1 cup [240 g] active Sourdough Starter (page 128)
¼ cup [55 g] unsalted butter, plus more for serving
2 large eggs
1 tsp salt
1 tsp baking soda
Pure maple syrup, for serving

SPECIAL EQUIPMENT
Waffle iron

The night before you plan to make waffles, in a large bowl, add the flours, sugar, kefir, and sourdough starter, mixing gently to combine. Cover the bowl tightly with plastic wrap and allow to sit at room temperature overnight.

In the morning, melt the butter in a small saucepan over low heat, then set aside to cool.

In a small bowl, whisk together the eggs, salt, baking soda, and cooled melted butter. Add this to the flour mixture, stirring to combine.

Coat the waffle iron with nonstick spray and heat until very hot. Following your machine's instructions, pour the batter into the waffle iron, spreading it to cover the surface and being careful not to overfill. Cook the waffles until golden brown and cooked through.

Serve immediately with maple syrup and more butter.

NOTE: Extra batter can be made into waffles, then frozen and wrapped in two layers of plastic wrap. Reheat in a toaster or oven. Our favorite alternative is to simply refrigerate any unused batter. It will continue to ferment, but at a much slower pace, and will be good for up to 5 more days with an even more sour and delicious taste.

GILDING THE LILY: In addition to butter and maple syrup, think about other delicious toppings, such as Crème Fraîche (page 177), whipped cream, Greek yogurt (page 168), fresh berries, Domestella (page 40), or homemade jam (page 100).

Spelt Pasta Dough

Homemade pasta tastes completely different than store-bought, whether fresh or dried. While there are many delicious imported varieties, nothing compares with your own freshly made pasta dropped into boiling water. This whole-grain version is made from spelt, an ancient heirloom grain with a uniquely nutty flavor and a hearty, rustic "tooth." It is excellent whether cut into linguini and served with a simple sauce (page 322) or turned into ravioli and stuffed with a rich, herb-laced ricotta (page 138). We include a no-machine method, with instructions for kneading, rolling, and cutting by hand, as well as a faster method that calls for a food processor and hand-cranked pasta machine. The good news: Both make superior pasta. **YIELD: ABOUT 1 LB [450 G]; SERVES 4 TO 6**

2½ cups [350 g] whole spelt flour
1 tsp fine sea salt
3 large eggs, at room temperature
3 Tbsp olive oil

Food processor (optional)

Pasta machine (optional)

Bench scraper (optional)

Fluted pastry cutter (optional)

METHOD 1:
FOOD PROCESSOR/PASTA MACHINE

Add the flour, salt, eggs, olive oil, and 3 Tbsp of water to the bowl of a food processor fitted with the metal blade and process until the dough comes together, 20 to 30 seconds. If, after 60 seconds of mixing, the dough is not coming together, add water, 1 tsp at a time (or if it is very wet, add flour, 1 tsp at a time) and pulse until the dough is tacky and elastic but not sticky.

Transfer the dough to a lightly floured work surface, then pat it into a ball and wrap tightly in plastic wrap. Allow to rest at room temperature for 15 to 20 minutes.

After resting, uncover the dough and knead for 5 to 10 minutes on a lightly floured work surface, pushing and folding the dough away from you and turning at quarter turns.

After kneading, the dough should feel firm but smooth and supple. Pat the dough into a ball, wrap tightly in plastic wrap, and allow to rest at room temperature for 30 minutes.

ROLLING OUT WITH A PASTA MACHINE

Divide the dough into quarters, setting one piece aside to work with and keeping the remaining pieces covered, tightly wrapped in plastic wrap.

Set the pasta machine to its widest setting (number 1). Use your fingers to flatten the piece of dough into a 3 by 4 in [7.5 by 10 cm] rectangle and feed the shorter side through the rollers. After running it through the machine once, fold the dough in half or in thirds (like a letter) and repeatedly roll it through on setting 1 until you have a rectangular sheet of dough approximately 4½ in [11.5 cm]

wide. If the dough is too sticky at any point, dust both sides very lightly with flour.

Turn the machine's dial to the next narrower setting. Pass the dough through the rollers once. Continue passing the dough through the machine, progressively using the next finest roller setting, and stopping when the sheet is slightly translucent but still easy to handle. You should end up with a long sheet of dough approximately 5 in [13 cm] wide. If the sheet becomes too long to handle, cut it in half at any time. If the sheet becomes tapered at one end, feed the wider side through first. If the sheet becomes tangled or ragged at any point, it can be kneaded back together and re-rolled.

Lay the pasta sheet on a lightly floured baking sheet and cover with plastic wrap or a clean, slightly damp kitchen towel and set aside. Repeat with the remaining portions of dough, placing a piece of wax paper or a dusting of flour between pasta sheets to prevent sticking. Pasta can be cut immediately (see following) or wrapped tightly in plastic wrap and refrigerated overnight.

CUTTING PASTA WITH A PASTA MACHINE

When ready to cut the pasta, feed one sheet of dough at a time through the machine's cutting die of your choice, gently guiding the dough through. Dust the pasta lightly with flour if it wants to stick to itself, then gently coil the noodles on a lightly floured baking sheet and repeat with the rest of the pasta sheets. Pasta can be cooked immediately after cutting (see Cooking Pasta, page 138) or stored in an airtight container in the refrigerator for up to 3 days.

METHOD 2:
TRADITIONAL WOODEN BOARD

Arrange the flour in a mound on a wooden board or countertop and sprinkle the salt over the flour.

Create a well in the center of the mound and break the eggs into it, using a fork to beat the eggs thoroughly while maintaining the walls of the well.

CONT'D

Add the olive oil and 3 Tbsp of water to the eggs, beating to combine, then slowly begin pulling in and incorporating flour from the sides with the fork, creating a paste in the center of the well. At the same time, build up and maintain the wall of flour with your other hand.

At any point, switch to your fingertips to continue mixing. When the dough becomes stiff, use a bench scraper to scrape up the remaining flour and knead just until the dough comes together and all the flour is incorporated. If the dough is not holding, add water 1 tsp at a time, or if it is very wet, add flour 1 tsp at a time, until the dough is tacky and elastic but not sticky.

Pat the dough into a ball, wrap tightly in plastic wrap, and allow to rest at room temperature for 15 to 20 minutes.

After resting, unwrap the dough and knead on a lightly floured surface for 10 minutes, pushing and folding the dough away from you and turning at quarter turns.

After kneading, the dough should feel firm but smooth and supple. Pat the dough into a ball, wrap tightly in plastic wrap, and allow to rest at room temperature for 30 minutes.

ROLLING OUT BY HAND

Divide the dough into quarters, setting one piece aside to work with and keeping the remaining pieces covered, tightly wrapped in plastic wrap.

Use your fingers to flatten the dough into a rectangle.

On a lightly floured work surface, roll the dough with a floured rolling pin until it is as thin as possible. Dust with additional flour as necessary to prevent it from sticking. It should be almost translucent, but still easy to handle. You should end up with a long sheet of dough approximately 5 in [13 cm] wide.

Lay the pasta sheet on a lightly floured baking sheet and cover with plastic wrap or a clean, slightly damp kitchen towel and set aside. Repeat with the remaining portions of dough, placing a piece of wax paper or a dusting of flour between pasta sheets to prevent sticking. Pasta can be cut immediately (see following) or wrapped tightly in plastic wrap and refrigerated overnight.

CUTTING PASTA BY HAND

When ready to cut the pasta, place one sheet at a time on a lightly floured work surface, dusting the top of the sheet with flour as well.

For small, narrow pastas such as spaghetti, fettuccine, or linguine, start with the short, narrow end of the sheet. Tightly roll up the sheet of dough into a tube. With a sharp knife dipped in flour, slice the pasta tube to your desired width.

Unroll the coils of pasta, placing them on a floured baking sheet while you proceed with cutting the remaining flat sheets.

For wider types of noodles, use a fluted pastry wheel or a sharp knife to create a crimped edge when cutting the pasta sheet to your desired width. The crimping helps sauce cling to the pasta.

Pasta can be cooked immediately after cutting (see following) or stored in an airtight container in the refrigerator for up to 3 days.

BOTH METHODS:
COOKING PASTA

To cook, bring a large pot of heavily salted water to a rolling boil. Add the pasta and boil until al dente, 1 to 2 minutes, depending on size and thickness. Drain well and serve immediately.

Ricotta Spelt Ravioli

Traditional ravioli pasta dough is brought (without kicking and screaming) into the whole grains movement, and you get the chance to use your homemade ricotta in the filling; a pesto made from a bunch of fresh herbs, pine nuts, and more cheese. Bonus: Ravioli freeze well and can be simply dropped into a pot of salted, boiling water after a hard day's work. A glass of Barbera d'alba anyone?

YIELD: 30 TO 40 RAVIOLI; SERVES 4 TO 6

HERB PESTO

4 garlic cloves, peeled

3 cups [110 g] chopped, lightly packed mixed fresh herbs (such as parsley, chives, and basil)

½ cup [60 g] pine nuts

½ cup [50 g] grated Parmesan cheese

3 Tbsp fresh lemon juice

½ tsp lemon zest

1 tsp fine sea salt

½ tsp freshly ground black pepper

½ cup [125 ml] olive oil

FILLING

⅔ cup [150 g] Herb Pesto

⅔ cup [160 g] Ricotta (page 164)

½ cup [40 g] grated mozzarella

1 egg yolk, lightly beaten

¼ tsp fine sea salt

1 batch Spelt Pasta Dough [1 lb or 450 g], rolled into sheets and uncut (page 136)

Parmesan cheese, for garnish

SPECIAL EQUIPMENT

Food processor

Pastry brush (optional)

Fluted pastry roller (optional)

MAKE THE PESTO

In a food processor with the motor running, drop the garlic cloves through the feed tube. Process until the garlic is minced, about 10 seconds. Add the herbs, pine nuts, Parmesan, lemon juice, lemon zest, salt, pepper, and olive oil and pulse until smooth, scraping down the sides of the bowl as necessary. Pesto can be used immediately, or stored in an airtight container, covered with a thin layer of olive oil, for up to 5 days in the refrigerator.

MAKE THE FILLING

In a medium bowl, add ⅔ cup [150 g] of the herb pesto, setting aside the remainder for the sauce. Add the ricotta, mozzarella, egg yolk, and salt to the bowl and mix well to combine. If not using

immediately, cover and place in the refrigerator until ready to fill the ravioli.

FILL THE RAVIOLI

Keep pasta sheets covered with plastic wrap or a slightly damp dish towel until ready to use, taking out one sheet at a time. Lay a sheet of pasta on a lightly floured work surface and use a pastry brush or a soft cloth to brush the top of the pasta sheet lightly with water.

Spoon the filling in heaping teaspoons [about 8 g] along the long edge of the sheet, about 1 in [2.5 cm] in from the edge and leaving 1½ in [4 cm] of space between each mound.

Fold the dough in half lengthwise to cover the filling, pressing with your fingers all the way around each mound to eliminate air pockets and seal.

Use a fluted pastry roller or sharp knife to cut filled pasta into individual ravioli squares, then transfer them to a lightly floured baking sheet in a single layer and cover loosely with plastic wrap.

Repeat with the remaining sheets of dough.

Ravioli can be cooked immediately or wrapped tightly in plastic wrap and refrigerated for up to 2 days, or frozen for up to 1 month. If freezing, freeze in a single layer on a baking sheet, then transfer to a resealable plastic freezer bag, making sure to remove as much air as possible.

COOK AND SERVE THE RAVIOLI

Bring a large pot of heavily salted water to a rolling boil. Add the ravioli and boil for 1½ to 2 minutes, or until al dente. If using frozen ravioli, do not thaw; add to the boiling water directly from the freezer and boil for an additional 2 to 3 minutes or until done. Drain immediately, reserving some of the pasta cooking water.

Make a sauce by combining 1 part reserved herb pesto and 1 part pasta cooking water, stirring to combine.

Transfer the ravioli to warmed plates or wide, shallow bowls and drizzle the pesto sauce over the top. Garnish with a sprinkling of Parmesan cheese and serve.

Corn Tortillas

Fresh tortillas made with masa harina are totally different from the ones your typical grocery store carries. Masa harina, similar to hominy, is made from corn that is soaked in an alkaline solution, then ground and dried into flour. You can use a rolling pin to make the tortillas, but using a tortilla press (see Equipment, page 112) is easy and produces fantastic results. Tortillas are great for quesadillas and tacos, but we're also happy just smearing a fresh tortilla with butter and placing it directly on a stove burner until the edges have charred, then inhaling it over the stove. **YIELD: 16 TORTILLAS**

2 cups [280 g] masa harina, plus more as needed
½ tsp kosher salt

SPECIAL EQUIPMENT
Cast-iron griddle (optional)
Heavy-duty 1 qt [1 L] resealable plastic bag
Tortilla press (optional)

In a medium bowl, combine all of the ingredients with 1¼ cups [310 ml] warm water and mix with your hands or a wooden spoon, then knead the mixture until a smooth dough forms. It should hold together without sticking to your hands. If the dough is not coming together, add water, 1 tsp at a time (or if it is very wet, add masa harina, 1 tsp at a time), until the dough is tacky and elastic but not sticky.

Divide the masa into 16 equal-size pieces and roll each into a smooth ball. Cover the portioned dough with a damp kitchen towel to keep it from drying out.

Preheat an ungreased, cast-iron griddle or heavy, ungreased skillet over medium-high heat. While it heats, cut the zipper top and sides off the plastic bag, leaving the bottom seam intact. Working one at a time, place each ball of masa between the two squares of plastic and flatten into a small disk 5½ in wide [14 cm] using a tortilla press, or by placing a heavy cutting board over the top and pressing down with even pressure.

Transfer the pressed tortillas to the preheated griddle as you make them, cooking as many as you can fit at one time. Cook for about a minute on each side, or until the bottom is lightly browned in spots and the edges begin to curl slightly.

Wrap the cooked tortillas in a clean dish towel, stacking them as you go, to keep them warm and moist as you proceed with the remaining balls of masa. Though best eaten immediately, while still warm, tortillas can be stored, tightly wrapped, in the refrigerator for up to 1 week, or frozen for up to 1 month.

Buckwheat Parmigiano Crackers

If Cheez-Its (or Goldfish) crackers have been one of your guilty pleasures since childhood, this is the respectable adult version. Nutty buckwheat flour replaces most of the white flour, while Parmesan cheese adds a salty-savory note. While your childhood self might want to sink these crackers immediately into a bowl of soup (not a bad idea), we at the Institute have not yet made a batch that we didn't just eat straight out of the oven with a glass of crisp white wine. **YIELD: ABOUT 10 DOZEN SMALL CRACKERS**

⅔ cup [90 g] buckwheat flour
½ cup [70 g] all-purpose flour
¾ cup [75 g] grated Parmesan cheese
1 tsp kosher salt
¼ cup [55 g] unsalted butter, softened and cut into small pieces
⅓ cup [80 ml] ice water

SPECIAL EQUIPMENT
Food processor (optional)
Fluted pastry cutter (optional)

Preheat the oven to 350°F [180°C]. Line two baking sheets with parchment paper and set aside.

In a large bowl, combine the buckwheat and all-purpose flours, Parmesan cheese, and salt, mixing with your hands. Add the butter and use your fingertips to pinch and rub the butter into the flour mixture until it is well incorporated and the mixture resembles coarse meal. Add the ice water and mix and knead with your hands until the mixture comes together into a smooth, soft dough. Alternatively, place the ingredients in a food processor and pulse until combined and the dough holds together when pinched between your fingers. Transfer to a bowl and knead until smooth.

Divide the dough into two equal portions, cover the bowl, and allow the dough to rest for 15 minutes in the refrigerator.

Lightly dust a work surface with buckwheat flour. Working with one portion at a time, use a rolling pin to thinly roll the dough into a rough rectangle, about 1/16 in [1.5 mm] thick, dusting lightly with more buckwheat flour as needed to prevent sticking.

Use a fluted pastry cutter or a sharp knife to cut the dough into 1¼ in [3 cm] squares, then use the tines of a fork to prick the center of each piece.

Transfer the crackers to the prepared baking sheets, leaving ½ in [12 mm] of space between them. Bake for 10 to 12 minutes, rotating the sheets halfway through baking, until the crackers are golden on top and browned on the bottom.

Remove from the oven and transfer the crackers to a cooling rack to cool completely before serving. Crackers will crisp up in the first few minutes of cooling and should have a firm snap when broken.

Crackers can be stored in an airtight container at room temperature for up to 5 days.

Matzo

The traditional, kosher method for making matzo dictates that no leavening may be used. This commemorates the Passover story, in which the enslaved Jews had to flee Egypt in such haste that there was no time for their bread to rise before setting out. This tradition has been literally baked into the present-day ritual of making matzo for Passover: The entire process, from mixing to baking, must be completed in no more than 18 minutes. Any longer, according to rabbinical law, and

the wheat will begin to ferment, creating a natural leavening.

Growing up, my family did not keep kosher, but we did celebrate Passover and we looked forward to all the ways we would use up the leftover matzo after our seder. We'd snack for days—sometimes simply spreading the flat crackers with butter and ample pinches of salt, other times making Matzo Brei (page 142), an eggy breakfast dish. If you are used to only store-bought, commercially produced matzo, as we were, making your own from scratch opens up a completely new experience of what matzo can be. The boxed versions are thicker, rectangular, and mostly tasteless, while our (non kosher) variation here is thin, free-form, and full of flavor, thanks to the addition of olive oil and salt. With practice, you can even make it in under 18 minutes, but we're not going to time you.

YIELD: 4 MATZOS

2½ cups [350 g] all-purpose flour, plus more as needed

1 tsp kosher salt, plus more for sprinkling

2 Tbsp olive oil

SPECIAL EQUIPMENT

Pizza stone (optional)

Place a pizza stone or a large, heavy baking sheet on the lowest rack in the oven and preheat the oven to 500°F [260°C] for 45 minutes.

In a medium bowl, add the flour, salt, and oil, stirring with a fork or wooden spoon to combine. Add ¾ cup [180 ml] of water to the bowl, mixing until the dough comes together into a ball. Transfer to a lightly floured surface and knead with your hands until the dough is soft and smooth. If the dough is very sticky, add more flour, 1 Tbsp at a time (or if very dry, add water 1 Tbsp at a time), and knead until the dough can be rolled out without sticking.

Divide the dough into four equal portions, covering them with a clean kitchen towel to keep them from drying out while you work.

Working one at a time, place a ball of dough between two sheets of parchment paper and use a

CONT'D

rolling pin to roll it as thin as possible, making a rough disk, 8 to 10 in [20 to 25 cm] in diameter. Remove the top parchment sheet and lightly sprinkle the dough with salt, then replace the parchment and give the dough a final pass of the rolling pin to embed the salt. Uncover the dough and use the tines of a fork to prick the dough thoroughly over its entire surface to prevent the matzo from puffing up in the oven.

Using your fingertips or a long spatula, transfer the dough to a lightly floured pizza peel or the back of an extra baking sheet, then transfer to the preheated pizza stone or baking sheet in the oven. Bake until the matzo is golden on top, about 2 minutes, then use tongs or a wide spatula to flip it over and bake for another 1 to 2 minutes, until the other side is golden and crisp. A few of the edges may burn or blister, which is the true tell of a matzo master.

Remove the matzo and place on a cooling rack to cool completely. Homemade matzo may warp as it cools, for a rustic look; you can mitigate this, if desired, by placing a heavy cooling rack on top as a weight.

Repeat with the remaining dough portions. (You've got 18 minutes—go!)

Matzos can be stored in a paper bag at room temperature for up to 1 week.

Max's Matzo Brei

It seems like every Ashkenazi Jewish family makes their own particular version of matzo brei (Yiddish for "fried matzo"). Most often, the matzo is broken up into small pieces and soaked in hot water, then drained before scrambling in a hot pan with butter and eggs. In my family, usually after Passover when we had an extra box of matzos lingering in the pantry, my father, Max, had his own French toast–adjacent technique in which he fried much larger pieces of matzo flat in the skillet. The family loved it, and I still make it the same way, smothered with syrup or jam. **SERVES 2**

4 to 6 sheets Matzo (page 141)
4 eggs
Salt
Freshly ground black pepper
2 to 4 Tbsp butter
Maple syrup, honey, or a good fruit jam for serving

Fill a large bowl with boiling water and set aside.

Break the matzo sheets into large pieces, about 4 to 5 in [10 to 13 cm] each. Working with a few pieces at a time, dip them in the hot water until the matzos are damp and pliable, about 30 seconds for store-bought matzo. Homemade matzo will take longer, depending on the thickness. Transfer the dipped pieces to a colander to drain, then remove to a baking sheet lined with a clean, dry dish towel and set aside. Repeat with the remaining matzo.

In a medium bowl, add the eggs and use a fork to beat lightly. Season with salt and pepper to taste.

In a large skillet over medium-high heat, add 1 Tbsp of butter and heat until melted. Carefully dip one sheet of soaked matzo into the beaten egg mixture to coat both sides, then place it into the skillet, using a spatula if needed. Continue with additional pieces of egg-dipped matzo until the skillet is covered in a single layer.

Fry the matzo on one side until golden brown, 4 to 5 minutes. Flip the pieces over and fry until the other side is golden brown, another 3 to 4 minutes. Transfer the cooked matzo brei to a platter or plate. Repeat with the remaining matzo and fry in batches, adding more butter as needed.

Serve immediately, topped with maple syrup, honey, or jam.

DOMESTICA

Beginning in 1926, the Institute began publishing Domestica, a one-sheet quarterly journal offering tips, recipes, and news. The front page of the October 1933 issue (see facing page) features an open letter from founder and first director Eliza Taylor Reynolds, in which she announces her imminent retirement. (We couldn't help but notice that her rather florid writing, standard for her generation, is full of mixed metaphors, for which she apparently had quite a weakness.) Note that class tuition at the time was $2! (That's the equivalent of about $38 today.) Also note the recipe, the Institute's version of a frugal dish made popular (and sadly necessary) by the Great Depression. The recipe's author, Mrs. Beulah Howell, may have been too polite to refer to it by its pejoratively popular name, "Hoover Stew."

DOMESTICA

The Quarterly Journal of the Institute of Domestic Technology

VOLUME 7   OCTOBER, 1933   ISSUE 3

From the Director's Desk

By Mrs. Eliza Taylor Reynolds

**DEAR STUDENTS OF
THE DOMESTIC ARTS,**

When I founded our Institute back in 1911, little did I know that it would still be here so many years later, a brightly shining beacon of light continuing to thrive and grow like a mighty tree, even after the crash of 1929.

It has been with the greatest satisfaction that I have presided over an ever-expanding roster of highly skilled teachers and enthusiastic students, eager to share, learn and preserve the irreplaceable knowledge of our grandmothers and great grandmothers. As many of you know, I have worked tirelessly to advance the cause of our increasingly threatened domestic arts that have, like an orphaned bird, struggled against the rising tide of prepared foods in boxes, cans and jars.

Nevertheless, it is to you, our students, that I owe a debt of gratitude. For without you, none of my efforts would have mattered. And I know there is so much more that the Institute can and will accomplish.

It is therefore with some sense of poignancy that I announce that it is time for me to step down from the helm of the Institute and hand over the reins to a new director, our well-regarded and esteemed colleague, Miss Melinda McCracken. Rest assured that I will be leaving you in good hands, and that no matter what Miss McCracken might have said about me behind

...CONTINUED ON PAGE 2

OUR CLASS SCHEDULE

AUTUMNAL OFFERINGS AT THE INSTITUTE

**A THRIFTY
THANKSGIVING MENU**

DATE: Saturday, November 4
TIME: 10:00 am – 4:00 pm
TUITION: $2

———

**SOAP-MAKING
WITH SPENT COOKING OIL**

DATE: Sunday, November 5
TIME: 10:00 am – 4:00 pm
TUITION: $2

———

**HOME BUTCHERING IV:
PIGEON PREPARATION**

DATE: Saturday, November 11
TIME: 10:00 am – 4:00 pm
TUITION: $2

———

**RENDERING SUET IN TIME
FOR CHRISTMAS**

DATE: Sunday, November 12
TIME: 10:00 am – 4:00 pm
TUITION: $2

RECIPE CORNER

By Mrs. Beulah Howell

FRANKFURTER STEW

Our recipe for Frankfurter Stew takes advantage of all those delicious beans and vegetables you "put up" this past summer! For stuffing the frankfurters, we recommend either sheep or hog casings for best results.

INGREDIENTS

1 box elbow macaroni
1 jar each, home-canned whole tomatoes, corn or beans
6 frankfurters

DIRECTIONS

1. Boil macaroni until soft.

2. While the macaroni is boiling, slice the frankfurters very thinly, into round "coins."

3. Open the canning jar(s), retaining all the liquid.

4. Combine the frankfurters and contents of each can (vegetables and liquid) in a large pot. Bring to a simmer, breaking the tomatoes up into small pieces with a wooden spoon.

5. Drain the macaroni, reserving the cooking water to add to the pot. Add the macaroni, and continue simmering until the frankfurters are thoroughly cooked.

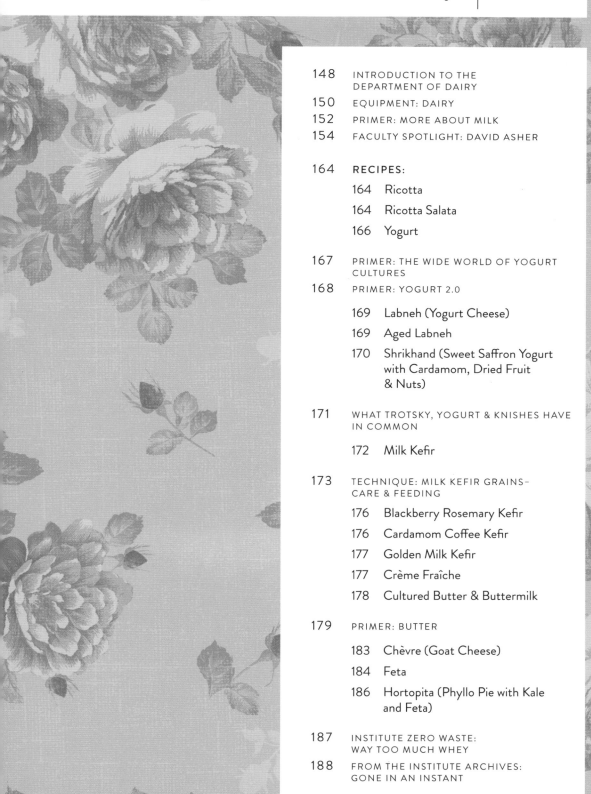

Department of Dairy | CH.05

THE DEPARTMENT OF DAIRY

The Institute's cheese and dairy classes are some of the most sought-after we offer. While we love all our classes equally (honest!), we do acknowledge the fascination and mystery of making your own cheese. Many of us have an understanding of how most ingredients are transformed into something new through culinary intervention. Flour and yeast become bread. Fruit and sugar become jam. But transforming milk into cheese just seems divorced from the contemporary home kitchen.

Homemade cheeses resemble none of the commercial products we're used to buying in the market, and many of them can be made at home with milk or cream that's in our refrigerators already. The process of making things from scratch not only gives us the opportunity to understand how they are made, but, if we pay attention, we are given a deeper appreciation of the ingredients we are using.

The Institute's first cheesemaking classes were taught by urban goat farmers Gloria Putnam and Steven Rudicel. They began making cheese in order to use up the excess milk from their small, backyard herd. Their cheese, made from fresh, raw milk straight from the day's milking, was amazing. But when they experimented with store-bought milk, both cow and goat, there were sporadic failures. They discovered that the way milk was commercially processed affected its ability to transform into cheese.

The more processed the milk, especially at higher pasteurization temperatures, the more likely that it would not transform into cheese. This informed our interest in researching the backstory on the store-bought milk we purchased for classes. Hopefully, you'll be curious to learn more about the milk you purchase. We've included a shorthand guide to get you started (see More About Milk, page 152).

When *The Art of Natural Cheesemaking* author and Dean of Dairy David Asher took over the cheesemaking program, we were introduced to his natural cheesemaking philosophy. David advocates for using raw milk* whenever possible and uses only natural bacterial cultures and rennet, eschewing laboratory-produced cultures and vegetarian GMO rennet. When raw milk isn't an option, David uses the natural bacterial cultures present in Milk Kefir (page 172) to inoculate milk and add flavor to cheeses and other fermented dairy products.

Once armed with this information, home cheesemakers can move on to discover how cheese and fermented dairy products are made and what the variances are that produce different types of cheese.

Almost all cheesemaking follows the same general steps. Milk is heated,

---

*For those wanting to avoid raw milk, or who live in areas that do not allow its sale, see More About Milk, page 152.

bacterial culture is added, followed by rennet. Once curds have formed, they are cut, possibly stirred, possibly heated again, then drained from the whey. They can be salted and eaten immediately or pressed into molds, air-dried, and aged. When any of these steps is altered, even slightly, a wildly different cheese is produced.

Other fermented dairy products are even simpler, involving only culturing milk at a certain temperature to produce yogurt, kefir, cultured butter, or crème fraîche. Our cheesemaking classes actually require a prerequisite of learning about dairy ferments first. It is the best introduction to transforming milk before moving on to cheese, and if you're new to cheesemaking, we encourage you to try dairy ferments like Crème Fraîche (page 177), Milk Kefir (page 172), and Yogurt (page 166) first.

One of the perks of having the Institute's early classes held on a goat dairy farm was that for the majority of the students, it was their first time meeting a goat, seeing her milked, and experiencing an udder-to-table cheese. But don't let not meeting a goat stop you from trying your hand at home cheesemaking. Armed with a bit of knowledge about the milk you source and after acquiring a natural culture or two, you will be well on your way to becoming a home cheesemaker. No backyard goat dairy farm required.

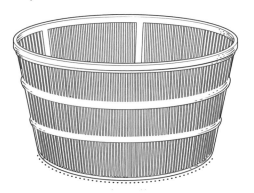

BUTTER MUSLIN

One of the most confusing pieces of equipment is the draining cloth known as butter muslin. Used to drain whey off of curds or other cultured dairy products, butter muslin's weave is finer than a metal fine-mesh sieve, but not as fine as traditional unbleached muslin found in fabric stores. Butter muslin has a 90-thread count, meaning that if you took a magnifying glass and a ruler, then counted across 1 in [2.5 cm] of the fabric, there would be 90 threads woven in each direction. It is possible to find other similar fabrics, such as gauze, voile, or even flour sack towels, that are the right weave; just bring your magnifying glass and ruler to the store—we have! The nice thing about butter muslin (as opposed to cheesecloth, see following) is that it's reusable. After using, rinse well with cool water and throw it in the wash. Avoid bleach, perfumed detergent, or scented dryer cloths, which could affect the flavor of your cheese. If you can't get them in the wash the same day you use them, soak them in a bucket of water until they can be washed.

CHEESE MOLDS

These come in multiple shapes and sizes. Most are basket-shaped with slits that allow the whey to continue to drain from the cheese. They also give cheese its shape, supporting the curds while they are knitting together. Commercially available molds are plastic, though we've commissioned ceramic artists to make them for us as well. We've also been known to upcycle strawberry baskets and plastic food containers drilled with holes when we're on the road.

CHEESECLOTH

While we acknowledge that this material has the word *cheese* in it, we rarely use it for cheese-making. It's great for draping over cheeses while they dry to keep dust and flies away, but in order to be used as a draining cloth, you'll need three to four layers of it to contain the curds. Then comes the worst part—you have to throw it away after one use.

YOGURT INCUBATOR

Yogurt needs to be incubated at a range hotter than room temperature, 110°F to 115°F [43°C to 46°C]. For the best results, maintain an even temperature during incubation and leave the yogurt in an undisturbed location where it won't be jostled.

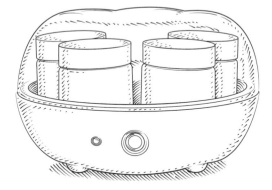

There are many yogurt makers on the market. They maintain the correct temperature simply by plugging them in. Some models are equipped with a timer, but they're all essentially an inoculation chamber with a heating element and a thermostat.

If you don't want to invest in a dedicated incubator, here are a few alternatives to try:

- An electric blanket, heating pad, or greenhouse seedling heat mat. Set your jars on the pads, then wrap with a towel or blanket to insulate and swaddle both the pad and jars.

- A sealed oven with the pilot light and/or oven light bulb left on.

- An insulated picnic cooler filled with enough warm (110°F to 115°F [43°C to 45°C]) water to submerge the jars halfway. Wrap the cooler in a blanket to maintain the heat. Check on the water temperature periodically, adding more warm water as needed.

Other ideas include a food dehydrator, electric pressure cooker, insulated soup thermos, or slow cooker with a low setting.

MORE ABOUT MILK

Those of us who shop at farmers' markets might know the provenance of our fruits and vegetables and maybe the names of our farmers, but we have no idea where store-bought milk comes from and what the differences in processing techniques are. We see the dancing cows, green pasture graphics, and the term *farm fresh* on the labels, but what does that really mean?

The Institute's beginner cheesemaking class starts with a blind milk-tasting exercise. Flights of shot glasses filled with different milks are set out, with each one described in detail as it is revealed. Here is a breakdown of what to look for when considering milk for cheesemaking.

RAW MILK

If you are lucky enough to live in one of a handful of states that legally allows the sale of raw milk, then keep reading. Raw milk has not been pasteurized or homogenized and therefore maintains all the integrity of the milk from the animal's udder. Raw milk contains healthy bacteria, normally killed during pasteurization, that give cheesemakers a leg up when it comes to developing flavor. Its calcium content has also not been altered, making it accessible for proper curd formation.

When following Professor David Asher's natural cheesemaking technique, we suggest the use of raw milk whenever possible. For those wanting to avoid raw milk (including young children and people with weakened immune systems), or who live in areas that do not allow its sale, we describe the other types of milk below.

SHELF LIFE

Shelf life is the length of time that milk can be held under recommended storage conditions—between 34°F and 38°F [1°C and 3°C]. Cheesemaking benefits from the freshest milk possible. I am not above being called a "Milk Maid," the character played by director Kevin Smith's mother, Grace, in the movie *Clerks*. In the dairy aisle, she pulls out all the bottles of milk in search of the freshest sell-by date—usually stocked behind the older bottles in front. The sell-by date listed on the container is voluntarily offered by the dairy, and while it is a good measure of the milk's shelf life, many products remain consumable for 2 to 5 days after the date. However, for cheesemaking, take a tip from Grace and seek out the freshest milk possible.

PASTEURIZATION

Pasteurization is the brief heating process that destroys raw milk's native microorganisms and any foreign bacteria that find their way into milk as it's handled. It also increases the milk's shelf life.

Here are the three most common pasteurization procedures:

Low Temp Long Time or LTLT
Milk is heated to 145°F [63°C] for 30 minutes, followed by a prompt chilling. Also called bulk pasteurization or vat pasteurization. Shelf Life: 8 to 14 days.

Next to raw milk, we've had the best results with non-homogenized LTLT milk.

High Temperature Short Time or HTST
Milk is heated to 161°F [72°C] for 15 seconds followed by a nearly instantaneous cooling to 40°F [4°C]. This is the procedure followed by most commercial brands and sometimes referred to as flash pasteurization. The container will be labeled as Grade A Pasteurized. Shelf Life: 10 to 21 days.

Due to the high temperature used in HTST pasteurization, the chemical structure of the milk changes, reducing the level of calcium, which is necessary for curd formation. A calcium chloride supplement can be added to the milk to compensate, but at the Institute, we do not advocate the use of HTST milk.

Ultra-High Temperature or UHT Milk is heated to 280°F [138°C] for 2 seconds. At this high temperature, the proteins in milk are destabilized and as a result, the calcium in the milk does not bond properly. UHT, also known as ultra-pasteurized milk, often has a cooked flavor when compared to LTLT or HTST pasteurized milk. Shelf Life: 30 to 90 days.

We do not recommend UHT or ultra-pasteurized milk for cheesemaking.

HOMOGENIZATION

Homogenization is the process by which the fat in milk is emulsified, preventing the cream from separating. It involves pumping hot milk at high pressure through a very small orifice, tearing the fat globules apart into smaller ones and evenly dispersing them in the milk. It also gives milk a longer shelf life.

Whenever possible, we recommend seeking out non-homogenized milk. It is also called cream-top, and you can actually see a plug of cream at the top of the bottle. Another advantage of non-homogenized milk is that the fat content will tend to be higher, producing cheeses with much more body and richness.

FAT CONTENT

During high-temperature short-time (HTST) pasteurization processing, milk first enters a heat exchanger. The heat exchanger heats the cold milk using the residual heat from milk that has previously been pasteurized. The milk fat is then separated out and, depending on the type of milk to be made, added back in at the minimum required level, all in the name of standardization. The USDA requires whole milk to have a minimum milk fat content of 3.25 percent. What's hidden behind that information is that when you look at, for example, two popular milk-producing cow varieties, you'll find they produce milk with more than 3.25 percent fat content: A Holstein cow produces milk with a 3.69 percent milk fat content. A Jersey cow produces milk with a fat content of 4.80 percent.

Where, you may ask, is the remaining fat percentage going? The excess cream is going toward making butter, ice cream, or cartons of heavy cream. You'll discover that the price of nonfat and skim milk is also the same price as whole milk. While this allows dairy farmers a chance to recoup some of their dwindling profits with a higher profit margin on those products, it also justifies the higher price of non-homogenized milk with a full fat content.

ORGANIC MILK

USDA organic milk standards prescribe that cows must be able to graze on plenty of fresh grass and spend at least four months a year grazing in pastures. The cows cannot be treated with hormones or antibiotics, and their feed must be grown without chemical fertilizers, pesticides, or genetically modified seeds.

Unfortunately, most large organic milk processors use ultra-high temperature pasteurization to prolong the shelf life due to organic milk's higher cost. If you can find non-homogenized organic milk, there's a good chance that the dairy uses low temp long time pasteurization methods, which is our method of choice when raw milk is not being used. Look for "LTLT," "bulk pasteurization," or "vat pasteurization" on the label or on the dairy's website.

DAVID ASHER
Dean of Dairy

Professor David Asher is an organic farmer, farmstead cheesemaker, and cheese educator based on the Gulf Islands of British Columbia, Canada. A guerrilla cheesemaker, David does not make cheese according to standard industrial philosophies—he explores traditionally cultured and more organic methods of cheesemaking.

David believes that making our own cheese naturally assures us that the ingredients used and the processes involved are up to our own exacting standards, and that making cheese reconnects us with the land, the livestock, and the farmers that feed us.

We connected with David while he was on tour promoting his book, *The Art of Natural Cheesemaking*. After he led a series of workshops for us, we adopted his natural cheesemaking approach, reinventing our fermented dairy and cheesemaking program based on his teachings.

How cheese is made already is a mystery to most people, but thankfully David's techniques have simplified the process. Eliminating complicated equipment and creating your own bacterial cultures has made teaching cheesemaking more approachable and exciting for students, as well as for Institute faculty.

TIPS FROM THE PROFESSOR

Consider that cheesemaking happens naturally inside the stomachs of young cows, goats, and sheep that drink their mothers' milk. Their stomachs produce enzymes and acids that curdle their milk into cheese, which makes the milk more digestible as a solid than as a liquid.

When you're making cheese, you'll want to take this context to heart. For instance: When a calf goes to drink its mother's milk, the milk goes right from the udder straight to its stomach. The milk isn't pasteurized, homogenized, or refrigerated along the way—if it were, the animal would have trouble digesting the milk, as it would have been changed by the processing and would lose much of its nutrition, as well as its essential structure. If you get milk that's as fresh as possible, and has been processed as little as possible, that milk will transform into cheese much more readily, and it will taste better, too.

RICOTTA (PAGE 164)

SHRIKHAND (SWEET SAFFRON YOGURT WITH CARDAMOM, DRIED FRUIT & NUTS) (PAGE 170)

FLAVORED MILK KEFIR (PAGE 176)

MILK KEFIR GRAINS (PAGE 173)

BUTTER HACKS (PAGE 179)

CHÈVRE (GOAT CHEESE) (PAGE 183)

FETA (PAGE 184)

HORTOPITA (PHYLLO PIE WITH KALE AND FETA) (PAGE 186)

Ricotta

Ricotta is one of the gateway homemade cheeses. It's so easy to make, and you can make it the same day you plan to serve it. Traditionally, ricotta is made by reheating leftover whey from other cheeses, hence its name in Italian means "recooked." At the Institute, we begin each cheesemaking series with this recipe. It's a shortcut that uses whole milk instead of whey since we figure most beginners are not going to have a few gallons of whey lying around. See the Ricotta Bar (facing page) for serving suggestions, and also consider taking the recipe a step further by pressing, salting, and aging it into Ricotta Salata (right). **YIELD: ABOUT 1 LB [450 G]**

1 gl [4 L] whole cow milk, not ultra-pasteurized (see Primer, page 152)
½ tsp fine sea salt, plus more for seasoning
¼ cup [60 ml] distilled white vinegar, plus more as needed

SPECIAL EQUIPMENT

Butter muslin

Instant-read thermometer

Line a colander with a piece of dampened butter muslin and place inside a larger bowl. Set aside.

In a heavy, 5 qt [5 L] nonreactive pot over medium-low heat, combine the milk and salt and heat to 190°F [88°C], stirring occasionally to prevent scorching on the bottom of the pot.

When the milk reaches temperature, gently stir in the vinegar. Cover the pot and turn off the heat, then let it sit undisturbed in order to allow curds to form, 8 to 10 minutes.

After resting, open the lid and you should be able to see the coagulated curds separated from the yellowish whey. If not, add an additional 1 to 2 Tbsp vinegar, stirring gently to incorporate. Replace the lid and allow to sit for another 10 minutes.

Once the curds have separated, use a finely slotted spoon or mesh skimmer to gently scoop the curds from the pan and transfer them to the butter muslin–lined colander. Discard the leftover whey, or see Way Too Much Whey, page 187.

Sprinkle additional salt over the curds, ¼ tsp at a time, tossing gently to incorporate and tasting as you go until satisfied with the flavor.

Let the curds drain at room temperature for 5 minutes to 1 hour, depending on how moist you prefer the final product.

Ricotta can be served immediately or transferred to an airtight container and stored in the refrigerator for up to 4 days.

Ricotta Salata

Ricotta salata is a hard, white cheese made by pressing, salting, and aging fresh ricotta. It's easy to make, but you'll need to be patient while it dries and ages in the refrigerator for 8 days. Make two batches and let one age for even longer, up to 2 months, for even more depth of flavor. When finished, it has a salty flavor similar to feta, but can be used in the same way you would use Parmesan or Pecorino Romano, shaving it over salads, pizzas, pastas, or vegetable dishes. **YIELD: ½ LB [225 G]**

1 batch Ricotta (left), about 1 lb [450 g]
Fine sea salt

SPECIAL EQUIPMENT

Butter muslin

4½ in [11.5 cm] wide by 3 in [7.5 cm] high cheese mold, or upcycle a 16 oz [473 ml] round, food-safe plastic container (such as a sour cream tub) with as many drainage holes drilled on the sides and bottom as possible

1 pt [500 ml] mason jar

Cheese paper (optional)

DRAINING & MOLDING

Make a draining tray by placing a wire cooling rack on a rimmed baking sheet. Line a round cheese mold with a piece of dampened butter muslin and place it on the tray.

Place the well-drained ricotta into the prepared mold, making sure to gently press it into the corners of the mold. Fold the overhanging flaps of muslin over the top of the curds.

Place a sealed, 1 pt [500 ml] mason jar filled with water on top of the cheese to act as a press.

After 1 hour, remove the weight and lift the wrapped cheese from the mold, unwrap it, and flip it over. Rewrap the cheese in the butter muslin, then place it back in the mold and replace the weight. Return the cheese to the draining rack, then transfer the whole setup to the refrigerator for 12 hours.

Remove the cheese from the mold, unwrap, and sprinkle with the salt, making sure to cover all surfaces. Rewrap the cheese with a clean piece of butter muslin, return it to the mold, and set it back on the draining rack without the weight. Refrigerate for another 12 hours.

DRYING & AGING

Take the cheese out of the butter muslin and rub salt over all of its surfaces. Flip it over and return it to the mold without the cloth, then place it back in the refrigerator.

Repeat, salting and flipping the cheese once a day for 3 more days, then remove the cheese from the mold and continue salting and flipping for an additional 4 days, allowing it to age directly on the draining rack in the refrigerator.

Once this initial aging process is complete, brush off any remaining salt from the surface and enjoy the cheese immediately or continue to age it, wrapped in cheese paper in the refrigerator for up to 2 months. If you encounter mold on the surface during this final aging process, wipe it off with a clean, damp cloth and give the surface another salting.

RICOTTA BAR

Fresh ricotta is called for in a few recipes throughout the book, but we love it so much at the Institute we wanted to include a few more serving suggestions to prove how versatile this easy-to-make cheese is to use. The other ricotta recipes in the book are Ricotta Coffee Cream (page 67) and Ricotta Spelt Ravioli (page 138).

Serve fresh ricotta on a thick slice of crusty bread with a few grinds of black pepper and a drizzle of fruity olive oil.

For dessert, mix ricotta with fresh figs and a drizzle of raw honey. Top with toasted pine nuts and a pinch of Maldon sea salt.

Purée mixed berries with powdered sugar and lemon juice and drizzle on top of ricotta served in dessert glasses.

Yogurt

With so much to say about yogurt, we're going to start with the basics: heat milk, cool, add yogurt culture, incubate till tangy, refrigerate. Set some aside for the next batch and repeat. This describes a rhythm performed for thousands of years through-out Yogurtistan (see The Wide World of Yogurt Cultures, facing page) and now in homes around the world. Supermarkets now have entire aisles dedicated to yogurt brands, many of them laden with sugar, thickeners, and, at worst, containing no live cultures. Making your own yogurt allows you to choose the quality of milk you start with, and, if you can source an heirloom culture, as we did with Yonah (see What Trotsky, Yogurt & Knishes Have in Common, page 171), you'll end up with something available only in your personal kitchen.

YIELD: TWO 1 PT [500 ML] MASON JARS

1 qt [1 L] whole cow milk, not ultra-pasteurized (see Primer, page 152)

1 Tbsp live yogurt culture (see Primer, facing page)

SPECIAL EQUIPMENT
Two 1 pt [500 ml] mason jars
Instant-read thermometer

Wash two 1 pt [500 ml] mason jars in warm soapy water, rinse well, then keep them warm while you prepare the milk.

In a heavy, nonreactive medium pot over medium heat, bring the milk to 180°F [82°C], stirring occasionally with a wooden spoon to prevent scorching on the bottom of the pan.

When the milk reaches temperature, remove from the heat and cool to between 110°F and 115°F [43°C and 46°C], stirring occasionally. This can take 30 minutes or longer at room temperature, but you can speed the process along by placing the pot in a sink full of cold water or an ice bath (a large bowl filled with roughly equal parts ice and water).

Place the yogurt culture in a small bowl. This is your "starter." Pour 1 cup [250 ml] of the cooled milk into the starter and whisk to dissolve thoroughly, then stir the dissolved starter mixture back into the pot of milk.

Carefully pour the inoculated milk into the warmed 1 pt [500 ml] jars and place the jars in the incubator of your choice (see page 151). Allow the milk to incubate, undisturbed, while maintaining a temperature between 110°F and 115°F [43°C and 46°C], being careful not to jiggle or shake the containers until the yogurt has transformed into a delicate, custard-like consistency. This can take anywhere from 4 to 8 hours depending on the strength of the yogurt culture, consistency of temperature, and quality of milk.

When the yogurt is ready, remove 1 Tbsp from one of the jars to save as the starter for your next batch. Store it, carefully labeled, in a separate airtight container in the refrigerator.

Yogurt can be stored, tightly sealed, in the refrigerator for up to 1 month.

THE WIDE WORLD OF YOGURT CULTURES

Sourcing a starter culture to begin your yogurt-making journey can be as simple as a trip to the supermarket, or as adventurous as tracking down obscure heirloom strains with rich, multigenerational stories attached. Each one will taste a bit different, ferment differently, and have its own story.

STORE-BOUGHT PLAIN YOGURT CONTAINING LIVE CULTURES
The supermarket is overflowing with all types of yogurt. The first step is to identify a plain yogurt that contains live cultures. Some brands of commercially produced yogurt have been pasteurized after the initial fermentation to prolong shelf life, essentially killing off the beneficial live cultures. Check the label to make sure it reads "contains live cultures." The advantages of store-bought yogurt are its easy availability and its price. The disadvantage is that, as you hold back 1 Tbsp of yogurt each time to start the next batch, after a few batches you'll begin to notice the "set" of the yogurt becoming weaker, producing a thinner final product. This is due to the fact that commercial producers add only a few bacterial yogurt strains to the milk, not enough to create a vibrant and diverse community of healthy bacteria strong enough to live from yogurt batch to yogurt batch. It's not a huge inconvenience, but you will need to periodically purchase a fresh container of yogurt to use as your new starter.

FREEZE-DRIED CULTURES
Available online, these are a handful of cultures grown in a laboratory, then freeze-dried. They last quite a while when kept in the freezer and contain a slightly more diverse population of concentrated cultures than supermarket yogurt. The advantages are that they are convenient and provide a consistent "set" every time. The disadvantages are that they are expensive and many varieties must be replenished over time if you develop a regular yogurt-making routine. They are also made in a laboratory and, depending on your thoughts and feelings about Man vs. Nature, you may not feel 100 percent excited about them.

HEIRLOOM CULTURES
These are the cultures that yogurt folklore is made of. Thousands of years ago, milk was being fermented throughout "Yogurtistan," a term coined by Anne Mendelson, author of *Milk: The Surprising History of Milk Through the Ages,* for a swath of the globe encompassing most of the Middle East and West Asia, which very likely may be the birthplace of yogurt. The warm weather–loving bacteria present in yogurt from these climates have mutated and adapted for centuries, making them incredibly resilient. They also like to live in diverse communities comprised of hundreds of different strains, just in case some of the weaker ones die off. Many of these heirloom cultures have survived for hundreds of years; therefore the advantage is that they are tough and do not need to be replaced after a few batches of yogurt making. They also have a more complex taste due to their diverse bacterial population, with varieties ranging in the hundreds, as opposed to the handful of bacteria varieties in the supermarket or laboratory versions.

Heirloom yogurt cultures can be found online, through fermentation groups on social media, and quite possibly from neighbors in your own community whose ancestors are originally from Yogurtistan.

YOGURT 2.0

FLAVORED YOGURT

Heat a few tablespoons of your favorite jam to 110°F [43°C], then spoon into the bottom of your yogurt-making container before adding the inoculated milk. You can also add maple syrup, vanilla, a mixture of cocoa powder and sugar, or Cold Brew Coffee Concentrate (page 66) and sugar to the milk when you add the culture. Proceed to incubate the jars as directed. (Be sure to make a small amount of plain yogurt as well, to ensure you have plain yogurt to start your next batch.)

SUPER RICH YOGURT

You only live once! Substitute ½ cup [125 ml] of heavy cream for ½ cup [125 ml] of the milk. Try to source non–ultra-pasteurized cream if you can. It will be labeled "pasteurized" or "Grade A."

GREEK YOGURT

Line a colander with a piece of dampened butter muslin and place inside a larger bowl. Pour the finished yogurt into the colander, straining the whey into the bowl. Let drain for about 30 minutes or until the whey has considerably slowed its dripping and the consistency of the yogurt is similar to a thick sour cream.

YOGURT WHEY

The whey that drains from the yogurt can be made into a refreshing drink. Combine 3 cups [750 ml] cold whey with the juice of 1 lemon or lime, 1 Tbsp maple syrup, and ¼ tsp ground cardamom. Or, use the whey to jump-start other fermentation projects, such as Fermented Ketchup (page 32) or Sauerkraut (page 278). (See also Zero Waste: Way Too Much Whey, page 187.)

Labneh (Yogurt Cheese)

Take your yogurt a step further by turning it into a thick, spreadable cheese called *labneh*. Labneh is made by draining much of the whey from yogurt and is a popular ingredient in the Middle East. Try spreading it on toast, topped with honey, jam, and chopped nuts. **YIELD: 2 CUPS [500 ML]**

1 qt [1 L] plain, whole milk yogurt (page 166)

SPECIAL EQUIPMENT

Butter muslin

Line a colander with a piece of dampened butter muslin and place inside a larger bowl. Pour the yogurt into the colander, allowing the whey to drain into the bowl until it has completely stopped dripping and the labneh is the texture of a thick spread, anywhere from 6 to 24 hours.

You can speed up the draining process by gathering the four corners of the butter muslin and tying them into a bundle that can be hung from the handle of a long wooden spoon set over a deep pot. Another technique is to place a clean weight on top of the yogurt as it sits in the colander (fold the flaps of the butter muslin over the yogurt first). With any method, the draining process will go faster at room temperature and a bit slower in the refrigerator.

Labneh can be used immediately or transferred to an airtight container and stored in the refrigerator for up to 1 month.

Aged Labneh

When regular labneh is drained even further, you get aged labneh, which is much thicker. In this version, aged labneh is rolled into balls and stored in herbed olive oil, ready to use as an appetizer with cocktails. **YIELD: 1 PT [500 ML]**

2 cups [500 ml] Labneh (left)
½ tsp fine sea salt
Olive oil
Herbs and flavorings of your choice (optional)

SPECIAL EQUIPMENT

1 pt [500 ml] mason jar

In a medium bowl, add the labneh and salt, mixing thoroughly to combine. The salt will facilitate the draining of even more whey.

Line a colander with a piece of dampened butter muslin and place inside a larger bowl. Transfer the labneh to the colander, folding the butter muslin flaps lightly over the top, and place the whole setup in the refrigerator. Allow the whey to drain until it has completely stopped dripping and the labneh is the texture of a spreadable cheese, 2 to 3 days. It should be firm and no longer tacky to the touch.

Lightly coat your hands and a plate with olive oil. Scoop up the labneh 1 Tbsp at a time and roll it into balls in the diameter of your choice; golf ball–size is traditional. Set the balls on the oiled plate as you roll them. Re-oil your hands as necessary.

If the balls are a bit sticky when you are done, briefly refrigerate the plate before carefully transferring the cheese balls to a 1 pt [500 ml] jar. If desired, add 1 to 2 tsp mixed flavorings of your choice, such as dried oregano, Za'atar (a sumac-thyme-sesame spice mixture), dried garlic, or Aleppo pepper powder. Bay leaves and dried chiles are also welcome.

Cover with enough olive oil to submerge the labneh balls.

Aged labneh balls can be enjoyed immediately or sealed tightly and stored in the refrigerator for up to 3 weeks. The oil will congeal around them, so be sure to let the jar sit at room temperature long enough to liquefy the oil before serving.

Shrikhand (Sweet Saffron Yogurt with Cardamom, Dried Fruit & Nuts)

Yogurt is such a versatile dairy product. It's delicious in both savory preparations and sweet dishes like this one, where it is the perfect vehicle for flavors like saffron, cardamom, rose water, and pistachios. Thick and creamy *shrikhand*, pronounced "Shree-kand," is a traditional Indian dessert, to which we've added crème fraîche for extra decadence. Feel free to experiment with other flavor combinations for the toppings and explore your own creative ideas using this recipe as a guide. **SERVES 6**

1 qt [1 L] plain, whole milk Yogurt (page 166)
Pinch of saffron threads, about 8 threads
1 cup [240 g] Crème Fraîche (page 177)
¼ cup [30 g] powdered sugar, sifted
1 tsp rose water
½ tsp ground cardamom

TOPPING

¼ cup [35 g] pistachios
3 large Medjool dates
6 dried apricots (page 321)
Two 1 by 3 in [2.5 by 7.5 cm] strips orange zest
½ tsp dried rose petals (optional)

SPECIAL EQUIPMENT

Butter muslin

Line a colander with a piece of dampened butter muslin and place inside a larger bowl. Pour the yogurt into the colander, folding the butter muslin flaps over the top, and place the whole setup in the refrigerator.

Allow the yogurt to drain in the refrigerator for several hours or overnight until you have roughly 3 cups [720 g] of very thick yogurt and about 1¼ cups [310 ml] of drained whey. The yogurt should be thicker than Greek yogurt but softer than cream cheese. You can speed up the draining process by gathering the four corners of the butter muslin and tying them into a bundle that can be hung from the handle of a long wooden spoon set over a deep pot.

Reserve 1½ tsp of whey, discarding the rest (or see Way to Much Whey, page 187), and place it in a small bowl with the saffron threads, allowing them to bloom in the liquid for 10 minutes.

In a medium bowl, combine the drained yogurt, crème fraîche, powdered sugar, rose water, cardamom, and bloomed saffron with threads, whisking well to incorporate the flavors and dissolve the sugar.

Cover and chill in the refrigerator, allowing the flavors to infuse for a minimum of 3 hours or up to overnight. The flavors, particularly the saffron, will continue to bloom and intensify as it rests.

Twenty minutes or so before you are ready to serve, prepare the topping. Place the pistachios in a dry, heavy-bottomed skillet over medium heat and toast, stirring frequently, until fragrant and lightly toasted. Transfer to a plate and allow to cool before coarsely chopping.

Chop the dates and apricots into a ¼ in [6 mm] dice. Stack the strips of orange zest on top of one another and finely slice crosswise into thin chiffonade strips. Crumble the dried rose petals, if using, between your fingers.

To serve, divide the chilled yogurt mixture evenly between six bowls and garnish with the toppings. Serve immediately.

WHAT TROTSKY, YOGURT & KNISHES HAVE IN COMMON

A wonderful story of an heirloom yogurt culture's resilient life span was passed along to Institute students by visiting professor Sandor Katz during one of his fermentation classes.

In 1917, the famous Marxist revolutionary Leon Trotsky was living in exile in the Bronx, and was rumored to love the yogurt served at a knishery he frequented on the Lower East Side of Manhattan, founded by a Romanian Jewish immigrant named Yonah Schimmel.

Schimmel opened his eponymously named restaurant in 1910, serving yogurt made from an heirloom culture he had brought over on the boat from Romania. Not only could Trotsky enjoy Schimmel's yogurt, but, as of the writing of this book, so can you. Yonah's knishery still exists in its original location on Houston Street and continues to make yogurt from the *very same* culture.

This story continues with a mention of Yonah Schimmel's yogurt in Sandor Katz's book *Wild Fermentation*. Eva Bakkeslett, a Norwegian friend of Sandor's, having read his account of Yonah Schimmel's heirloom yogurt culture, went to the knishery while visiting New York, ordered the famed yogurt, and took home a sample in a jar. Years later, Eva brought some of her Yonah Schimmel culture to an event in England where she and Sandor were teaching together. Sandor decided to bring some back home with him to Tennessee, experimenting with a method he had heard about: dipping a clean handkerchief into the yogurt and allowing it to dry. Once home, the hanky got buried on his desk and forgotten. More than a year later, Sandor rediscovered it and, undaunted, continued the experiment by rehydrating it to inoculate fresh milk. Years later, he is still using the revived culture, as well as passing samples of it on to his students.

While this may seem like a romantic sidebar, it begs us to pause and contemplate the unlikely notion that a strain of yogurt traveled from Romania in the nineteenth century to New York via boat; Leon Trotsky went nuts ordering it at a knishery that still exists; it then traveled to Norway in a jar; came back to the United States in a handkerchief; was shared with the Institute by Sandor Katz; and, in turn, has been shared with our students ever since.

At the Institute, we make a big batch of yogurt weekly with great results and lovingly refer to the few tablespoons we hold back each time as "Yonah."

Milk Kefir

While culturing kefir is the foundation for most of the cheese recipes in this chapter, it is also a probiotic, fermented milk beverage, refreshing enough to drink on its own. Similar to yogurt, but cultured at room temperature, kefir is most interesting to us because the kefir "grains" used to inoculate fresh milk are alive and you, their caretaker, can see them growing. As with any living organism, you are also responsible for nurturing and encouraging them to grow. For more information and instructions for long-term storage when not actively making kefir, see Milk Kefir Grains: Care & Feeding, facing page.

YIELD: 1 CUP [250 ML]

1 cup [250 ml] whole cow or goat milk, not ultra-pasteurized (see Primer, page 152)

1 tsp active milk kefir grains (see Technique, facing page)

SPECIAL EQUIPMENT
1 pt [500 ml] mason jar

Pour the milk into a 1 pt [500 ml] mason jar, add the kefir grains, and cover.

Allow to ferment at room temperature, preferably around 71°F [21°C], for 12 to 24 hours, or until it thickens slightly and has a tangy taste. You may notice that the fermentation has created a bit of CO_2, producing a slight hissing sound (like opening a soda bottle) when you unscrew the jar. Though not necessary, the jar may be gently agitated once or twice during the fermentation time to help distribute the microflora on the grains and in the milk. Undisturbed milk may separate or have a lightly curdled texture, which is fine and will end up integrating during the straining process.

Strain the kefir through a fine-mesh sieve, stirring to coax all the liquid through. Reserve the kefir grains for culturing the next batch of milk or cream.

Drink the cultured milk kefir plain, or see page 176 for flavor ideas. Milk kefir can be consumed immediately at room temperature or stored in an airtight container and chilled in the refrigerator for up to 1 week, where it will continue to ferment at a slower pace and develop an even tangier flavor.

MILK KEFIR GRAINS: CARE & FEEDING

TAKE ME TO YOUR LEADER

Milk kefir is a mystery to most people. Whenever kefir is mentioned in class, hands are raised, asking what it is and where it came from. As a matter of course, we give students our sci-fi-fantasy theory first—kefir grains came from outer space. They arrived on Earth via an asteroid that crash-landed on a Jersey Cow dairy just outside of what is now Ann Arbor, Michigan.

Now that we've gotten that out of the way, the actual origins are not as clear. Milk kefir is generally thought to have originated over a thousand years ago in the Caucasus Mountains, which are contained by the Black Sea to the west and the Caspian Sea to the east.

Before refrigeration, milk kefir was used to culture and preserve milk for consumption. The added benefit was that it also turned fresh milk into a healthy probiotic food. Milk kefir is different from water kefir, which looks similar but cannot be used interchangeably. We now know that kefir is a SCOBY, an acronym for Symbiotic Culture of Bacteria & Yeast. The kefir SCOBY manifests itself as a white mass of grain-like shapes that cluster together to resemble a cauliflower floret. They are referred to as "grains" because of their appearance, though many people find this term confusing. At the Institute, we tried to remedy this by referring to them as florets, only adding to the confusion before we gave up. Two students of ours named theirs "The Sutherlands," inspired by the actor Kiefer Sutherland. We encourage you to name yours as we did with Yonah, our yogurt culture.

Commercially available kefir products are inoculated with only a handful of laboratory-grown bacteria, whereas live kefir grains contain more than thirty different kinds of yeast and bacteria, which work symbiotically in a precise relationship to grow, divide, and multiply.

What intrigues us the most about kefir is that it is a living organism that changes its environment. Most organisms are adaptive; they adapt to their environment. But kefir is transformative; it changes the environment it inhabits. Once the transformation is complete, it doesn't die or get consumed, like yeast in a loaf of sourdough bread, but strengthens and multiplies.

CONT'D

MILK KEFIR GRAINS: CARE & FEEDING, CONT'D

KEFIR CARE & FEEDING FOR NEW KEFIR PARENTS

When placed in fresh milk at room temperature, kefir grains feed off the milk sugars and proteins, producing a yogurt-like beverage. The grains are then strained out and placed into fresh milk to repeat the process all over again. Over time, they will grow and increase in volume, changing the milk-to-kefir grain ratio. At this point, the excess grains can be eaten, given away to new homes, or dried and stored for future use.

When you want to take a break from making kefir or, say, go on a vacation, there are a few ways to hit the pause button.

SHORT-TERM STORAGE: UP TO 1 WEEK

Place kefir grains in a sealed jar with fresh milk as you usually would when feeding them. Label the container and store in the refrigerator.

MEDIUM-TERM STORAGE: 2 TO 3 MONTHS

Place kefir grains in a jar with fresh milk, as you usually would when feeding them. Label the container and store in the refrigerator. Drain and repeat this process each week.

LONG-TERM STORAGE (FROZEN): UP TO 1 YEAR

Unlike Walt Disney, who was rumored to be cryogenically preserved, kefir grains actually can be frozen. Drain the grains, wash them with filtered water, and gently pat them dry. Place in an airtight, resealable plastic bag or glass jar and cover them completely with dry powdered milk to avoid freezer burn, then freeze.

LONG-TERM STORAGE (DEHYDRATED): 1 TO 4 YEARS

Dehydrating kefir grains for long-term storage not only keeps them in suspended animation longer, but also removes the risks of power outages and freezer temperature fluctuations. Drain the grains, wash them with filtered water, and gently pat them dry. Lay them on a piece of parchment or wax paper, cover with a piece of cheesecloth, and dry them at room temperature, no higher than 85°F [29°C], for 3 to 4 days, depending on humidity and room temperature. A dehydrator will speed things up a bit, just keep it set at 85°F [29°C] or below. Once fully dried, they will turn yellow, which is perfectly normal. Place them in an airtight resealable plastic bag or glass jar and cover them completely with dry powdered milk.

WAKE ME UP BEFORE YOU GO-GO

Waking up refrigerated grains: Drain off the milk they were sleeping in (discard, or use for baking), then give them a shallow milk bath in fresh milk, just enough to wash off the old milk and mucilage. Swish them around gently with your fingers, then pour the bath milk off and drink or use for baking. Put the grains back in the jar and add ½ cup [125 ml] fresh milk. Seal with a lid, leaving it out on the counter. Drain off and discard the milk every 24 hours, and add another ½ cup [125 ml] fresh milk. Repeat this process until you notice the milk coagulating within 24 hours. It should thicken slightly and have a pleasantly tangy taste. You may also notice that the fermentation has created a bit of CO_2, producing a slight hissing sound (like opening a soda bottle) when you unscrew the jar. This may take 3 days or longer. Once reestablished, begin increasing the amount of milk in ½ cup [125 ml] increments with each feeding until you reach the desired amount.

Waking up frozen grains: Take the grains out of the freezer and thaw. Wash off any powdered milk with cool, filtered water. Place in a jar and add ½ cup [125 ml] fresh milk for every 2 Tbsp of grains, then seal the jar and leave at room temperature. Drain off and discard the milk every 24 hours, and add ½ cup [125 ml] fresh milk. Repeat this process until you notice the milk coagulating within 24 hours. It should thicken slightly and have a pleasantly tangy taste. You may also notice that the fermentation has created a bit of CO_2, producing a slight hissing sound (like opening a soda bottle) when you unscrew the jar. This may take a week or longer. Once reestablished, begin increasing the amount of milk in ½ cup [125 ml] increments with each feeding until you reach the desired amount.

Waking up dehydrated grains: Wash off any powdered milk with cool, filtered water. Place in a jar and add ½ cup [125 ml] fresh milk for every 2 Tbsp of grains, then seal the jar and leave at room temperature. Drain off and discard the milk every 24 hours, and add ½ cup [125 ml] fresh milk. Repeat this process until you notice the milk coagulating within 24 hours. It should thicken slightly and have a pleasantly tangy taste. You may also notice that the fermentation has created a bit of CO_2, producing a slight hissing sound (like opening a soda bottle) when you unscrew the jar. This may take 1 to 2 weeks or longer. Once reestablished, begin increasing the amount of milk in ½ cup [125 ml] increments with each feeding until you reach the desired amount.

FLAVORED MILK KEFIR: Milk kefir requires regular feeding, producing a new batch every day. In an effort to keep things interesting, we suggest a few ways to flavor your daily batch.

Blackberry Rosemary Kefir

YIELD: ABOUT 2 CUPS [500 ML]

One 5 in [13 cm] sprig of fresh rosemary
2 Tbsp granulated sugar
1½ cups [180 g] blackberries, fresh or frozen
2 Tbsp fresh lemon juice
1½ cups [375 ml] chilled Milk Kefir (page 172)

In a small saucepan over medium-high heat, combine the rosemary, sugar, and ½ cup [125 ml] water. Bring to a boil, then lower the heat to low and simmer for 5 minutes. Transfer the syrup to a medium bowl and allow to cool for 20 minutes, then discard the rosemary.

In the same saucepan, combine the berries and lemon juice and cook over medium heat until the berries begin to soften, about 10 minutes. Transfer to a fine-mesh sieve set over the bowl of rosemary syrup and press the berries through with the back of a spoon. Discard the remaining seeds and pulp.

Chill the blackberry mixture for 15 to 30 minutes, then add the kefir and stir to combine. Pour into glasses and serve.

Cardamom Coffee Kefir

YIELD: ABOUT 2 CUPS [500 ML]

6 Tbsp [50 g] roasted coffee beans (see page 62)
5 or 6 cardamom pods
1 cup [250 ml] filtered water
2 Tbsp granulated sugar
1 cup [250 ml] chilled Milk Kefir (page 172)

SPECIAL EQUIPMENT
Burr coffee grinder
1 pt [500 ml] mason jar
Butter muslin or paper coffee filter

Using a coffee grinder, grind the coffee beans and cardamom pods together to a medium coarseness, about the size of kosher salt granules, and place in a 1 pt [500 ml] mason jar. Add filtered water, cover, and steep for 12 hours at room temperature.

Strain the cardamom coffee through a fine-mesh sieve lined with clean, damp butter muslin or a paper coffee filter, discarding the grounds. Use immediately or cover and chill in the refrigerator for 15 to 30 minutes (or up to 1 week). When ready to use, add the sugar and kefir, stirring to combine. Pour into glasses and serve.

Golden Milk Kefir

YIELD: ABOUT 2 CUPS [500 ML]

1 Tbsp peeled and grated fresh ginger
1 Tbsp peeled and grated fresh turmeric, or 1½ tsp ground turmeric
¼ tsp ground cardamom
¼ tsp freshly ground black pepper
2 Tbsp honey
2 cups [500 ml] chilled Milk Kefir (page 172)

SPECIAL EQUIPMENT
Blender

Place all of the ingredients into a blender and blend until smooth.

Pour into glasses and serve.

Crème Fraîche

You might think crème fraîche, with its fancy-schmancy French name, is above your pay grade to make yourself. But look below—there are only four steps and two of them are simply pouring it into jars. Crème fraîche is really only cultured fresh cream, thickened slightly and imbued with a layer of natural flavor. And by the way, it's the first step to making a European-style Cultured Butter (page 178). Use as a topping for tarts, pies, or a bowl of berries. Add some sugar for sweetness or a dash of Madagascar vanilla, rose water, or orange flower water to elevate it from sublime to exotic.

YIELD: 1 PT [500 ML]

1 pt [500 ml] heavy cream
1 Tbsp active milk kefir grains
(see Technique, page 173)

SPECIAL EQUIPMENT
1 pt [500 ml] mason jar

Pour the cream into a 1 pt [500 ml] mason jar, add the kefir grains, and cover.

Allow to ferment at room temperature for 12 to 36 hours, or until it thickens to the consistency of sour cream.

Strain the mixture through a fine-mesh sieve, gently pushing the thickened cream through with a soft spatula. Reserve the kefir grains and reuse them for culturing more milk or cream.

Use immediately or return the crème fraîche to the mason jar and store, tightly sealed, in the refrigerator for up to 1 week.

Cultured Butter & Buttermilk

After growing up with margarine, I couldn't believe my taste buds when I finally tasted butter for the first time in college. I had no idea how it was made, or the multitude of ways it can transform a dish. I was also unaware of the incredible ways it can itself be transformed through clarifying and browning (see Primer: Butter, page 180). Years later, however, I take the bold liberty of pronouncing that the most amazing way of transforming the taste of butter is to culture it with bacteria before churning. After all, Europeans have been doing this for ages, knowing that it not only tastes better, but also lasts longer—even when kept out at room temperature. The other benefit of culturing butter is its by-product, cultured buttermilk. It's nothing like the substance available in the grocery store, so don't throw it out. **YIELD: ABOUT 1 LB [450 G]**

2 pt [1 L] Crème Fraîche (page 177)
Kosher or sea salt (optional)

SPECIAL EQUIPMENT
2 qt [2 L] mason jar or food processor

In a large bowl, prepare an ice bath with roughly equal parts ice and water, then submerge a colander in the middle, nestling it in the ice. Set aside.

Transfer the crème fraîche to a 2 qt [2 L] jar, seal tightly, and shake vigorously for 5 to 10 minutes, until you can see distinct clumps of butter separate from the buttermilk. Alternatively, place the crème fraîche in a food processor and pulse until the buttermilk visibly separates from the butter clumps.

Strain the mixture through a fine-mesh sieve placed over a medium bowl to separate the clumps of butter, reserving the buttermilk for another use.

Transfer the strained butter to the colander submerged in the ice water bath in order to chill the butter quickly.

Gather the clumps of butter together and knead gently with your hands, or two wooden spoons or paddles, to remove as much of the remaining buttermilk as possible. Keep the butter submerged in the ice bath, since the warmth of your hands can prevent the butter from solidifying.

Change the ice bath water as needed to keep it very cold and knead until the water runs clear, indicating you have squeezed out all of the buttermilk.

Transfer the butter to a medium bowl and add salt, if desired, ¼ tsp at a time, kneading it into the butter gently until incorporated, tasting as you go until you're satisfied with the flavor.

Pack the butter into a crock or ramekins. Store salted or unsalted butter tightly wrapped in the refrigerator for up to 1 month or in the freezer for up to 3 months. Salted butter may also be stored at room temperature for up to 1 week.

BUTTER HACKS: SOFTENING BUTTER QUICKLY

Once you've decided to make your own butter, why not go ahead and make a few pounds at a time? Butter stores well in the freezer and ensures a backup supply in a pinch. The trouble is that if you haven't planned and thawed in advance, you're stuck with a frozen block of unspreadable butter.

HACK #1

A box grater is your friend. Frozen butter grates easily and produces light, fluffy shreds with lots more surface area than one solid block. Exposed to room temperature for a few minutes, the grated butter warms up nicely, ready to be spread on toast.

HACK #2

Just had a manicure and don't want to risk it with a box grater? Create an instant spa-adjacent warming chamber. Place butter on the counter in a small saucer. Fill a mason jar with boiling water, wait 30 seconds, dump out the water, and invert the warm jar over the butter until softened.

STORING BUTTER

I'm pretty sure that everyone has a different way of storing butter at home. Most of these habits, I'm also pretty sure, stem from our childhoods. Questions, and fears, about storing butter in the fridge vs. on the counter are a constant source of discussion in every cheesemaking class, so here are our definitive answers.

COUNTER APPROVED

Cultured butter (see facing page) contains lactic acid bacteria, which lowers the butter's pH and acts as a preservative. Salted butter, whether cultured or uncultured, will spoil more slowly than unsalted due to its ability to reduce bacterial growth. Both cultured butter and salted uncultured butter may be left out on the counter at temperatures below 70°F [21°C] for up to a week before going rancid.

THE FRIDGE IS YOUR FRIEND

Use the freezer for long-term butter storage, but the best place for shorter-term storage is in the fridge. Consider storing butter in the warmest section of the fridge, usually the door, which gets the most exposure to room temperatures since it's opened repeatedly. It will be safe and spreadable for up to 1 month.

CONT'D

CLARIFIED BUTTER

While fresh butter is our favorite fat flavor-bomb to cook with, it lacks in the long shelf-life department, and also falls short when heated to high temperatures. A solution that remedies both issues is to render it into clarified butter. The process involves removing the milk proteins, which can go rancid over time with exposure to heat and air, and water from the butter, leaving you with pure butterfat that can be heated to 450°F [230°C] (as opposed to 325°F [160°C] for unclarified butter), and can be stored for months in the fridge. We like to make clarified butter, ghee, and brown butter in 1 lb [450 g] batches, but if you prefer to start small, we suggest using a minimum of 8 oz [220 g] for each preparation.

1. Melt unsalted butter in a light-colored, heavy-bottomed saucepan over low heat. As the butter melts, it will bubble lazily and the water will sink to the bottom as the milk protein solids foam and float to the surface.

2. Once melted, the butter will begin to simmer gently as the water evaporates. Fat globules suspended in golden liquid will be visible as it bubbles. The milk solids will gradually sink to the bottom and the foam on top will start to break up and dissipate.

3. As the foam begins to break up, use a fine-mesh skimmer to continuously skim and discard the remaining foam from the surface. This makes it easier to see what is happening below.

4. After the butter has been cooking for 15 to 20 minutes, the simmering will begin to slow down and a layer of clear yellow liquid will be visible between the milk solids at the bottom of the pan and any remaining foam above. Watch closely to make sure the milk solids don't begin to brown. When the bubbles become smaller and more like champagne bubbles, remove immediately from the heat.

5. Carefully and quickly pour the clear, liquid butter into a heatproof container, making sure to leave the milk solids in the pan. If desired, or if you accidentally transfer any milk solids, you can strain the butter further by pouring it through a fine-mesh strainer lined with butter muslin or several layers of cheesecloth, or through a paper coffee filter. Discard the solids (or spread on a piece of toast) and allow the clarified butter to cool to room temperature. Clarified butter may be stored in an airtight container in the refrigerator for up to 3 months.

GHEE

Ghee is ubiquitous in Indian cooking and very similar to clarified butter, only heated a bit more until the milk solids are browned, giving it a nuttier flavor. It differs as well by not requiring refrigeration.

1. Follow steps 1 through 4 for Clarified Butter, but instead of removing from the heat at the end of step 4, increase the heat to medium. Continue simmering until the butter foams a second time and begins to smell nutty and toasted. When the milk solids turn dark golden brown and the butter is a rich golden color, remove immediately from the heat.

2. Carefully and quickly pour the clear, liquid butter into a heatproof container, making sure to leave the milk solids in the pan. If desired, or if you accidentally transfer any milk solids, you can strain the butter further by pouring it through a fine-mesh strainer lined with butter muslin or several layers of cheesecloth, or through a paper coffee filter. Discard the solids (or spread on a piece of toast) and allow the ghee to cool to room temperature. Ghee may be stored in an airtight container at room temperature for up to 1 month or in the refrigerator for up to 3 months.

BROWN BUTTER

Brown butter, or what we call "liquid gold," is butter that has been cooked until the milk protein solids separate from the butterfat and become nutty as they toast. Unlike clarified butter or ghee, the solids are left in, rather than strained out, for a serious flavor boost. Brown butter is your secret weapon when stored in the fridge and can be spread over grilled fish, scallops, and pasta or added to omelets, frittatas, or simply fried eggs to add an extra savory depth of flavor. On the sweet side, substitute brown butter when baking cookies, pie fillings, or tarts to add an irresistable *je ne sais quoi* to your favorite recipes. Brown butter can be used in its melted state, or chilled until solid and creamed like regular butter.

CONT'D

BUTTER, CONT'D

1. Melt unsalted butter in a light-colored, heavy-bottomed saucepan over medium-high heat, stirring occasionally with a silicone spatula as it melts. At first, the butter will bubble vigorously as the water sinks to the bottom and the milk protein solids foam and float to the surface.

2. As the butter continues to cook, begin stirring more frequently, using the spatula to scrape along the sides and bottom of the pan. The foam will dissipate as the milk solids sink to the bottom and the butter will start sizzling as the water begins to evaporate. Keep a close eye on the butter, as it can burn in a matter of seconds. As the butter nears completion, bits of browned milk solids may appear around the edges of the pan. The sizzling will start to quiet down and the butter will start to smell nutty and toasted. When the milk solids turn the butter a rich, chestnut-brown color, remove immediately from the heat and pour directly into a heat-proof container, making sure to scrape all the brown bits in.

3. Use right away (stir it first) or allow to cool to room temperature before covering tightly and refrigerating. Stir every 30 minutes while chilling until the butter solidifies to distribute all the flavorful solids. Brown butter may be stored in an airtight container in the refrigerator for up to 1 month.

VARIATION:
SAGE BROWN BUTTER
Add a few fresh sage leaves to every 8 oz [220 g] of butter as it browns.

BUTTER EQUIVALENTS

1 TBSP	½ OZ [15 G]		
4 TBSP	2 OZ [55 G]	¼ CUP	
8 TBSP	4 OZ [110 G]	½ CUP	1 STICK
16 TBSP	8 OZ [220 G]	1 CUP	2 STICKS
24 TBSP	12 OZ [330 G]	1½ CUPS	3 STICKS
32 TBSP	1 LB [440 G]	2 CUPS	4 STICKS

Chèvre (Goat Cheese)

The word for goat in French is *chèvre*. However, in English, *chèvre* is the name for goat cheese. Chèvre is the creamy, spreadable cheese we want to serve at any party, accompanied by slices of bread and crackers, sprinkled with a fancy finishing salt, and washed down with a glass of chilled Sancerre. You'll also be able to brag, "By the way, I made it myself."

YIELD: 1½ LB [680 G]

4 qt [4 L] whole goat milk, not ultra-pasteurized (see Primer, page 152)

¼ cup [60 ml] Milk Kefir (page 172)

1⁄16 to 1⁄8 tablet WalcoRen calf's rennet

¼ cup [60 ml] filtered water

Kosher or sea salt

SPECIAL EQUIPMENT

Butter muslin

Instant-read thermometer

In a heavy, 5 qt [5 L] nonreactive pot over medium-low heat, gently warm the milk to 90°F [32°C], stirring occasionally with a wooden spoon to prevent scorching on the bottom of the pot. Keep a close eye; remember that 90°F [32°C] is below our body temperature and this temperature may be reached quickly.

Turn off the heat and add the kefir, stirring to incorporate thoroughly.

In a small bowl, crush and dissolve the rennet in the filtered water, then add to the milk, stirring first in a circular motion, then from the bottom to the top of the pot to incorporate thoroughly.

Cover the pot and allow to sit undisturbed at warm room temperature (72°F to 78°F [22°C to 25°C]) for 12 to 24 hours, until a mass of curd shrinks away from the sides of the pot and clear whey is visible around the edges.

When the curd is ready, line a colander with a piece of dampened butter muslin and place the colander inside a larger bowl. Gently ladle the curd into the lined colander, allowing the whey to drain into the bowl. Empty the whey from the bowl often, making sure it does not rise up to the level of the curds. Discard or reserve the whey for another use (see Way Too Much Whey, page 187).

Cover and continue to drain the curds in the colander for 10 to 12 hours at room temperature, until your preferred consistency is achieved, somewhere between spreadable and crumbly. You can speed up the draining process by gathering the four corners of the butter muslin and tying them into a bundle that can be hung from the handle of a long wooden spoon set over a deep pot.

Transfer the drained curds to a medium bowl and gently stir in salt, ½ tsp at a time, making sure to incorporate it well and tasting as you go until you're satisfied with the flavor.

Chèvre can be served immediately or transferred to an airtight container and stored in the refrigerator for up to 5 days.

Feta

We love feta cheese at the Institute. We can source multiple varieties at the same Middle Eastern markets where we find our spices, but like everything else, we get immense satisfaction from making it ourselves. Try it in our Hortopita (page 186) or simply smear on toast with a drizzle of olive oil.

YIELD: ½ LB [225 G]

4 qt [4 L] whole goat or cow milk, not ultra-pasteurized (see Primer, page 152)

¼ cup [60 ml] Milk Kefir (page 172)

¼ tablet WalcoRen calf's rennet

¼ cup [60 ml] filtered water

6 Tbsp [60 g] kosher salt, plus more for aging

SPECIAL EQUIPMENT

Instant-read thermometer

Butter muslin

Rectangular cheese mold, 5 in [13 cm] wide by 3½ in [9 cm] high, or upcycle two plastic strawberry baskets, stacking them together for extra support

1 pt [500 ml] mason jar

INOCULATING THE MILK

In a heavy, 5 qt [5 L] nonreactive pot over medium-low heat, gently warm the milk to 90°F [32°C], stirring occasionally with a wooden spoon to prevent scorching on the bottom of the pot. Keep a close eye; remember that 90°F [32°C] is below our body temperature and this temperature may be reached quickly.

Turn off the heat and add the kefir, stirring to incorporate thoroughly. Cover and allow to sit, undisturbed, for 1 hour, maintaining the temperature of the pot at 90°F [32°C]. (See Note on Maintaining Milk Temperature.)

In a small bowl, crush and dissolve the rennet in the filtered water, then add to the milk, stirring first in a circular motion, then from the bottom to the top of the pot to incorporate thoroughly. Cover the pot and allow to sit for 1 hour, maintaining the temperature of the pot at 90°F [32°C].

CURD FORMATION

After 1 hour, check for a "clean break" of the curd by inserting your finger straight down into the milk, curling it, then lifting it straight up out of the pot. The curds should "break," revealing a clean line of curd on either side, similar in look and feel to silken tofu. If a clean break has not been achieved after 1 hour, replace the lid and check every 30 minutes, maintaining the temperature at 90°F [32°C], until you have success.

Using a long-bladed knife, such as a bread knife, cut the curds, holding the knife vertically and making parallel slices ¾ in [2 cm] apart, all the way through the curd mass. Begin at the far edge of the pot and draw the blade through the curds toward you. Next, make another series of cuts from left to right, ¾ in [2 cm] apart, forming a grid. Finally, make a series of cuts ¾ in [2 cm] apart, holding the knife at a 45-degree angle and drawing it from left to right, effectively making your cuts as close to horizontal as possible. Rotate the pot 180 degrees and repeat.

Cover and allow the curds to rest, undisturbed, for 10 minutes, while maintaining a temperature of 90°F [32°C].

After the resting period, use a long-handled wooden spoon to give the curds a gentle stir every 5 minutes for the next 30 minutes, continuing to maintain a temperature of 90°F [32°C]. This allows the curds to release more whey and keeps them from matting together. At the end of the 30 minutes, the curds should have developed a firm but springy consistency.

Let the curds rest for another 5 minutes. They should settle to the bottom of the pot.

DRAINING & SALTING

Line a colander with a piece of dampened butter muslin and place inside a larger bowl. Gently ladle the curds into the lined colander, allowing the whey to drain into the bowl. Empty the whey from the bowl often, making sure it does not rise up to the level of the curds.

Reserve 1 qt [1 L] of the whey to make a brine, stirring 4 Tbsp of the salt into it while still warm. Cool the brine to room temperature and transfer to an airtight container, then store in the refrigerator until ready to use. Discard or reserve the remaining whey for another use (see Way Too Much Whey, page 187).

Sprinkle the remaining 2 Tbsp of salt over the curds and gently mix with your hands or a wooden spoon to incorporate thoroughly. Allow to drain for another 2 hours or until the curds feel firm and the whey has slowed or stopped dripping.

MOLDING & PRESSING

Make a draining tray by placing a wire cooling rack on a rimmed baking sheet. Line a rectangular cheese mold with a piece of dampened butter muslin and place it on the tray.

Transfer the well-drained curds into the prepared mold, making sure to gently press them into the corners of the mold. Once all the curds have been transferred, fold the overhanging flaps of muslin over the top of the curds.

Place a sealed 1 pt [500 ml] mason jar filled with water on top of the cheese to act as a press.

After 10 minutes, remove the weight, lift the cheese from the mold, unwrap it, and flip it over. Rewrap the cheese in the butter muslin, then place it back in the mold and replace the weight. Repeat, flipping it and rewrapping it every 10 minutes for 30 minutes.

DRYING & AGING

Remove the cheese from the mold, unwrap it, and sprinkle it with salt, making sure to cover all the surfaces.

Place the cheese, unwrapped, directly on the draining tray and allow to air dry for 1 to 2 days in the refrigerator, flipping it a few times to ensure even drying.

Transfer the cheese to a plastic or glass container deep enough to be able to cover the cheese completely in brine, and pour in the prepared salt brine. You may need to place a weight, such as a small resealable plastic bag filled with extra brine or even water, on top in order to keep the feta completely submerged.

Cover tightly and allow the feta to age in the refrigerator for at least 2 weeks, or up to 2 months, before using. To serve, first drain off the brine. If the feta is too salty for your taste, soak it in fresh water for 30 minutes to 1 hour, then allow to drain before using.

MAINTAINING MILK TEMPERATURE WHILE FERMENTING: Keep the pot on the stovetop and wrap with a towel or blanket if no burners are going. You may need to periodically turn the heat on to low for a minute or two (remove the towel or blanket first) if the temperature drops. Check the temperature occasionally without disturbing the curds, keeping in mind that you lose heat whenever you remove the lid. Heavier pots, such as ceramic-coated cast iron, retain heat longer than thinner-walled pots, such as stainless steel.

Hortopita
(Phyllo Pie with Kale and Feta)

Phyllo, the same dough used for baklava and those delicious triangle-shaped hors d'oeuvres, is put into action here as one whole savory pie. This classic Greek dish is filled with sautéed dark leafy greens, fresh herbs, and feta cheese. Baked in the oven till browned, it produces a crispy, flaky crust that complements the moist, herby filling. **SERVES 6 TO 8**

2 large leeks

½ cup [125 ml] olive oil

11 oz [300 g] dandelion greens, coarsely chopped

9 oz [250 g] kale, stems removed, coarsely chopped

3 Tbsp chopped fresh dill

3 Tbsp chopped fresh mint

2½ cups [350 g] crumbled Feta (page 184)

½ tsp freshly ground black pepper

15 sheets phyllo dough (smallest side at least 12 in [30.5 cm] wide)

1 Tbsp white sesame seeds

SPECIAL EQUIPMENT

Pastry brush

9 in [23 cm] springform cake pan

Kitchen shears (optional)

Place a rack in the center of the oven and preheat the oven to 350°F [180°C]. Use a pastry brush to oil a 9 in [23 cm] springform cake pan with 1 tsp of the olive oil and set aside.

Trim the root end and dark green tops from the leeks, then slice the white and pale green stalk in half lengthwise, leaving 1 in [2.5 cm] intact at the base. Rinse the leeks thoroughly under running water, using your fingers to separate the layers at the top to flush out any clinging dirt. Thinly slice the leeks crosswise and set aside.

In a wide, shallow pan over medium heat, heat 2 Tbsp of the olive oil. Add the leeks, dandelion greens, kale, dill, and mint and sauté until the greens are wilted and the liquid has evaporated, about 10 minutes.

Transfer the cooked greens to a large bowl and add the crumbled feta and black pepper, tossing gently to combine. Set aside.

Prepare the phyllo dough: Remove from the package and use kitchen shears or a sharp knife to trim the sheets to 12 in [30.5 cm] square. Cover the sheets with a slightly damp kitchen towel when not in use, to keep them from drying out.

Lay a sheet of phyllo in the prepared cake pan, gently lifting and guiding it into the inside edges of the pan. Brush the surface with olive oil and repeat with five more sheets of phyllo, brushing olive oil over each one and leaving an overhang on the sides of the pan.

Evenly spread a third of the greens mixture (about 2 cups [120 g]) into the pan, gently spreading the mixture to the edges of the pan.

Layer three more sheets of phyllo on top, brushing each surface with olive oil, again gently lifting and guiding them into the inside edges of the pan and allowing excess dough to overhang the pan.

Repeat with another third of the greens mixture and three more sheets of phyllo brushed with olive oil, then top with the last third of greens and the remaining three sheets of phyllo brushed with olive oil.

Trim the overhanging phyllo sheets, or crimp them up and over the top edge of the pan.

Brush the top of the pie with olive oil and sprinkle the sesame seeds on top. With a sharp knife, lightly score only the top phyllo layers, not cutting all the way through the pie, to divide the pie into 6 to 8 pieces.

Bake for 45 minutes or until the top is dark golden brown. Remove from the oven and transfer to a wire rack to cool for at least 20 minutes before unmolding.

Unmold the hortopita from the springform and cut it into slices, using your score marks as a guide. Serve warm or at room temperature.

WAY TOO MUCH WHEY

When you make cheese, you produce whey—lots of it. Students hate to see it go down the drain, and in fact, municipal laws in certain areas forbid large, commercial cheesemaking operations from dumping it down the municipal drain due to its high acidity. Home cheesemakers dumping only a few cups down the drain have nothing to worry about except the guilt of having it go to waste. Whey still has lots of protein, plus some fat and lactose sugars. Sounds good to us! Besides inflicting whey too many terrible jokes on our students (sorry, we can't control ourselves), we have a bunch of unexpected uses. Any kind of whey can be used for most of these ideas, but note that when "active" whey is called for, it refers specifically to whey that has been inoculated with a live culture, such as from yogurt or long-fermented cheeses like chèvre.

- Substitute whey for milk in béchamel sauce.

- Tenderize chicken before cooking. Marinate in 1 cup [250 ml] whey for at least 1 hour.

- Add whey to boiling pasta water.

- Replace the water used for making oatmeal, polenta, or rice with whey.

- Boil potatoes in whey. If making mashed potatoes, add additional whey to adjust the consistency.

- Substitute whey for the water or milk called for in bread recipes, pizza dough, quick breads, pancake or waffle batter, cornbread, muffins, or biscuits.

- Soaking grains or beans overnight before cooking improves their digestibility. The addition of several tablespoons of active whey to the soaking water will supercharge the process.

- Add some whey to a pot of soup or stew as it cooks.

- Jump-start the lacto-fermentation process of pickles (page 281), Sauerkraut (page 278), or condiments by adding a few tablespoons of active whey.

- Add whey to homemade fruit smoothies to turn them into protein shakes.

- Make lacto-fermented whey lemonade. In a 1 gl [4 L] container, mix 1 cup [200 g] sugar, juice from 2 lb [900 g] of lemons, and 1 cup [250 ml] active whey. Top with filtered water, leaving 1 in [2.5 cm] of headspace, seal, and ferment at room temperature for 2 to 3 days. Chill before drinking.

- Traditionally, farmstead cheesemakers also raise chickens and pigs, if only to feed them all the leftover whey. Pigs raised on a diet of whey are prized, and chickens will finish off any leftovers.

- Looking to add more nitrogen to a compost pile? Whey will balance out the carbon from dried leaves and twigs.

GONE IN AN INSTANT

It's 1965, and the postwar romance with all things plastic is in full swing. Prepackaged, prepared, and chemically enhanced foods are quickly replacing that old-fashioned stuff that your mother used to buy at her grocer's and will usher in a bright new day in which every family will eat like the Jetsons. The Institute, over fifty years old at this point, was clearly struggling in this changing environment, as you can see from this letter sent to Nellie Archer by Theodore J. Hoover III, the Institute's sixth (and last) director. (Ms. Archer was then the owner of the Institute and daughter of its founder, Eliza Taylor Reynolds.) Ironically, under Hoover's direction, the Institute closed its doors for the last time on January 1, 1966, just missing the hippie "Natural Food" reaction against "plastic food" that might have saved it. As it turned out, it would be another forty-five years before the Institute would be revived and begin to reclaim all that had been lost.

July 29, 1965

Dearest Nellie,

It is with great reluctance that I write to you today with what will surely be unwelcome advice.

You know that, as the Director of IDT, I have followed in the footsteps of my predecessors and dedicated myself wholly to the Institute. I have, indeed, made its mission — to preserve our vanishing domestic arts — my very raison d'être for the past 13 years. [...] with no possibility of being accused [...] I tell you that I believe the time [...] to close our beloved Institute of Dome[...]

"Why now," you may ask, after all the var[...] that have come our way for over a dec[...] Isaac Newton, they say, had his grea[...]

The Institute of Domestic Technology
511 S. Main St.
Los Angeles, California

Nellie Archer
310 S. Irving Blvd.
Los Angeles, Cal.

LOS ANGELES
JUL 30
1965
CA.

July 29, 1965

Dearest Nellie:

It is with great reluctance that I write to you today with what will surely be unwelcome advice.

You know that, as the Director of IDT, I have followed in the footsteps of my predecessors and dedicated myself wholly to the Institute. I have, indeed, made its mission—to preserve our vanishing domestic arts—my very *raison d'être* for the past thirteen years. It is thus with no possibility of being accused of flippancy that I tell you that I believe the time may have at last come to close our beloved Institute of Domestic Technology.

"Why now?" you might ask, after all the various "slings and arrows" that have come our way for over a decade now? Well, Sir Isaac Newton, they say, had his great insight regarding gravity when an apple fell on his head. My own epiphany occurred last week in a doctor's waiting room, leafing through the pages of *McCall's Magazine*.

There, right in front of me, was a full-page advertisement for something called "Carnation Instant Breakfast." (Yes, there is now such a thing.) It's basically a foil packet containing some kind of "nutritional" powder with artificial flavoring. You apparently mix it with milk and gulp it down to avoid the unimaginable torture of having to make some toast, scramble an egg, or squeeze some orange juice. I'm sure you would agree that if your dear mother weren't already deceased, the knowledge of such an abomination (and the utter collapse of civilization it signals) would have surely killed her. As I finished reading the ad—"Now—when your family doesn't have time to eat a balanced breakfast, they can drink it"—I felt as if I were reading the Institute's epitaph.

For some time now, we have had to cope with declining attendance and interest in a world which increasingly values convenience over quality, a world, moreover, where seemingly every conceivable dish has been packaged and whose preparation seems to require nothing more than a toaster (the inedible "Pop Tarts" springs to mind) or a pot of boiling water. But the "drinking" of an entire meal? Really? What's next? Will we soon be drinking steak and potatoes? Are we all to live like cosmonauts? What is the point?

And so it has come to this. We have fought the good fight, Nellie, but as any good general will tell you, it is important to know when to surrender. I submit to you that "Carnation Instant Breakfast" is the proverbial writing on the wall. Let us close our doors now, with dignity, and concede the battle. As George Eliot said, "Failure after long perseverance is much grander than never to have a striving good enough to be called a failure."

Yours very truly,
Teddy

Department of Meat & Fish | CH.06

THE DEPARTMENT OF MEAT & FISH

Preserving meat, fish, and fowl was a common and necessary skill in the "Before Refrigeration Era" (B.R.E.). Back in the early days of the B.R.E., hunters and farmers discovered that drying, curing, brining, and smoking meats kept them safe to eat for months. Lucky for us, it also transformed them into something uniquely delicious. These early preservation methods involved either removing water from the meat via dehydration; curing and brining with high levels of salt; or smoking over wood, with the compounds in smoke acting as both antioxidants and antimicrobial preservatives. If all of this sounds familiar, it's because these same techniques are used today, even in our modern Refrigeration Era (R.E.)—not out of necessity, but because cured and smoked meats taste so good.

The Institute's Department of Meat & Fish was established with the same sustainability principles we've applied to every other department, starting with the obvious: Source the best ingredients, purchase the freshest product, and get to know your supplier. That said, of all the day-to-day ingredients we regularly stock in our kitchens, we tend to be the farthest removed, psychologically, from the sources of our meat. Unlike making your own bread or roasting your own coffee, curing your own meat has more of a "primal" feel to it, and handling raw meat might even make us a little squeamish. There's a (once-living) animal involved and we are less inclined to look at (or want to know) how it was raised, handled, and slaughtered—it's practically an unspoken taboo. At the Institute, we believe this is all the more reason to rediscover the techniques of meat preservation. After all, making and preserving your own meat products is the only way to truly know what does and does not go into them. With many of today's highly processed commercial products, it's virtually impossible to tell.

The recent resurgence of backyard chicken coops illustrates this issue and the subsequent search for homegrown solutions. The proliferation of urban coops has become so great in many areas that municipalities have had to rewrite ordinances prohibiting roosters (due, no doubt, to complaints from sleep-deprived neighbors). It's exciting to see people raising chickens in an urban environment, treating their birds with care, and providing them with healthful feed in order to produce better-than-store-bought eggs. For some urban homesteaders, however, there is an unforeseen hiccup. As the hens age and stop producing eggs, their owners are faced with a conundrum: continue buying them expensive feed or slaughter them for meat? We actually tried to address this issue at the Institute, organizing a class for backyard chicken newbies on how to cull their chickens. The class sold out, but after a protest threat from PETA, and rain, we ultimately decided to cancel it. (Did we mention that the subject is taboo?)

If you don't happen to feel comfortable butchering your own meat, chickens or otherwise, then selecting the best meat means finding a good butcher. Unless you know a rancher personally, establishing a relationship with a reputable butcher is the best way to know where your meat comes from. With a little bit of effort, it's possible to find out how the animals you eat were raised and fed. Ask your butcher these questions; her answers may surprise you.

When working with fresh ingredients, there is always a concern about food safety, and that goes double duty for meats. Please give our refresher course on Meat Food Safety (page 196) a read before you explore the recipes. Based on the USDA's guidelines, these are good, commonsense practices to follow, with recommendations for cleaning tools and surfaces and the best ways to avoid cross contamination between ingredients.

And while we're on the subject of safety, we want to point out that we've chosen to focus on some of the more accessible meat-curing techniques that can be done at home, in your refrigerator. This includes brined meats such as Corned Beef (page 210); cured and smoked meat (with Bacon, page 208, as the star); and the cured fish gravlax (page 224), a Scandinavian salmon dish that's one step away from lox. But wait, there's more! In addition, we show you how to preserve egg yolks in a salt cure (see page 223), transforming them into a Parmesan-adjacent umami bomb for grating on pasta. You'll also be empowered to break down a whole chicken (see page 219), which is both economical and rewarding, and to make your own fresh sausage (see page 211), which can be made and served the same day—no waiting!

MEAT & FISH

Most cured meats require nothing more than bowls and pans to brine or smoke in. Sausage making, however, benefits from a few time-saving tools.

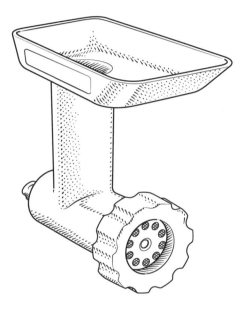

MEAT GRINDER

There are many hand-cranked meat grinders on the market, but we prefer the electric models. Even with the electric versions there are many options available of varying price, size, capacity, and horsepower. Generally, the lower-priced models are good for grinding small amounts of meat at a time, which is not a problem if you plan on making only small amounts of sausage on an occasional basis. Some models combine a meat grinder with a sausage stuffer, though often with mixed results. Some meat grinders come with multiple plate attachments; ¼ in [6 mm] is the standard grind size, but finer and coarser die plates are also available.

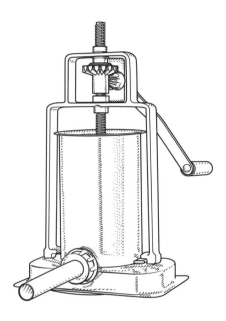

SAUSAGE STUFFER

Stuffing sausage benefits from having two people, one to load the meat and control the pressure and the other to control the output. That said, you'll also want a decent stuffer, one that is sturdy and easy to operate. Two of the more common types are vertical stuffers and horizontal stuffers. Both operate under the same basic principle: A plunger is depressed through a cylinder containing the meat mixture, which is extruded through an interchangeable stuffing tube and into the sausage casing. Stand-alone sausage stuffers, whether electric or manual hand-crank ones, are generally an investment. For information about sausage casings, see All About Casings (page 213).

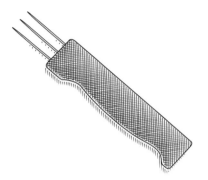

SAUSAGE PRICKER

Essentially a piece of plastic with a few sharp needles sticking out, a sausage pricker is exactly what it sounds like. It's used to remove air bubbles between the meat and the casing when forming sausages, preventing the sausages from bursting when cooked. If you have a sharp, sterilized awl or even a corn cob holder (you know, the ones shaped like tiny ears of corn), they work just as well.

PINK CURING SALT

Curing salt is used to prevent spoilage when curing meat by inhibiting bacterial growth. There are only two types but, perplexingly, each type is known by several different names. Both salts are dyed pink (hence the name *pink salt*) so they won't be confused with common table salt. Also note that cures are not interchangeable. If following a recipe from another source, make sure it specifies which salt to use.

INSTA CURE #1
(aka Prague Powder #1 or Pink Curing Salt #1)

One of the most common curing salts, it contains 6.25 percent sodium nitrite and 93.75 percent sodium chloride (table salt). It's used when curing meats that will cure in a short period of time; that require cooking, brining, or smoking; and that will be eaten relatively quickly. This includes poultry, fish, bacon, and corned beef.

Insta Cure #1 is the only curing salt used in the recipes in this chapter. We are focused only on cured meats with short curing times that do not require special equipment to control temperature and humidity.

CURING SALTS DECONSTRUCTED

Sodium nitrite: A naturally occurring compound also found in small amounts in vegetables like carrots, celery, and spinach. Sodium nitrite prevents the growth of bacteria, including *Clostridium botulinum*, the cause of botulism.

Sodium chloride: Common table salt works as a preservative to draw out water from within bacterial cells, thereby killing them.

THE CELERY QUESTION

Many Institute students ask about the naturally occurring nitrates contained in celery and wonder if they can substitute celery powder for Insta Cure #1. There *are* naturally occurring nitrates contained in celery but only in small and varying amounts, and they dissipate quickly when left at room temperature. The sodium nitrate in celery can be exposed to certain types of bacteria that will convert the nitrate to sodium nitrite, but this process is possible only under laboratory conditions and then produces a product so close to Insta Cure #1 that you might as well start there in the first place.

MEAT FOOD SAFETY

When purchasing, handling, cooking, and storing meat, it's important to use common sense along with these basic food-handling guidelines to prevent food-borne illness.

You can't see, smell, or taste harmful bacteria that may cause illness, so at the Institute, we follow these five steps when handling meat:

1. Wash hands with warm water and soap for 20 seconds before and after handling raw meat. We sing "Row, Row, Row Your Boat" twice, which clocks in handily at 20 seconds.

2. Don't cross contaminate. Keep different meats and seafood separate from each other, as well as from vegetables, dairy, and eggs. We use different colored food-grade plastic cutting mats, designating one color for each category. After cutting raw meats, we wash cutting boards and utensils with hot, soapy water. We also keep our work surfaces clean and sanitized using a fresh solution of bleach and water (1 Tbsp : 1 gl [15 ml : 4 L]), spraying surfaces down both before and after handling raw meat.

3. Don't rinse. Many older recipes instruct you to rinse raw meat, especially chicken, with cold water before preparing for cooking. This practice has since been rejected by the USDA as transferring more harmful bacteria (to your sink and counters, via splashing) than it eliminates. As long as you select and store your meat carefully and cook it to the safe minimum internal temperature, there is no need to worry about excess bacteria on raw meat and poultry.

4. Refrigerate raw as well as cooked and leftover meat promptly if not using. Cook and consume promptly, too.

5. Cook all meat to the minimum internal temperature shown on the chart on the facing page. Use an instant-read food thermometer before removing meat from the heat source. After removing meat from the grill or oven, its internal temperature will remain constant or will continue to rise for several minutes, helping to destroy more harmful bacteria. You may want to rest meat for even longer after cooking to improve the texture, but be sure to follow the chart and allow the cooked meat to rest for the specified amount of time at minimum.

SHOPPING & STORAGE

Use these guidelines when shopping and once you get home.

- Never purchase meat or poultry in packaging that is torn or leaking.

- Follow the "Sell-By," "Use-By," or other expiration dates. We always select products with the most recent packing dates or ask the butcher for something that just came in.

- Refrigerate your purchase as soon as possible, preferably within 2 hours, or 1 hour on hot days when the ambient temperature is above 90°F [32°C].

- Check the temperature of your refrigerator and freezer with an appliance thermometer. The refrigerator should be at 40°F [4°C] or below and the freezer at 0°F [-18°C] or below. If you've never checked your refrigerator, you may be shocked. It's a good idea to check once a year.

- If there is no "Use-By" date listed, cook or freeze fresh poultry and fish within 2 days of purchase; beef, lamb, and pork, within 3 to 5 days.

- Wrap meat and poultry tightly in plastic wrap to maintain quality and to prevent meat juices from getting onto other food while in the refrigerator.

- When freezing raw meat and poultry, keep them in their original packaging, then wrap the package again with foil or plastic wrap that is recommended for the freezer.

- Thawing frozen meat and poultry in the refrigerator allows for a slow, safe thawing time. Keep tightly wrapped to prevent juices from dripping onto other food or surfaces. A faster method is to place the food in a leakproof plastic bag and submerge it in cold tap water. Change the water every 30 minutes. Cook immediately after thawing. Do not thaw raw meat on the counter at room temperature.

- Meat and poultry defrosted in the refrigerator may be refrozen before or after cooking, though the texture may be affected. If thawed in cold water or in the microwave, cook before refreezing.

SAFE MINIMUM INTERNAL COOKING TEMPERATURES

Food	Min. Temperature	Min. Rest Time
Ground Beef, Pork, Lamb	160°F [71°C]	None
Poultry	165°F [74°C]	3 minutes
Whole Beef, Pork, Lamb	145°F [63°C]	3 minutes

RASHIDA PURIFOY

Dean of Meat & Fish

Professor Rashida Purifoy's relationship with the Institute dates back many years to when we met her at a guerilla farmers' market selling homemade bacon. We immediately latched on to her, knowing that her accessible approach to making bacon would spill over to her teaching style when she took over the Department of Meat & Fish.

Rashida grew up in the South with a mother fluent in southern cuisine and a father with impressive grilling skills. Farms and backyard vegetable gardens are integral to southern cuisine and had a huge influence on Rashida growing up, and on how she cooks today.

She launched her bacon business, Cast Iron Gourmet, inspired by an "aha" moment involving a craving for a BLT. Rashida had gone to the store for fixings and wasn't excited by the bacon selection. She decided she could make much better bacon herself, and a week later, invited friends to try the results, which were a smash hit.

Teaching students her curing techniques has given Professor Purifoy immediate feedback on flavor profiles for her own products. It has also given her a window into her students' passion for developing their own flavors, learning new processes firsthand, and gaining an awareness of what's in their food.

TIPS FROM THE PROFESSOR

When brining meat such as corned beef, keep a detailed log of the process and label the brining containers with a piece of masking tape noting the date, weight, and number of days to go before removing from the brine.

Use a round, food-safe container for brining. It allows for even coverage of the meat.

Whether you're a novice or seasoned home curer, search out others curing and preserving meat and fish in your city. They will be as eager to talk to you about their process as you are to talk about yours. Find charcuterie shops at home or when you travel and taste as many varieties as you can. You'll discover ideas for spices and flavors to use in your own projects.

BACON (PAGE 208)

CORNED BEEF (PAGE 210)

SAUSAGE STUFFING (PAGE 211)

SOUP FEATURING CHORIZO VERDE (GREEN CHORIZO) (PAGE 214)

MERGUEZ SAUSAGE WITH BUCKWHEAT POLENTA AND KALE (PAGE 216)

MOROCCAN CHICKEN TAGINE WITH PRESERVED LEMONS AND OLIVES (PAGE 222)

CURED EGG YOLKS (PAGE 223)

Bacon

Nothing makes meat lovers (and some wayward vegans) swoon like the smell and taste of bacon. (Vegans don't call it the "gateway meat" for nothing.) Transforming raw pork into something as otherworldly as bacon is an act of alchemy. Brining and smoking the meat is easy and doesn't require an elaborate smoker, though by all means, use one if you have one. Our method requires only a roasting pan, a rack, and aluminum foil. Once you've made your bacon, cook it straight up for breakfast with one of our three favorite cooking methods (see facing page). **YIELD: 3 LB [1.4 KG]**

One 3 lb [1.4 kg] slab skinless pork belly

BRINING CURE

¼ cup [80 g] maple syrup

¼ cup [60 ml] bourbon

¼ cup [45 g] packed brown sugar

¼ cup [40 g] kosher salt

¼ cup [28 g] coarsely ground black peppercorns

1 tsp pink curing salt, Insta Cure #1 (see Pink Curing Salt, page 195)

SPECIAL EQUIPMENT

2 gl [8 L] freezer-safe resealable plastic storage bag

13 by 16 in [33 by 41 cm] roasting pan or disposable aluminum foil roasting pan

18 in [46 cm] wide heavy-duty aluminum foil

4 cups [175 g] smoking chips, such as apple, cherry, or hickory wood

Roasting rack

Instant-read thermometer

CURING INSTRUCTIONS

Use a sharp knife to trim or "square off" the pork belly until you have a nice rectangular piece.

In a small bowl, add all of the brining cure ingredients, stirring to combine.

Coat the pork belly with the brining cure mixture, evenly rubbing it in to cover all sides.

Place the pork belly in the plastic storage bag and seal, then place on top of a tray or other container to catch drips. Refrigerate, flipping the bag every other day, until the belly is fully cured and all surfaces are firm to the touch, 7 to 10 days.

SMOKING INSTRUCTIONS

Remove the pork belly from the bag, rinse under cool water, and pat dry with paper towels. Allow to sit at room temperature for 1 hour.

Arrange a rack in the lowest position in the oven, removing the rest of the racks, and preheat the oven to 200°F [95°C].

Thoroughly line a roasting pan with heavy-duty aluminum foil, making sure that the bottom and sides of the pan are completely covered.

Scatter the wood chips in an even layer across the bottom of the pan.

Place the roasting rack over the chips, making sure there is enough space between the chips and the bottom of the rack for the smoke to flow freely.

Place the pork belly on the rack.

Make a tent of aluminum foil to cover the roasting pan like a lid, leaving 2 to 3 in [5 to 8 cm] of room above the top of the pork belly for the smoke to circulate. Crimp the foil along the edges of the pan to ensure a tight seal. The more tightly the foil is sealed, the more the smoke flavor will penetrate the meat.

Place the roasting pan on the stove across two burners over medium-high heat until you notice a steady stream of smoke venting from the seams of the foil lid, 3 to 5 minutes.

Move the pan to the preheated oven and smoke until the internal temperature of the pork belly reaches 150°F [65°C] on an instant-read thermometer, 2 to 2½ hours.

Carefully remove the foil tent, then transfer the bacon to a wire cooling rack and allow to cool to room temperature.

To firm up the bacon and make slicing easier, wrap the bacon tightly in plastic wrap and place in the freezer for 1 hour. Remove promptly and slice against the grain of the meat to your desired thickness. Bacon can be cooked immediately or stored tightly wrapped in the refrigerator for up to 1 week. To freeze for longer-term storage, up to 1 month, spread the bacon slices in a single layer on a sheet pan lined with wax paper and freeze until frozen solid. Promptly remove from the freezer and restack the slices on top of each other, interleaving each with wax paper, then wrap the whole stack with foil and place in a freezer-safe resealable plastic storage bag and return to the freezer. Remove individual slices as needed and cook directly from frozen, or thaw at room temperature for 5 minutes before using.

THREE WAYS TO COOK BACON

PAN FRY
The classic method: Place the bacon in a preheated skillet over medium heat, turning occasionally to cook evenly, until crispy. Drain on paper towels.

WATER METHOD
To reduce splattering, place bacon in a cold skillet with just enough water to coat the bottom of the pan. Bring the water to a boil over medium-high heat, then continue to cook until the water has evaporated. Lower the heat to medium and cook the bacon, turning as needed, until crispy. Drain on paper towels.

OVEN
Place a rack in the upper third of the oven and preheat the oven to 425°F [220°C]. Place bacon strips directly on a foil-lined sheet pan and bake for 15 to 20 minutes until crispy. Drain on paper towels.

Corned Beef

"Corning" is a way of preserving beef by brining it in a salt cure. The term comes from the traditional use of large-grained rock salt called "corns." Brining beef in salt enables fresh meat to be preserved for long periods, though today this method is used less for preservation and more for flavor and texture. A staple of delicatessens everywhere, corned beef is also synonymous with St. Patrick's Day and boiled cabbage—inspiring us to cook the corned brisket in a delicious bath of Guinness Stout. **SERVES 8 TO 10**

BRINING CURE

½ cup [80 g] kosher salt

3 Tbsp mustard seeds

3 Tbsp coriander seeds

3 Tbsp Garlic Powder (page 326)

3 Tbsp Onion Powder (page 327)

2 Tbsp firmly packed brown sugar

2 Tbsp black peppercorns

1 Tbsp Ginger Powder (page 326) or ground ginger

2 tsp pink curing salt, Insta Cure #1 (see Equipment, page 195)

1 tsp allspice berries

1 tsp ground nutmeg

4 bay leaves, crumbled

6 cloves

One 5 lb [2.3 kg] beef brisket
64 oz [1.9 L] Guinness Stout

SPECIAL EQUIPMENT

8 qt [8 L] freezer-safe resealable plastic storage bag

MAKE THE BRINE

In a large bowl, add all of the brining cure ingredients and 2 qt [2 L] of water, stirring to combine, and set aside.

MAKE THE BRISKET

Place the brisket in a 2 gl [8 L] freezer-safe resealable plastic storage bag, then pour the brining cure mixture into the bag, making sure the brisket is fully submerged; if not, add more water to cover.

Seal the bag and place on top of a tray or other container to catch drips. Refrigerate for 7 days, flipping the bag every other day to ensure even brining.

When ready to cook, rinse the brisket and discard the brine. Transfer the brisket to a 2 gl [8 L] stockpot or Dutch oven and add the Guinness Stout. If the brisket is not fully submerged in the liquid, add water to cover.

Bring to a boil over high heat, then turn the heat down to low. Cover and gently simmer for 2½ to 3 hours or until the meat is very tender and pulls apart easily when pierced with a fork.

Remove the brisket from the pot, discarding the liquid, then trim away any excess fat. Slice against the grain into pieces about ¼ in [6 mm] thick and serve. Store leftovers in an airtight container in the refrigerator for up to 4 days.

MEAT GRINDING & SAUSAGE STUFFING

MEAT GRINDING

SPECIAL EQUIPMENT

Meat grinder

For the tastiest ground meat, start with cuts that have some visible marbling, since fat = flavor. Aim for about 20 percent fat when making something like a burger or meat loaf, or 30 percent for sausages. Shoulder cut is a good choice for lamb and pork, while chuck is a solid option for beef (or try a blend of cuts, including sirloin, short rib, and brisket). Additional pure fat from the butcher may be added if using a leaner cut of meat.

Cut the meat into 1 to 2 in [2.5 to 5 cm] chunks, then spread it in a single layer on one or more baking sheets lined with wax paper or parchment. Transfer to the freezer and chill until the meat is firm but not completely frozen, about 1 hour. Also chill a large bowl (preferably stainless steel) and all of the grinder parts in the freezer until very cold, about 1 hour.

Assemble the grinder and run the meat through on high speed, 3 or 4 pieces at a time, into the chilled bowl. Garlic, onion, and herbs may be processed through the grinder at the same time if desired, or chopped separately and added later. If grinding more than a few pounds of meat, keep half of it in the freezer until ready to use. As the meat warms up, it will be more prone to clogging, so it is helpful to keep everything as cold as possible. If the ground meat starts to clog, turn off the machine and clean the die and cutter before continuing, or use the reverse button if available. Re-grind the clogged meat along with some fresh pieces.

Freshly ground meat should be tightly sealed and stored in the refrigerator for up to 2 days. To freeze ground meat, double wrap in plastic wrap, then cover tightly with aluminum foil. Store for up to 4 months.

SAUSAGE STUFFING

SPECIAL EQUIPMENT

Sausage casings (see All About Casings, page 213)
Sausage stuffer
Sausage pricker, awl, or corn cob holder
Kitchen shears

STEP 1 Rinse the casings well under running water, then place in a fresh bowl of cool water and soak at room temperature for 1 hour. Cut into smaller lengths if desired, then use a stuffing tube to hold the casings, one at a time, against the sink faucet, gently running water through the entire length of the casing to flush out any excess salt or impurities. (If using collagen casings, no need to soak or flush.)

STEP 2 Select a stuffing tube size to match the size of your casings, then attach the tube to the front of the sausage stuffer. Slide one length of casing onto the stuffing tube, feeding it on and pushing it down to the end of the tube so that it compresses like a scrunched stocking. Leave a 6 in [15 cm] overhang without tying the end. Place a large baking sheet or tray in front of the tube, so that the sausage has a landing pad as it comes out of the stuffer.

STEP 3 Gently pack the sausage mixture into the stuffer. Using one hand to operate the plunger,

CONT'D

push the meat through the stuffing tube and into the casing. Use the other hand to grip the sausage as it comes out of the tube, regulating the pressure inside the casing. It helps to have a partner who can slowly pull the sausage away from the nozzle and wind it onto the baking sheet as it is extruded.

STEP 4 Fill the casing firmly but be careful not to overstuff, as this can cause bursting later. It is easy to add a few extra twists to tighten a sausage, but more work to loosen one. As the casing fills up, prick any air bubbles that form with a sausage pricker. Leave at least 6 in [15 cm] of empty casing at the end, sliding it off the end of the tube, then make a knot at each end of the casing flush against the meat.

STEP 5 To form links, start from the first knot end and pinch off a 6 in [15 cm] length of sausage, squeezing the meat to keep it firmly packed inside the casing, and twist it toward you two to four rotations. Pinch off another length 6 in [15 cm] from the end of the previous one, then squeeze and twist it away from you two to four rotations. Repeat, twisting in alternate directions each time, until you can't form another 6 in [15 cm] sausage.

Squeeze out the extra meat and return it to the stuffer, then tie off the end of the casing flush with the last sausage. Prick each sausage several times with a sausage pricker to prevent bursting when cooking.

STEP 6 Repeat steps 2 through 5 with the remaining casing and sausage mixture.

STEP 7 Spread the links in a single layer on one or more baking sheets lined with wax or parchment paper, then transfer to the refrigerator and chill, uncovered, for at least 12 hours to dry out the casings.

STEP 8 Use kitchen shears to cut the casing between the links. Use immediately or store tightly sealed in the refrigerator for up to 2 days, or in the freezer for up to 2 months.

TROUBLESHOOTING

If the casing bursts while forming the sausages, cut the casing in two at the tear and squeeze out several inches of meat on both ends of the cut. Tie off the casing on both ends and begin again.

ALL ABOUT CASINGS

NATURAL VS. COLLAGEN

There are abundant options for sausage casings, but the two most common varieties are natural casings, made from the cleaned intestines of sheep, pigs ("hogs" in sausage-making lingo), and cows, and collagen casings, made from processed cow hides. Whereas all-natural casings are edible, some collagen casings are and some are not. In general, collagen casings are less expensive, provide a more uniform product, and, because they do not require soaking, come "ready to use." They are also more delicate than natural casings and can tear easily, so when making links should be twisted only two times or tied off with twine. Here at the Institute, we prefer natural casings for their durability as well as their distinctive "bite" or "snap" and flavor. It's easiest to find casings, both natural and collagen, online.

SIZING

Sausage casings are sized in metric measurements based on diameter. Different animals produce different size casings; lamb are the smallest in diameter, and also the most fragile, whereas beef casings are the largest. Hog casings are the most common and come in varying diameters and lengths depending on what part of the intestine (large, middle, small) is used. Some sausage blends can be used interchangeably with different casing sizes, but as a rule of thumb, consider that cocktail sausages are 18 to 20 mm; breakfast and Merguez sausages are 19 to 22 mm; bratwurst, kielbasa, and Italian sausages are 29 to 35 mm; and dry salami is often in the 40 to 42 mm range. Sausage stuffers come with variously sized stuffing tubes (also known as stuffing horns or nozzles) through which the ground meat is extruded into the casing. Use the largest stuffing tube that your casing will easily slide over.

PREPARATION

Natural casings are usually packed in a wet salt brine, though they may also be dry salt packed. Always rinse them well first, then soak in fresh water for 1 hour before using. Dry salt packed casings should be soaked longer, for 2 to 4 hours, to fully hydrate. Unless the casings come "pre-flushed," they should also be flushed with water by attaching the casing to a sink faucet and running water all the way through. Casings can be purchased preloaded or "tubed," meaning they have a long plastic spacer running through them, which helps to keep them from tangling and makes them easy to load. "Hanks" and "home packs" are multiple casings tied together in a bundle. They must be separated, rinsed, soaked, and flushed. Casings may be cut into 2 to 4 ft [61 cm to 1.2 m] lengths for ease of working.

STORAGE

Once you open a package, store unused casings in an airtight container, packed in liquid brine or kosher salt. They will last longest when stored in the refrigerator, 6 months to 1 year; never freeze natural casings, as this weakens them and can lead to bursting.

Chorizo Verde (Green Chorizo)

Chorizo, a fresh pork sausage found throughout Mexico, is traditionally made with red chiles, but we're fond of a green version specific to Toluca, a city about an hour's drive west of Mexico City. *Chorizo verde*, as the name implies, features a variety of fresh and green ingredients; we use pumpkin seeds, serrano chiles, spinach, cilantro, and oregano to balance out the richness of the pork. We also added a splash of tequila, because why not? A popular way to serve chorizo is in a breakfast taco with sautéed potatoes, but don't stop there—see our other suggestions in the FlavorBar (facing page).

YIELD: 2½ LB [1.1 KG]

2 Tbsp pepitas (hulled green pumpkin seeds)

1½ tsp black peppercorns

¾ tsp cumin seeds

3 bay leaves, roughly crumbled

1 Tbsp kosher salt, plus more as needed

3 oz [85 g] fresh spinach

2 or 3 garlic cloves, peeled

5 serrano chiles, halved, stems and seeds removed

½ cup [20 g] chopped cilantro, leaves and stems

1½ tsp chopped fresh oregano

1 Tbsp tequila or water

1 Tbsp fresh lime juice

Zest from ½ lime

2½ lb [1.1 kg] ground pork (see Technique: Meat Grinding, page 211)

SPECIAL EQUIPMENT

Spice mill or mortar and pestle

Food processor

In a dry, heavy-bottomed skillet over medium heat, toast the pepitas until fragrant, about 5 minutes. Transfer the seeds to a plate to cool.

Use a spice mill or mortar and pestle to grind the peppercorns, cumin seeds, bay leaves, and pepitas, then transfer to a small bowl. Add the salt and set aside.

Blanch the spinach in a pot of boiling salted water until wilted, about 15 seconds, then drain and run under cold water to stop the cooking. Drain well, squeezing out as much liquid as possible, and set aside.

In a food processor with the motor running, drop the garlic cloves through the feed tube. Process until the garlic is minced, about 10 seconds. Add the blanched spinach, chiles, cilantro, oregano, tequila, lime juice, and lime zest. Pulse until the mixture forms a paste, scraping down the sides as needed. Add the spice and pumpkin seed mixture and pulse just until combined. Transfer to a large bowl.

Add the ground pork to the bowl, mixing gently with your hands until all the ingredients are well integrated. Use a light touch when handling the ground meat to prevent a dense texture when cooked.

To test for seasoning, form a small ball of the sausage mixture into a patty and cook in a lightly oiled frying pan over medium-high heat until cooked through. Taste, then adjust the seasoning of the remaining sausage mixture, if desired, before proceeding.

Cover and chill uncooked chorizo in the refrigerator for a minimum of 3 hours to allow the flavors to meld.

Cook the chorizo in a skillet over medium-high heat, breaking it up into small pieces with a spatula and stirring occasionally, until browned, crumbly, and cooked through, 5 to 7 minutes. Alternatively, chorizo can be stuffed into casings (see page 211 for instructions) or formed into patties, then grilled or cooked in a skillet over medium-high heat until the internal temperature reaches 160°F (71°C).

Uncooked chorizo can be stored tightly wrapped in the refrigerator for up to 2 days, or in the freezer for up to 2 months.

Merguez Lamb Sausage

We are totally smitten with the spices and flavors of North Africa, where merguez sausage originates. Made from ground lamb and heavily spiced with cumin, harissa, sumac, fennel, and garlic, merguez is typically stuffed into lamb sausage casings, and we encourage you to try your hand at this technique. Its signature red tint comes from chile-forward harissa, and its smoky notes from Spanish *pimentón* (smoked paprika). Merguez is traditionally grilled, but it's also delicious sautéed, in link form or in patties—really, it's just delicious, period. Serve it over couscous, in pasta, on top of buckwheat polenta with sautéed kale (page 216), or go rogue and eat it on a toasted hot dog bun with more harissa, coarse ground mustard, and sauerkraut.

YIELD: 2½ LB [1.1 KG]

1½ tsp coriander seeds

1½ tsp black peppercorns

1 tsp cumin seeds

1 tsp fennel seeds

2½ Tbsp Harissa (page 32)

1 Tbsp kosher salt

2½ tsp smoked paprika

1 tsp ground sumac

¾ tsp ground cinnamon

3 or 4 garlic cloves, finely chopped

3 Tbsp finely minced mint

3 Tbsp finely minced parsley

2½ lb [1.1 kg] ground lamb (see Technique: Meat Grinding, page 211)

SPECIAL EQUIPMENT

Spice mill or mortar and pestle

Using a spice mill or mortar and pestle, grind the coriander, peppercorns, cumin, and fennel and transfer to a large bowl. Add the harissa, salt, paprika, sumac, cinnamon, garlic, and herbs and stir to combine.

CONT'D

Add the ground lamb to the bowl, mixing gently with your hands until all the ingredients are well integrated. Use a light touch when handling the ground meat to prevent a dense texture when cooked.

To test for seasoning, form a small ball of the sausage mixture into a patty and cook in a lightly oiled frying pan over medium-high heat until cooked through. Taste, then adjust the seasoning of the remaining sausage mixture, if desired, before proceeding.

Cover and chill the uncooked sausage mixture in the refrigerator for a minimum of 3 hours to allow the flavors to meld.

The sausage mixture can be stuffed into casings (see page 211 for instructions) or formed into patties, then grilled or cooked in a skillet over medium-high heat until the internal temperature reaches 160°F [71°C].

Uncooked merguez sausage can be stored, tightly wrapped, in the refrigerator for up to 2 days, or in the freezer for up to 2 months.

Merguez Sausage with Buckwheat Polenta and Kale

This hearty and healthy dish combines three of our favorite food groups: meat, grains, and vegetables. Traditional polenta is awarded an upgrade with the addition of kasha, toasted buckwheat groats. Buckwheat, which is actually the seed of a fruit, pairs incredibly well with merguez, the spicy North African lamb sausage (page 215) flavored with harissa, smoked paprika, coriander, cumin, and fennel seed. With the addition of sautéed kale, you've got a complete meal your grandmother would be proud of. **SERVES 4**

¼ cup [45 g] raw buckwheat groats
1 qt [1 L] Chicken Stock (page 221)
1 cup [250 ml] whole milk
Eight 1 by 3 in [2.5 by 7.5 cm] strips lemon zest
1½ tsp kosher salt, plus more as needed
12 large fresh sage leaves
½ tsp freshly ground black pepper
1 cup [140 g] polenta (not quick-cook)
¼ cup [55 g] unsalted butter
3 Tbsp olive oil, plus more as needed
16 large garlic cloves, peeled and thinly sliced
1 lb [450 g] lacinato kale, stems removed, leaves torn into pieces
1 Tbsp balsamic vinegar
8 Merguez Lamb Sausages (page 215)

SPECIAL EQUIPMENT

Spice mill or mortar and pestle

Instant-read thermometer

In a dry, heavy skillet over medium heat, toast the buckwheat groats until aromatic, about 5 minutes. Transfer to a plate to cool, then coarsely grind using a spice mill or mortar and pestle and set aside.

In a medium saucepan over medium-high heat, add the stock, milk, 1 cup [250 ml] of water, the lemon zest, and 1 tsp of the salt. Finely chop 6 of the sage leaves and add to the saucepan along with the pepper. Bring the mixture to a boil, then turn the heat to low and stir constantly while adding the polenta in a slow, steady stream, followed by the buckwheat.

Simmer, stirring the mixture every few minutes, until thick and creamy and the grains are tender, 35 to 40 minutes. Add more water in 1 Tbsp increments if the mixture becomes too thick.

Remove from the heat and add the butter, stirring to incorporate. Taste and adjust the seasoning, then cover the pan and set aside in a warm place.

While the polenta is cooking, prepare the kale. In a large sauté pan over medium heat, heat 2 Tbsp of the olive oil, then add half of the sliced garlic. Cook for 30 seconds, then add the kale and the remaining ½ tsp of salt and cook for 6 minutes, stirring occasionally, until wilted and soft. Add the vinegar to the pan and cook, stirring, for 1 minute more. Taste and adjust the seasoning, then remove from the heat and set aside in a warm place.

In a large, heavy-bottomed skillet over medium-high heat, heat the remaining 1 Tbsp of olive oil, then add the sausages and sauté until nicely browned on all sides and the internal temperature registers 160°F [71°C]. Transfer the sausages to a plate, leaving the juices in the pan, and keep warm.

Stack the remaining 6 sage leaves and roll them up like a cigar, then thinly julienne them. Add the sage and the remaining garlic slices to the pan with the meat juices, adding additional oil if needed, and cook over medium heat for 30 seconds, until lightly golden and aromatic, being careful not to burn them.

To serve, remove the lemon peel from the polenta, stirring until smooth and reheating it over low heat if needed, then divide between four plates. Top with the kale and then the sausage, sliced on the diagonal. Garnish with the fried garlic and sage and drizzle with any oil left over from the pan.

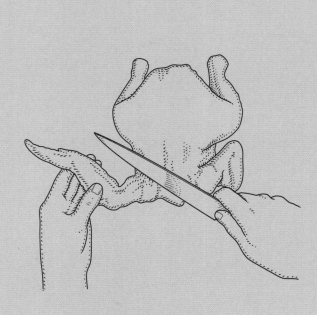

REMOVING THE WINGS

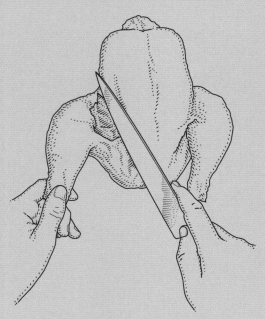

CUTTING A SLIT THROUGH THE SKIN
BETWEEN ONE BREAST AND THIGH

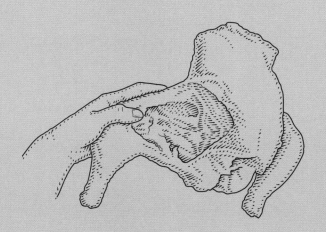

POPPING OUT THE JOINT BETWEEN
THE LEG AND BODY

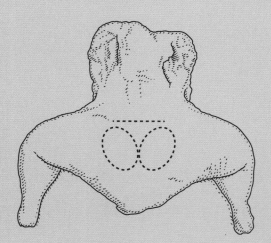

CUTTING THE CHICKEN STRAIGHT ACROSS THE
BACK AND ALONG THE TOP OF THE OYSTERS

Home Butchery:
Cutting Up a Whole Chicken

Purchasing chicken that has already been butchered into parts is not only more expensive, but you can also miss out on so much of the chicken. A whole chicken, butchered at home, gives you both white and dark meat (expand your horizons!) and the chicken's backbone, which you can use for making stock (page 221) from scratch. This means a lot more bang for your buck—and your taste buds—than a package of boneless, skinless chicken breasts in a Styrofoam tray. Jered Standing, the Institute's in-house butchery instructor and owner of Standing's Butchery here in Los Angeles, offers his preferred method for breaking down a whole chicken. His technique for including the "oysters," the two small, oyster-shaped pieces of dark meat residing on either side of the chicken's backbone, is a pro move that will elevate your home butchery skills. Don't sweat it if your first attempt takes a little extra effort; with time and practice you'll get the hang of it.

1 whole chicken

SPECIAL EQUIPMENT

Kitchen shears

REMOVING THE WINGS

Orient the chicken so that it is breast-side down and the drumsticks are pointing away from you. Grab a wing, lifting it up and twisting it away from the chicken to identify where the joint is between the wing and the chicken's back. Cut through the joint to remove the wing, hugging the wing bone with your knife and being careful to avoid the breast meat.

Repeat with the other wing.

If desired, remove the wing tips: Find the joint nearest the tip of the wing and cut straight down through it, leaving only the meatiest parts of the wing. Reserve the tips for stock.

REMOVING THE LEGS

Turn the chicken on its back with the legs pointing toward you. Cut a slit through the skin between one breast and thigh, then grab the thigh firmly in one hand and twist it out while pushing up with your fingers to break the joint between the leg and the body. You should feel a crunch or pop, and the leg will feel less firmly connected to the body.

Repeat with the other leg.

Turn the chicken over so that the breast now faces down. Identify the oysters, which will appear as two meaty pads midway up the back, flanking the spine. (This is an important landmark, perhaps the most delicious little morsel, and removing it whole with the leg is the mark of a good job breaking down the chicken.)

Cut the chicken straight across the back and along the top of the oysters, cutting down to the bone and connecting with the cuts you made previously on the other side of the chicken.

Starting from the cut you made across the back, use your fingers to dig underneath the oysters and push them down toward the rear of the chicken, effectively scraping them off the bones.

Cut the skin that attaches each oyster to the back, being careful to hug the spine with your knife and pulling the leg gently away from the body as you cut. This will help show you where to put the knife.

Find the ball-and-socket leg joint you broke. Continue the cut you made while freeing the oyster and get your knife into that joint. Again, pull gently while you do this, as things will open up and become clearer as you cut. Complete this cut all the way down to the rear of the chicken, keeping the knife against the backbone the entire time, and detach the leg.

Repeat with the other leg.

CONT'D

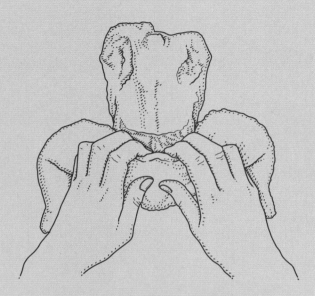

USING YOUR FINGERS TO DIG UNDERNEATH
THE OYSTERS AND PUSH THEM DOWN

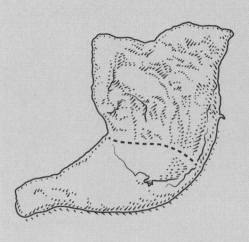

SEPARATING THE DRUMSTICK
FROM THE THIGH

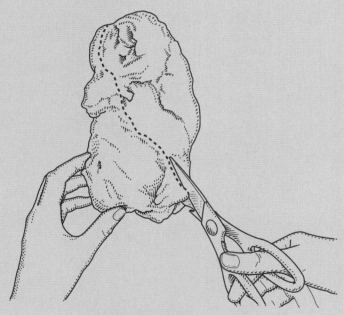

REMOVING THE BACKBONE

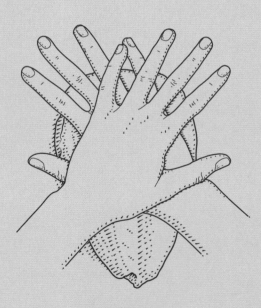

CRACKING THE BREASTBONE

SEPARATING THE DRUMSTICK FROM THE THIGH

Place one whole leg skin-side down. Look for a thin stripe of fat near the bend in the leg; the joint is directly behind it. Cut through that line, severing the joint and separating the thigh from the drumstick. Hold the skin taut around the thigh as you make the cut to prevent the skin from falling off.

Repeat with the other leg.

REMOVING THE BACKBONE

Place the chicken on its side with the neck pointing away from you. Look for a thin, diagonal stripe of fat outlining the breast and disappearing near the neck. Use kitchen shears to cut along this line, cutting through the membrane, ribs, and the thicker bone at the shoulder.

Turn the chicken on its other side and repeat, detaching the backbone completely from the body.

SPLITTING THE BREASTS

Place the breast skin-side down, with the wide end pointing away from you. Make a slit down the middle of the breastbone, then flip the breast over and apply pressure to the center of the breast, pressing firmly with your hands until you feel the bone crack in half.

Cut down the middle of the breast, forcing the knife through the cracked breastbone and splitting it in two.

VARIATION: SPATCHCOCK

Another alternative to cooking a whole bird is to spatchcock, or "butterfly," the chicken first. This method has several advantages: It's less work than boning a whole chicken; a spatchcocked chicken cooks faster than one left whole; and it makes for an attractive presentation.

Start with a whole chicken and remove the backbone by using kitchen shears to cut along the sides of the spine, keeping the shears close to the spine and cutting through the ribs and membranes. Reserve the backbone for stock.

Spread the chicken out in a single layer with the breast meat up, legs pointing inward, and the cavity side pressed flat against the work surface. Apply pressure to the center of the breast, pressing firmly with your hand. This will break the cartilage around the breast bone and allow the chicken to lie flat in a roasting pan.

Chicken Stock

If you're used to store-bought chicken broth, try homemade and you may never go back—it elevates everything from soups to braises. We leave it unsalted to have more control over the salt content when using it in dishes, but keep in mind it may taste a little flat on its own. **YIELD: 2 TO 3 QT [2 TO 3 L]**

2 to 3 lb [0.9 to 1.4 kg] chicken parts (backbone, neck, wing tips, etc.)
2 Tbsp olive oil
1 large onion, roughly chopped
1 celery stalk, roughly chopped
2 carrots, roughly chopped
Kosher or sea salt (optional)

Preheat the oven to 425°F [220°C]. Place the chicken parts on a baking sheet and roast for 45 minutes to 1 hour, until deeply browned.

In a large, heavy-bottomed stockpot, heat the oil over medium-high heat. Add the vegetables and sauté for 10 to 12 minutes, until browned.

Pour off any excess oil from the pot, then add the roasted bones and cover with 4 qt [4 L] of water. Bring to a boil, then turn down the heat to low and simmer uncovered for 3 to 5 hours, adding water as necessary to keep the ingredients submerged.

Remove from the heat and allow to cool. Strain, discarding the bones and vegetables. Taste and add salt, if desired. Transfer the stock to a container with a lid and refrigerate. A layer of fat will accumulate on the top of the stock as it cools, which can be scraped off and reserved for another use.

Store fresh chicken stock in an airtight container in the refrigerator for up to 3 days, or in the freezer for up to 6 months.

Moroccan Chicken Tagine with Preserved Lemons and Olives

This North African–inspired meat, vegetable, and fruit stew traditionally would be cooked in a tagine, a shallow clay pot with a conical lid, after which this type of dish is named. Though a clay tagine is a beautiful object that enables the dish to be cooked slowly over a fire, you do not have to use one to prepare this recipe—but feel free to tell those at the table you did! We prefer using bone-in chicken with the skin intact to add layers of flavor to this savory dish. Reducing the spiced stock and drippings at the end of cooking will produce a flavorful and unctuous sauce to spoon over the chicken and couscous when serving. **SERVES 4**

CHICKEN

One 3½ to 4 lb [1.6 to 1.8 kg] chicken, cut into 8 pieces (see Home Butchery: Cutting Up a Whole Chicken, page 219)

Kosher salt

2 Tbsp olive oil

1 large onion, sliced

3 garlic cloves, peeled and crushed

One 1 in [2.5 cm] piece fresh ginger, peeled and grated

1 Tbsp ground coriander

2 tsp ground cumin

2 tsp sweet paprika

½ tsp ground turmeric

½ tsp ground cinnamon

½ tsp freshly ground black pepper

½ tsp cayenne powder

Pinch of ground saffron (optional)

2 cups [500 ml] Chicken Stock (page 221)

1 bay leaf

3 Preserved Lemons (page 36), rinsed, rind cut into strips, pulp removed and discarded

1 cup [140 g] green olives, pits removed if desired

COUSCOUS

1 cup [250 ml] Chicken Stock (page 221)

1 Tbsp olive oil

¼ tsp kosher salt

1½ cups [240 g] couscous

Chopped cilantro, for garnish

MAKE THE CHICKEN

Pat the chicken pieces dry with paper towels, then season lightly with salt and set aside.

In a large, deep skillet, heat the oil over medium-high heat until shimmering. Working in batches if necessary, add the chicken pieces to the skillet, skin-side down, and allow to cook undisturbed until golden brown, 5 to 6 minutes, then flip and repeat on the other side. Transfer the chicken to a plate and set aside.

Pour off half of the oil left in the skillet, lower the heat to medium, and add the onion, sautéing until soft and lightly browned, 8 to 10 minutes. Stir in the garlic, ginger, coriander, cumin, paprika, turmeric, cinnamon, black pepper, cayenne, and saffron, if using, and cook for 1 to 2 minutes more.

Return the chicken pieces to the skillet, stirring to coat them with the onion-spice mixture before arranging them skin-side up in the pan. Pour the chicken stock into the skillet, add the bay leaf, and bring to a simmer. Lower the heat to medium-low, cover, and simmer for 15 minutes.

Stir in the preserved lemon peels and olives, cover, and continue to simmer until the chicken is cooked through, about 10 minutes.

If desired, reduce the sauce: Remove the chicken from the skillet, increase the heat to high, and cook, uncovered, until the sauce is slightly thickened, about 5 minutes.

MAKE THE COUSCOUS

In a medium saucepan over medium-high heat, combine the chicken stock, olive oil, salt, and 1 cup [250 ml] of water. Bring to a boil, then stir in the couscous. Remove from the heat, cover, and let stand for 5 minutes. Fluff with a fork before serving.

Serve the chicken on a bed of couscous, topped with the sauce and olives, and garnished with cilantro.

Cured Egg Yolks

What happens when you take a common ingredient like a fresh egg yolk and bury it in a salt-and-sugar cure for weeks? The yolk dry-cures, miraculously becoming hard and easily grated, producing a deep umami flavor similar to Parmesan cheese. Use the best-quality eggs you can find—backyard, pasture raised, and/or organic—as these will produce the most beautiful, jewel-like results. Grate them finely with a rasp-style grater and use them as you would any hard, Italian grating cheese, or try one of our ideas (following). **YIELD: 6 TO 12 YOLKS**

2 cups [480 g] fine sea salt
1⅓ cups [265 g] granulated sugar
6 to 12 eggs

SPECIAL EQUIPMENT
8 by 8 in [20 by 20 cm] glass or ceramic baking dish
Cheesecloth

In a large bowl, add the salt and sugar, stirring to combine.

Place half of the mixture into an 8 by 8 in [20 by 20 cm] glass or ceramic baking dish, smoothing the surface evenly.

Using a whole egg in its shell, make 6 to 12 divots (depending on how many egg yolks you want to cure) ½ in [12 mm] deep in the mixture, allowing space between each one and making sure to not hit the bottom of the dish.

Separate the eggs, reserving the whole yolks and saving the whites for another use.

Carefully place one yolk into each divot. Cover the yolks with the remaining salt-sugar mixture, making sure the yolks are completely buried. Cover the dish and place in the refrigerator, allowing the yolks to cure for 1 week, or until the yolks hold their shape but still have some give when squeezed.

Gently lift the yolks out of the baking dish, brushing off as much of the curing mixture as you can.

Fill a medium bowl with water and dip each yolk into it, rubbing the surface ever so gently to rinse off the remainder of the curing mixture. Pat dry with a towel.

Place a wire cooling rack on a baking sheet, cover with a layer of cheesecloth, and place the rinsed and dried yolks on top without touching each other. Cover with a second layer of cheesecloth and place in the refrigerator to dry further. Flip the yolks once a day, removing and replacing the cheesecloth, for 2 to 3 weeks or until firm and no longer tacky to the touch.

Cured egg yolks can be used immediately or transferred to an airtight container and stored in the refrigerator for up to 1 month.

SIX IDEAS FOR CURED EGG YOLKS

1. Grate on top of pasta or a pizza.

2. Add to soups to enhance body and flavor.

3. Grate over cooked vegetables such as asparagus or Brussels sprouts.

4. Sprinkle on top of a Caesar salad.

5. Grate on top of avocado toast.

6. Use as a baked potato topping.

Gravlax

The Scandinavians have a way with preserved fish, and there's nothing as elegant and easy to prepare as gravlax, which is similar to lox, but without the additional step of smoking. Fresh salmon is flavored with dill fronds and spices and treated to a salt-and-sugar cure, which draws out some of the fish's moisture, giving it a firm and velvety texture. We've also included a generous pour of juniper-forward gin in place of the traditional caraway-flavored Aquavit liquor. Gravlax is a showstopper, perfect for making a splash at a weekend brunch. It calls out to be thinly sliced and served open face on a slice of whole-grain bread or an "everything" bagel. Gravlax will benefit even further from sliced radishes, a dab of crème fraîche, and a gin and tonic. We said brunch, didn't we? **YIELD: 2 LB [900 G]**

2 tsp coriander seeds

1 tsp black peppercorns

1 tsp yellow mustard seeds

1 tsp fennel seeds

½ tsp celery seeds

½ tsp red pepper flakes

3 Tbsp kosher salt

1 Tbsp granulated sugar

¼ cup [60 ml] gin

1 tsp lemon zest

One 2 lb [900 g] salmon fillet, preferably a 1 in [2.5 cm] thick center cut

1 bunch [21 g] fresh dill, plus more for garnish

Crème fraîche (page 177), for garnish (optional)

SPECIAL EQUIPMENT

Spice grinder or mortar and pestle

Coarsely crush the coriander seeds, peppercorns, mustard seeds, fennel seeds, celery seeds, and red pepper flakes in a spice grinder (or crush with a mortar and pestle), then transfer to a small bowl and add the salt, sugar, gin, and lemon zest, stirring to combine.

Cut the salmon in half against the grain and place the pieces on one large sheet of plastic wrap, skin-side down. Spread the spice mixture over the surface of both halves, lightly massaging it in.

Spread the dill sprigs evenly on top of one salmon half, then sandwich the second half on top, skin-side up.

Wrap the salmon tightly in two layers of plastic wrap and place on a rimmed tray or pan to collect any drips.

Place a second small tray, pan, or cutting board on top of the salmon, weighting it down with a heavy can or other weight, and place in the refrigerator overnight.

The next day, remove the fish and the weight from the refrigerator, keeping the plastic wrap tightly sealed, and drain any liquid that has accumulated on the tray. Flip the fish over, replacing the weight, and return to the refrigerator. Repeat once a day for 2 more days.

After 3 days, remove the weight and discard the plastic wrap. Gently scrape off the dill and spices from the surface of both fillets and discard.

To serve, use a long, very sharp knife to slice each fillet as thinly as possible, cutting against the grain and on the diagonal for the greatest surface area, and leaving the skin behind.

Serve gravlax immediately, garnished with fresh sprigs of dill and/or a dollop of crème fraîche, if you feel like being fancy.

Leftovers can be transferred to an airtight container and stored in the refrigerator for up to 3 days.

COUNTY FAIR MEDALS AND RIBBONS

The establishment of the Los Angeles County Fair in 1922 was a real boon for the Institute. Over the years, the Institute's students made up an increasingly disproportionate share of winners at the fair, dominating nearly every culinary category. In this photo, IDT students Jessie Winthrop (far left) and Maria Wojciechowski (center) stand alongside an unknown fellow jam-maker while proudly displaying their winning entries at the 1924 LA County Fair's marmalade competition. Wojciechowski herself went on to join IDT's teaching staff and eventually rose to the level of Dean of Pickles and Preserves and, after that, the Institute's directorship. (Kevin West, the current Dean of Pickles and Preserves, says he was inspired by Wojciechowski's legacy when coming up with his own marmalade recipe on page 102.)

Apparently, fair medals and ribbons won by both IDT students and instructors were prominently displayed in a trophy case that stood in the Institute's lobby, but they were lost after the Institute closed in 1966. Many years later, a few of these relics from the Institute's heyday were discovered at the bottom of a disintegrating cardboard box full of canning lids that had somehow escaped notice among a pile of IDT records in the back of Nellie Archer's garage.* Sic transit gloria mundi!

*Nellie Archer was the daughter of the Institute's Founder and Director, Eliza Taylor Reynolds. See From the Institute Archives, page 188.

Department of Spirits | CH .07

THE DEPARTMENT OF SPIRITS

It doesn't always occur to people that the Institute would extend its interest in all things made from scratch to the pursuit of the perfect cocktail. In fact, spirits play a significant role at the Institute. What's more, while its starring role in cocktails tends to be front and center for most of us, alcohol has also fulfilled a number of other useful functions throughout history.

As is so often the case, it all starts with fermentation—specifically, with transforming the carbohydrates and sugars in various substances into alcohol. Then comes preservation. Alcohol has a much longer shelf life than the grains and fruits used to make it. For instance, perishables like summer fruit, herbs, and roots have been turned into wine, distilled spirits, and liqueurs for centuries, a transformation that allows them to last for years without spoiling. In addition to being used to make various liqueurs, bitters, and fortified wines, neutral spirits (unflavored grain alcohol) have a long history as an antibacterial (think battleground surgeries before the development of modern antiseptics). You can use vodka, in fact, to make a household cleaning spray or to prevent unwanted mold from growing on miso during its long fermentation.

Still, for all its pleasures and practical applications, civilization's relationship with alcohol has sometimes been a little complicated due to its intoxicating effects. One of the more interesting historical events in the United States involving alcohol, drinking, and byzantine legal loopholes was the adoption in 1920 of the Eighteenth Amendment to the Constitution—otherwise known as Prohibition—which banned the production, sale, and drinking of alcohol. Contemporaneous concerns about alcohol's impact on society notwithstanding, it's well known that Prohibition was a huge failure. Even before its repeal in 1933, illegal alcohol, while risky, was always relatively easy to procure, even during those thirteen supposedly dry years. You could even get a doctor to prescribe it for you as a "medicinal tonic" or "stimulant," much like medical marijuana in some states today. (The liquor section commonly found in modern drugstores dates from Prohibition. Now you know.)

But let's get back to the bar! Just as we're now seeing the third wave of coffee culture, we're also in the midst of a "Golden Age of Cocktails" revival. We see a connection between the Golden Age of the 1930s through 1950s—a period when many now-classic cocktails were invented—and Prohibition, the repeal of which set off a virtual explosion of pent-up cocktail creativity. Whatever it was that gave rise to still-popular drinks like the Vesper and Black Russian, we think the current interest in cocktails draws its inspiration from these vintage drinks.

Like so many of our cooking ingredients that have been subjected to standardized, commercial production, the component parts that go into making cocktails have suffered an unfortunate loss of quality and flavor as well. That's one of the reasons we find the current cocktail revival so exciting. Bars everywhere are getting the same Institute-style makeover that home and professional kitchens have gotten: handmade ingredients, innovative versions of authentic recipes, and the availability of ingredients like amaro and bitters that had become hard to find. Today's creators of unadulterated, small-batch cocktail ingredients employ a more culinary approach to creating their concoctions and have unleashed an obsessive interest among enthusiastic home bartenders.

For those who'd like to join in, we supply you with plenty of recipes for building your own homemade bar ingredients from scratch in this chapter, like Amaretto (page 250), Dry Vermouth (page 250), Tonic Syrup (page 249), and Luxardo Maraschino Cherries (page 251). We also unravel the mysteries of cocktail-making tools. And while there are plenty of shiny gizmos and gadgets out there and it's easy to become an obsessive collector (we're guilty!), remember that a decent drink can be assembled using almost anything from your own kitchen.

With all there is to learn about spirits, we're fortunate to have an expert like Daniel Kent as our guide. Professor Kent established the Institute's Coffee Lab, which quickly grew into an entire Department of Beverages, including both coffee as well as spirits. It authorized him to keep our students both caffeinated *and* lubricated. Many of the spirit recipes in this chapter take their cues from Professor Kent's sensibility of restraint—"Don't use too many ingredients in one drink; allow each ingredient to shine on its own as well as together in concert with others." The resulting assemblage of both familiar and unusual drinks in the following pages, adapted from Professor Kent's popular Cocktail Crafting classes, should please even the most sophisticated connoisseur.

Spirits and cocktail culture are not only a part of the Institute's mission; it could be said that they are central and emblematic to what we do here: rescuing forgotten traditions, resurrecting old standards of quality, and rediscovering simple pleasures for all five senses. Cheers!

230

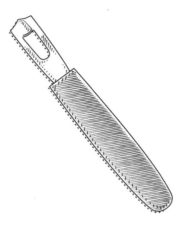

BARTENDER'S CHANNEL KNIFE

This tool, the size and shape of a small vegetable peeler, has a wooden handle and a V-shaped metal blade, often with a small hollow in the center. It's used to cut long strips of citrus peel for cocktail garnishes.

THREE-PIECE COCKTAIL SHAKER

Consisting of a metal tumbler with a perforated, domed lid and a small cap on top to contain the liquid while shaking, a cocktail shaker is the most efficient and user-friendly way to shake a drink. When ice is added, it chills the cocktail ingredients thoroughly. You can even strain the drink after chilling using the shaker's perforated lid. Alternatively, you can use a two-piece cocktail shaker (lid and base only) along with a Hawthorne strainer: a flat disk, usually with a handle, affixed to a coiled spring. When placed on top of a shaker rim, it traps and keeps chunks of ice from ending up in the drink.

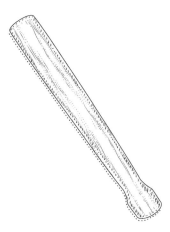

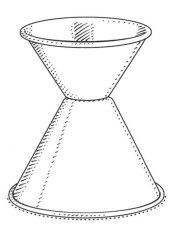

MUDDLER

This cylindrical, wooden pestle has a flat, rounded bottom, sometimes with a rasped surface on its blunt end. It's used to crush the aromatics at the bottom of the glass or shaker before adding other drink ingredients.

JIGGER

This hourglass-shaped, stainless steel measuring cup is used when mixing cocktails. The two-in-one tool has two distinct cups: one larger and one smaller. The larger cup is usually 1½ oz [45 ml], or "one jigger" exactly. The smaller one is a "half jigger," or ¾ oz [22 ml].

COCKTAIL GLASSES 101

While we'll gladly accept just about any cocktail offered to us, we do appreciate someone who gives a little extra thought as to how it's served. Using the right glass for the right drink can transform what may be a perfectly decent cocktail into a truly high-end experience. What's more, the way in which a cocktail's flavors reach your nose and tongue (or even the roof of your mouth) changes depending on the shape, depth, and thickness of the glass, so it isn't just about looks. All of which is to say, purchasing a few of these specialized glasses for your favorite cocktails is a smart investment.

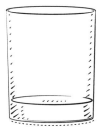

Old Fashioned or Rocks
A short, wide-brimmed tumbler with a thick base
VOLUME: 6 to 10 oz [180 to 300 ml]

Double Old Fashioned
Similar to an Old Fashioned or Rocks glass, but double the volume
VOLUME: 12 to 16 oz [360 to 480 ml]

Martini
A triangular bowl with a long stem
attached to a round base
VOLUME: 4 to 12 oz [120 to 360 ml]

Cordial
A small, thin-stemmed glass used
for after-dinner liqueurs
VOLUME: 1 oz [30 ml]

Punch Cup
Basically a fancy teacup with a handle
VOLUME: 4 oz [120 ml]

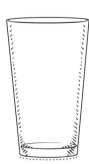

Highball
A straight-sided tumbler, taller than
an Old Fashioned
VOLUME: 8 to 12 oz [240 to 360 ml]

Beer
A heavy, 1 pt [500 ml] tumbler,
smaller on the bottom, wider on
the top
VOLUME: 16 oz [480 ml]

POLISHING A COCKTAIL OR WINE GLASS: VIRGO EDITION

Cocktail glasses spotted with hard water deposits after washing are a common cocktail-hour eyesore, the result of putting them away without drying and polishing first. This can necessitate an awkward, emergency wash-and-dry when serving guests. For sparkling, ready-to-use glassware, we suggest hand washing with warm water and just a drop of liquid dish soap, followed by drying and polishing with a lint-free, microfiber cloth before storing. (When drying fragile stemware, such as martini or cordial glasses, hold the glass by the bowl or flute when drying in order to avoid breaking off the stem.) If you have spotted glasses that were washed and put away without being polished first, use our remedial technique below. Your inner Virgo will thank you.

Fill a medium pot halfway with water and bring to a simmer over medium heat.

As the water begins to steam, place the glass upside down over the pot, without touching the hot water, until the mouth of the glass fogs up.

Remove the glass from the steam and wipe carefully with a lint-free, microfiber cloth.

NAME YOUR POISON: THE INGREDIENTS AND METHODS OF MAKNG ALCOHOL

Beer
Grains + hops + fermentation

Bourbon
Minimum of 51 percent fermented corn + distillation + aging in new, charred oak barrels in Kentucky

Brandy
Grapes + fermentation + distillation

Gin
Grains + fermentation + distillation + juniper berries and other botanicals

Rum
Sugar cane + fermentation + distillation (may be aged in oak)

Light = Silver or white, not aged in wood, has a clear color

Golden = Dark, aged in wood (commercial brands may use caramel coloring)

Spiced = Dark rum with spices added

Rye Whiskey
Minimum of 51 percent fermented rye + distillation in new oak barrels + aging

Tequila
Agave + fermentation + distillation

Blanco = Silver, aged 2 months

Reposado ("Rested") = Aged in oak barrels for 2 to 12 months

Anejo ("Old") = Aged 1 year or more in barrels

Vermouth
Wine + neutral spirits with aromatized botanicals and a bitter element

Vodka
Grains (traditionally potatoes, but most vodka is made from grains, such as corn or rice) + fermentation + distillation

Wine
Grapes + fermentation

A cocktail garnish is like a scarf or a pocket square—something that isn't entirely necessary but that adds the perfect finishing touch to an outfit. Does a cocktail really need a garnish? No. Could you skip it entirely if you had to? Absolutely. And do we encourage you to use them here at the Institute? *$%# yes! The garnish on a drink can hint at what ingredients might be hidden inside. Or, it can simply announce the fact that the drink got dressed up for you. In either case, you can think of a cocktail with a garnish as a date that's put his or her best foot forward to impress you.

Citrus Zest
Use a vegetable peeler or sharp paring knife to remove a 1 by 3 in [2.5 by 7.5 cm] strip of citrus zest from a washed (and preferably unwaxed) lemon, lime, grapefruit, or orange, using only the outermost part of the rind and avoiding the white pith.

Classic Lemon Peel Spiral
Drag a bartender's channel knife (see Equipment, page 230) through the peel of a lemon, starting at the top and spiraling your way around the fruit to create long, narrow spirals.

Lime Wedge
On a cutting board, place a whole lime on its side and cut off both ends. Stand the lime on one of the cut ends, then cut the lime into eight wedges by slicing through the fruit from top to bottom.

OLEO SACCHARUM SYRUP (PAGE 248)

MARTINI (PAGE 254)

WHITE RUSSIAN (PAGE 254)

INSTITUTE PUNCH (PAGE 255)

Simple Syrup

Simple syrup is just a fancy name for dissolved sugar water, but it's the perfect medium for sweetening drinks. If you were to add granulated sugar directly to a drink, we guarantee that you wouldn't be pleased with the result, as the sugar wouldn't incorporate properly. Dissolving the sugar in hot water first transforms it into a smooth, clear syrup that will seamlessly blend itself into any drink. A batch of simple syrup will keep in your refrigerator for up to 1 month, ready when needed for spur-of-the-moment cocktail making. **YIELD: 1½ CUPS [375 ML]**

1 cup [200 g] granulated sugar
1 cup [250 ml] filtered water

SPECIAL EQUIPMENT
1 pt [500 ml] mason jar or 16 oz [500 ml] glass bale-top bottle

In a small saucepan over medium heat, combine the sugar and water, stirring until the sugar is dissolved. Remove from the heat and allow to cool completely.

Use immediately or transfer the syrup to a 1 pt [500 ml] mason jar or 16 oz [500 ml] bale-top bottle. Store, tightly sealed, in the refrigerator for up to 1 month.

> ### VARIATIONS
> The following versions, using more or less sugar, can be used interchangeably in most recipes that call for simple syrup, depending on your sweet tooth.
>
> **"LITE" SIMPLE SYRUP:**
> Use ½ cup [100 g] sugar and 1½ cups [375 ml] water.
>
> **"HEAVY" SIMPLE SYRUP:**
> Use 1 cup [200 g] sugar and ½ cup [125 ml] water.

Oleo Saccharum Syrup

Oleo saccharum (OS) is Latin for "sugar oil" and is essentially what it sounds like: an ingredient that uses sugar to extract oil from citrus peels. Grapefruits, oranges, lemons, and limes all work well. In fact, you can experiment with a mix of different citrus fruit to make your own, personalized OS flavors. Use OS for a bittersweet addition in cocktails or try combining it with juice, liquor, bitters, and ice in our world-famous Institute Punch (page 255). **YIELD: ½ CUP [125 ML]**

9 oz [250 g] citrus zest strips (from 8 to 16 citrus fruits, depending on size)
1 cup [200 g] granulated sugar

SPECIAL EQUIPMENT
1 qt [1 L] mason jar
Muddler (optional)
½ pt [250 ml] mason jar

Use a vegetable peeler to peel away the zest from the citrus fruits in strips, using only the outermost part of the rind and avoiding the white pith.

In a 1 qt [1 L] mason jar, combine the strips of zest and sugar, then use a muddler or a wooden spoon to pound the peels until they are well bruised and all the sugar is worked into them.

Cover and leave at room temperature to macerate for 3 to 24 hours.

Once the oils have been extracted from the zest and liquid is visible at the bottom of the jar, strain the mixture through a fine-mesh sieve, pressing on the peels to extract as much liquid as possible.

Discard the spent peels and transfer the syrup to a ½ pt [250 ml] jar. Use immediately or cover tightly and store in the refrigerator for up to 1 week.

Tonic Syrup

Don't even think about comparing the Institute's Tonic Syrup with store-bought tonic water, because there is, quite literally, no comparison. Professor Daniel Kent's recipe bears no similarity whatsoever to that clear, quinine tonic in plastic bottles you're used to seeing at your liquor store or supermarket. First of all, there's the color. Look at the raw, unprocessed bark of the Peruvian cinchona tree, from which we get quinine, and you'll notice it's a deep, burnt-orange color, not colorless like commercial tonic water produced in a laboratory. Then there's the taste. Commercial tonic water is made with corn syrup or other processed sweeteners and some kind of lime flavoring. In all, it's not a pretty sight. Fortunately, you can switch to our handmade Tonic Syrup. Unlike the usual, ho-hum tonic water that's designed to blend into the background like a wallflower, with little to no distinct flavor of its own, IDT Tonic Syrup isn't shy at all. In fact, it's the life of the party, infused with an attention-getting blend of citrus, spices, and bitter cinchona. To use it in place of commercial tonic water in any recipe, simply add sparkling water in a 1:1 ratio. It'll also keep in the refrigerator, so you'll have it on hand whenever the mood strikes. (To locate cinchona bark and other tonic syrup ingredients, see Resources, page 340). **YIELD: ABOUT 4 CUPS [1 L]**

2¼ tsp powdered cinchona bark

⅔ cup [160 ml] 80-proof vodka

1 qt [1 L] filtered water

¼ cup [55 g] citric acid

Zest, peeled into strips, and juice of 3 limes

Zest, peeled into strips, and juice of 1 grapefruit

9 allspice berries

2 cinnamon sticks

⅛ tsp cardamom seeds

1½ cups [300 g] granulated sugar

1 tsp orange flower water

SPECIAL EQUIPMENT

Paper coffee filter

Two 16 oz [500 ml] glass bale-top bottles

In a small bowl, add the cinchona bark and vodka, stirring to combine, then allow to steep for 1 minute before straining the infusion through a fine-mesh sieve lined with a paper coffee filter. Discard the cinchona and set the infused vodka aside.

In a medium saucepan over medium heat, add the filtered water, citric acid, citrus zest and juice, allspice, cinnamon, and cardamom. When the mixture comes to a boil, turn the heat to low and simmer for 20 minutes. Remove from the heat and, while still warm, strain the liquid through a fine-mesh sieve into a large, heatproof pitcher or bowl, discarding the solids. Add the sugar, stirring until dissolved.

Add the cinchona infusion and orange flower water to the pitcher, stirring once more to combine.

Allow to cool, then use or decant the tonic syrup into two 16 oz [500 ml] bale-top bottles. Seal tightly, then store the tonic syrup in the refrigerator for up to 3 months.

Bitters

High-proof alcohol infused with botanical ingredients has been used for ages. Bitters were originally concocted in order to extract the essences of bitter roots, bark, and leaves for medicinal purposes, but at some point, ingenious drinkers found that adding a dash of bitters to a cocktail rounded out the flavors of both spirits and sugary liqueurs. They also discovered that imbibing bitters before a meal stimulated the appetite, and that a glass containing the same bitters after a large meal acted as an effective digestive. Use your own homemade bitters as you would store-bought bitters (who needs Angostura?) for mixed drinks, or to make a bottle of Dry Vermouth (page 250). (To locate wormwood and other bitters ingredients, see Resources, page 340.) **YIELD: ABOUT 1 CUP [250 ML]**

2½ tsp dried wormwood

¼ tsp crushed chamomile flowers

¼ tsp crushed dried sage

⅛ tsp cardamom seeds

¼ tsp coriander seeds

1½ cinnamon sticks

CONT'D

3 juniper berries

Peel of ½ orange (zest and white pith)

Peel of ½ lemon (zest and white pith)

1 cup [250 ml] 100-proof inexpensive vodka, such as Smirnoff

SPECIAL EQUIPMENT

1 pt [500 ml] mason jar

Paper coffee filter

Two 4 oz [120 ml] dark glass bottles with rubber dropper

In a 1 pt [500 ml] jar, combine all of the ingredients. Cover tightly and allow to infuse at room temperature for 5 to 6 days, shaking the jar gently once a day to distribute the mixture.

Strain the infusion through a fine-mesh sieve lined with a paper coffee filter, discarding the solids. Decant the bitters into two 4 oz [120 ml] dark glass bottles. Use immediately or store, tightly sealed, at room temperature for up to 1 year.

Dry Vermouth

If you like your martinis on the dry side and have been using only a thimble-full of vermouth at a time, chances are the bottle you've had in your bar forever went bad a long time ago. Vermouth is a wine and has the same limited shelf life as any other wine. To make homemade vermouth, you'll start with your own botanical bitters before "fortifying" them with wine. The result? A vermouth with so much flavor and personality, it's refreshingly drinkable over ice all by itself. **YIELD: ABOUT 4 CUPS [1 L]**

¾ cup [180 ml] Bitters (page 249)

3 cups [750 ml] crisp white wine, such as a Sauvignon Blanc or Grüner Veltliner

1½ Tbsp honey, gently warmed

SPECIAL EQUIPMENT

Two 16 oz [500 ml] glass bale-top bottles

In a large pitcher or medium bowl, add all of the ingredients, stirring to combine and until the honey is dissolved.

Decant the vermouth into two 16 oz [500 ml] bale-top bottles. Serve immediately, chilled over ice as a spritz with sparkling wine, or in a martini with gin or vodka (page 254). Or seal tightly and store in the refrigerator for up to 3 months.

Amaretto

Italian for "a little bitter," Amaretto is a sweet Italian liqueur best known for its almond flavor. The irony is, no actual almonds are used in making Amaretto. Its almond flavor instead involves a bit of alchemy that transforms the flavor found in the inner kernels of fruit pits. Cocktail alchemist Joshua McIver, an early instructor at the Institute, supplied us with this Amaretto recipe in the form of a pirate tale he penned (with a quill, no doubt) entitled "The Story of Little Bitter."

"Get ye bottles of 100-proof neutral spirits.

"Gather yourself 'bout 13 apricots.

"Pick ye 'bout 7 cherries.

"Scrape up a quarter stick of cinnamon (careful—it's explosive).

"Barter for some cloves and steal 1 Meyer lemon.

"Get yer hands on some apricot kernels, usually found 'bouts the island of health food stores.

"Ye needs to perform a light pulverization of the apricot meats in order to release their ornery oil.

"Smother all these unlikely companions in booze, then shake the crap out of them.

"Put them in a dark closet like a bitter secret for two months—occasionally poking them with a big stick.

"After the months have become unbearable—open, strain, and put this blend of bittersweet once more in the closet. Forget about it, only to be remembered again in another month or even another year or so. It only gets better with age."

To make your own Amaretto, you can try deciphering McIver's "Little Bitter" story or you can use our modern version, translated from the original Pirate. Then "after the months have become unbearable," open yer bottle and use ye some in an Amaretto Sour (page 253). Arrgh!

YIELD: ABOUT 6 CUPS [1.4 L]

7 cherries

13 apricots

4 oz [110 g] apricot kernels (see Note)

1 cinnamon stick

3 cloves

Zest of 1 Meyer lemon, peeled into strips

Two 750 ml bottles 100-proof vodka, such as Smirnoff

1½ cups [300 g] raw cane sugar

SPECIAL EQUIPMENT

Nutcracker or small hammer

Mortar and pestle

2 qt [2 L] mason jar

Paper coffee filter

Remove the pits and stems from the cherries, discarding both, and set the fruit aside. Remove the pits from the apricots and reserve, setting the fruit aside.

Using a nutcracker, crack open the apricot pits and remove their kernels, discarding the hard shell fragments. Alternatively, place the pits into a heavy cloth bag and pound with a hammer to crack, then remove the kernels. Place these kernels, along with the additional 4 oz [110 g] of apricot kernels, in a mortar, coarsely pulverizing the kernel meats with a pestle to release their oils.

In a medium, dry sauté pan over medium heat, add the apricot kernels, cinnamon, and cloves and toast, stirring, until the spices are fragrant, 1 to 2 minutes. Remove from the heat and transfer to a 2 qt [2 L] jar, along with the apricots and cherries. Add the strips of lemon zest, then pour the vodka over the mixture and stir to combine.

Seal the jar tightly and store in a cool, dark place for 2 months, occasionally giving the jar a shake to redistribute the ingredients.

After 2 months, strain the mixture through a fine-mesh sieve lined with a paper coffee filter, discarding the solids. Rinse out the jar and pour the Amaretto back in, along with the raw sugar. Stir to combine, then seal the jar tightly and return to a cool, dark place to age for an additional month, occasionally giving the jar a shake. Amaretto can be served after 1 month, but will improve with age, and can be stored for up to 1 year.

NOTE ON APRICOT KERNELS: Apricot kernels can be sourced online, in bulk and pre-cracked for convenience (see Resources, page 340)!

Luxardo Maraschino Cherries

The Luxardo maraschino cherry has a storied past. In 1821, Girolamo Luxardo founded a distillery in Dalmatia (Croatia) to produce a liqueur called maraschino made from Marasca sour cherries. By the early 1900s, the distillery also began producing the famed jars of whole cherries steeped in the distillery's maraschino liqueur. World War II and the Nazi invasion of Croatia put an end to the distillery's production there, but Girolamo's descendant, Giorgio Luxardo, fled to Italy along with the recipe, and the family has been producing the liqueur and bottled cherries ever since.

During Prohibition, the United States discovered a way to make nonalcoholic "maraschino" cherries by brining, bleaching, and adding red food coloring to American cherries. While nostalgic for some, these nuclear-red versions bear no resemblance to Luxardo's deep, dark, boozy version we love so much.

We made our first handcrafted Luxardo maraschino cherries during one of Dean of Pickles and Preserves Kevin West's "Saving the Season" workshops at the Institute, and we've continued to experiment and refine the recipe ever since. Unlike store-bought Luxardo cherries, which we find a bit too cloying, our version is lighter, boozier, and perfect for garnishing. Making these cherries is also a great way to preserve the fleeting cherry season, assuring you'll have them on hand all year long.

YIELD: TWO 1 PT [500 ML] MASON JARS

CONT'D

1 lb [450 g] fresh cherries, preferably sour

½ cup [100 g] granulated sugar

1 star anise pod

½ cinnamon stick

⅛ tsp nutmeg

One 1 by 4 in [2.5 by 10 cm] strip lemon zest

3 Tbsp fresh lemon juice

½ vanilla bean

1 cup [250 ml] Luxardo Maraschino Liqueur

SPECIAL EQUIPMENT

Two 1 pt [500 ml] mason jars

Remove the pits and stems from the cherries, discarding both, and set the fruit aside.

In a medium saucepan over medium-low heat, combine the sugar, spices, lemon zest, and lemon juice. Use a sharp paring knife to split the vanilla bean lengthwise, then use the tip of the knife to scrape the seeds into the pan, and add the pod.

Bring the mixture to a simmer, stirring frequently, and cook until the sugar has dissolved, about 5 minutes.

Add the cherries and liqueur, stirring to combine, then return to a simmer and cook for an additional 3 minutes. Remove from the heat and allow the mixture to cool completely.

Use a slotted spoon to transfer the cherries to two 1 pt [500 ml] jars, dividing them evenly. Remove and discard the vanilla bean pod and whole spices, then pour the syrup over the cherries, leaving ½ in [12 mm] of headspace. Seal the jars tightly before transferring them to the refrigerator to infuse for at least 2 weeks before using. Store maraschino cherries in the refrigerator for up to 6 months.

NOTE: For longer storage, up to 1 year, the cherries may be canned immediately after being transferred to jars. Follow the water bath canning instructions on page 79, processing for 15 minutes. Allow to sit for at least 2 weeks before using and store unopened jars at cool room temperature.

Gin & Tonic

Tonic water was originally conceived as a "medicinal" preventative against malaria due to the addition of quinine, derived from the bark of the Peruvian cinchona tree. Since quinine is extremely bitter, gin and sweetener were added to make it more palatable, essentially creating the Gin & Tonic, or G&T for short. Any type of gin can be used in a G&T, but we prefer the modern flavor of new American gins, distilled using a variety of locally sourced botanicals, over the more traditional London dry gins.
YIELD: 1 DRINK

2 oz [60 ml] gin
1 oz [30 ml] Tonic Syrup (page 249)
3 oz [90 ml] sparkling water
Crushed ice
Lime slice, for garnish

SPECIAL EQUIPMENT
Highball glass

In a highball glass, combine the gin and tonic syrup.

Add the sparkling water and stir gently.

Add the crushed ice, then garnish with a slice of lime. Serve.

Gin & Jam

We enjoy just saying the words *gin* and *jam* together, let alone actually drinking this cocktail equivalent of a PB&J. The botanical, resin-y taste of gin matches up perfectly with the sweetness of jam, inviting you to mix and match different types of both gin and jam (there they are again!) for endlessly interesting flavor combinations. We also couldn't resist adding a quintessentially "Institute" theatrical touch: We balance the spoon of jam on the rim of the glass when presenting the drink to each guest, inviting them to stir in as much or as little jam as they like. **YIELD: 1 DRINK**

2 oz [60 ml] gin
¾ oz [22 ml] fresh lemon juice
¾ oz [22 ml] Simple Syrup (page 248)
Ice
1 tsp Sweet Tomato Conserve (page 102) or other fruit jam

SPECIAL EQUIPMENT
Cocktail shaker with strainer
Old Fashioned or rocks glass

In a cocktail shaker, combine the gin, lemon juice, and simple syrup with a handful of ice.

Cover and shake vigorously, then strain into an Old Fashioned or rocks glass.

When serving, rest a teaspoon filled with the jam on top of the glass to allow guests to stir it into their drink, to taste.

Amaretto Sour

A slightly ironic craze involving vintage, classic cocktails seems to sweep the nation once every few years. (Think Appletinis or Cosmopolitans.) Made with Amaretto (page 250), lemon juice (or sour mix if you're at a dive bar), and a beaten egg white for froth, the Amaretto Sour is actually quite delicious, evoking the sophisticated elegance of an undiscovered, wood-paneled hotel bar. We hereby nominate this underappreciated cocktail as the Next Big Thing. **YIELD: 1 DRINK**

1 oz [30 ml] Amaretto (page 250)
1 oz [30 ml] Simple Syrup (page 248)
1 oz [30 ml] fresh lemon juice
1 egg white, approximately 1 oz [30 ml]
Ice
One 1 by 3 in [2.5 by 7.5 cm] strip lemon zest, for garnish
1 Luxardo Maraschino Cherry (page 251), for garnish

CONT'D

Cocktail shaker with strainer

Old Fashioned or rocks glass

In a cocktail shaker, combine the Amaretto, simple syrup, lemon juice, and egg white. Cover and shake vigorously, about 10 seconds.

Fill the shaker with ice and shake again. Strain into an ice-filled Old Fashioned or rocks glass. Garnish with the lemon zest and maraschino cherry.

Martini

When it comes to movies and martinis, we think of Bond. James Bond. It was 007, after all, who forever altered the martini lexicon with his famous maxim that a martini should always be "shaken, not stirred." Incidentally, he also gave us the recipe for the Vesper (gin and vodka, Lillet Blanc, and a lemon peel twist instead of an olive). Our martini recipe here is straight, direct, and true to Bond's explicit instructions, shaken and never stirred. As Bond villain Pussy Galore might say as she points her gun, "Good day, Mr. Bond . . . and good-bye!"
YIELD: 1 DRINK

2½ oz [75 ml] gin or vodka
½ oz [15 ml] Dry Vermouth (page 250)
Ice
1 olive, for garnish

SPECIAL EQUIPMENT

Cocktail shaker with strainer

Martini glass, well chilled in the freezer

In a cocktail shaker, combine the gin (or vodka) and vermouth with a large handful of ice.

Cover and shake vigorously, then strain into a chilled martini glass.

Garnish with the olive and serve.

Maraschino Cherry Cordial

Now that we can replace those nuclear-red, commercial maraschino cherries with our own handcrafted version (page 251), the Institute's maraschino ban has officially been lifted and this boozy cordial, a mash-up between a sipping drink and a Manhattan, can be enjoyed once more. The rye and bitters temper the sweetness of the cherry syrup, and of course, it's *de rigueur* for a maraschino cherry to be plunked into the glass before serving.
YIELD: 1 DRINK

Ice
2 oz [60 ml] rye
¾ oz [22 ml] cherry syrup, from store-bought or homemade Luxardo Maraschino Cherries (page 251)
¼ oz [8 ml] Simple Syrup (page 248)
Dash of Bitters (page 249)
One 1 by 3 in [2.5 by 7.5 cm] strip orange zest, for garnish
1 Luxardo Maraschino Cherry (page 251), for garnish

SPECIAL EQUIPMENT

Cordial or rocks glass

Fill a tall, deep mixing glass or large measuring pitcher with ice. Add the rye, cherry syrup, simple syrup, and bitters and stir with a long-handled spoon until well mixed and chilled.

Strain into a chilled cordial glass with a large cube of ice.

Garnish with the orange zest and Luxardo maraschino cherry and serve.

White Russian

In the movie *The Big Lebowski*, The Dude (Jeff Bridges) downs twelve of these Mexican coffee-flavored liqueurs (which he calls "Caucasians") adding, "Careful, man, there's a beverage here!" There's a drinking game among Lebowski fans in which they drink a Caucasian in a Dixie cup every time The Dude has one on screen. If that's the way it's going to go down, they'd better be good and homemade! **YIELD: 1 DRINK**

Ice
2 oz [60 ml] vodka
1 oz [30 ml] KahLúLú Domestica (page 66)
or store-bought Kahlúa liqueur
Heavy cream
Finely ground coffee, for garnish

SPECIAL EQUIPMENT
Old Fashioned or rocks glass

Fill an Old Fashioned or rocks glass with ice.

Pour in the vodka and KahLúLú Domestica.

Add a splash of heavy cream and stir.

Garnish with a dusting of finely ground coffee and serve.

Institute Punch

When making Caribbean rum punch in Barbados, they have a handy rhyme—a kind of unofficial Barbadian National Anthem—to help you remember the recipe: "One of Sour, Two of Sweet, Three of Strong, Four of Weak." (That's lime juice, sugar, rum, and water or black tea, in that order.) We've tweaked the traditional recipe a bit here, letting homemade Amaretto and oleo saccharum stand in for "Sweet," and using ginger beer for our "Weak." We've also added fresh citrus and a floating, fancy, frozen punch bowl ring as a showoff-y finishing touch.

A few days before your big punch-party shindig, freeze the Punch Bowl Ice Float (right) using filtered water and/or another nonalcoholic liquid (since alcohol would slow down the freezing process). Choose items that will harmonize with the punch ingredients (such as limes and oranges, both juiced and sliced) or add your own creative flourishes (berries, sliced stone fruit, or even citrus blossoms). Remember that as the party winds down, so will the ice block, slowly dissolving into the punch, so make sure your ice ring ingredients will enhance the punch's flavor as it melts.

We specify 5 oz [150 ml] teacups for imbibing, mostly because we like the vibe of their delicate "pinky" handles. Those rarely used teacups you inherited from your mom or grandmother (or the ones you bought at a flea market ten years ago but have never used) will be thrilled to find themselves liberated from a dark cupboard to serve as vessels for this festive drink. **SERVES 10**

½ cup [125 ml] lime juice (One of Sour)
1 cup [250 ml] Amaretto (page 250; Two of Sweet)
1½ cups [375 ml] gold rum (Three of Strong)
2 cups [500 ml] ginger beer (Four of Weak)
½ cup [125 ml] fresh orange juice, strained of any pulp
½ cup [125 ml] Oleo Saccharum Syrup (page 248)
1 orange, thinly sliced, for garnish
1 lime, thinly sliced, for garnish
1 Punch Bowl Ice Float (below)

SPECIAL EQUIPMENT
Punch bowl
Ten 5 oz [150 ml] teacups

In a large punch bowl, add the lime juice, Amaretto, rum, ginger beer, orange juice, and oleo saccharum, stirring to combine. Add the orange and lime slices to the bowl, then the Punch Bowl Ice Float, and serve immediately, ladling punch into 5 oz [150 ml] teacups.

Punch Bowl Ice Float

As a seven-year-old, I believed that a punch bowl of 7-Up, sherbet, and canned pineapple juice was an absolute must when inviting friends to a birthday party. Now that I'm a bit older, I've decided it's time to set my inner punch bowl free, but with updated ingredients. While even an unadorned punch bowl will immediately add a dash of vintage irony to your festivities, this floating ice ring, filled with fruit, herbs, and booze, will put the whole thing over the top.

CONT'D

Select a mold (or several) that will be small enough to float freely in the punch bowl you've chosen, rummaging your kitchen drawers for items that will freeze safely without cracking. Traditional ice float molds are round with a center hole, the perfect use for a decorative Bundt ring with fluted edges. That said, if you don't have a big Bundt, don't let that rain on your punch parade; feel free to think outside the bowl. **YIELD: 1 OR MORE ICE FLOATS**

Fresh fruit, chopped or whole, such as thinly sliced citrus, whole berries, sliced melon, or stone fruit

Fresh herbs and edible flowers, such as mint, rosemary, or citrus blossoms

Filtered water

SPECIAL EQUIPMENT

1 or more ice molds, such as a Bundt pan or tube pan, gelatin molds, fluted baking pans, muffin tins, or loaf pans

Clear a space in your freezer for the mold where it can sit flat until frozen solid.

Arrange whole or chopped fruit at the bottom of the mold, then scatter a handful of fresh herbs and/or edible flowers over the top.

Fill the mold with filtered water since it will eventually melt into the punch. Alternatively, try using mineral water or the soda of your choice instead of water. (You could even try 7-Up if you're feeling particularly ironic.) Because you're not a seven-year-old anymore, you might think about adding a splash of liqueur or other spirits for good measure. You don't have to go overboard, though, since (a) the ring won't freeze if there's too much alcohol, and (b) you can always add a little extra splash to the punch.

Carefully transfer the filled mold to the space you've cleared in your freezer. Be patient—the large size of the mold means it may take 1 to 2 days to freeze solid, so be sure to plan accordingly.

The day of your shindig, remove the mold from the freezer and dip it in a sink full of warm water until the ice ring loosens from the mold. Invert into a punch bowl and let the punch flow!

THE "GREAT LOS ANGELES PRUNE BUST"

During Prohibition (1920–1933), the Institute was raided for violations several times. The most dramatic incident came in 1924 when instructor Helga Vanderloop was arrested after locking herself in the Institute's pantry with what was apparently a large number of Armagnac prunes (see Prunes in French Armagnac, page 104). The Los Angeles Evening Express ran a short, sarcastic notice: "Great Los Angeles Prune Bust." As you can see from the "Report of Violation of Prohibition Law," page 258, Deputy Sheriff Kirkpatrick had a little trouble spelling "Armagnac."

SHERIFF'S OFFICE, LOS ANGELES COUNTY, CALIFORNIA

REPORT OF VIOLATION OF PROHIBITION LAW

Name of the accused Helga Vanderloop   No. 5693

Warrant issued by Brazier T. Small   Justice of the peace for
Downtown   district, Los Angeles County, Cal., 5/13/1924

Arrested at Inst. of Domestic Technology, 511 S Main St, 5/11/1924

Persons arrested Helga Vanderloop

Officers making arrest Robert Brady , State Prohibition Officer and K.
Kirkpatrick, Deputy Sheriff

Liquor and other articles found on premises or taken from persons arrested
38 1-gallon jars Armijac "Armaniyak prunes"; five bottles of
Armaniyak four full, one about three fourths full, eleven bottles
of Bordeaux wine

Charge filed unlawful possession of intoxicating liquor

Date 5/13/1924   Private prosecutor Stanton T. Gibson
Disposition of prisoner Pleaded guilty
Date of trial 5/13/1924   Fine imposed 50.00   Jail sentence none
Date released 5/13/1924   Fine paid 50.00   Date 5/13/1924

Remarks Received anonymous tip re liquor being stored and consumed at
the "Institute of Domestic Technology" on South Main. During raid on
premises, defendant locked herself in the pantry. After forced entry,
defendant was discovered pouring wine, grain alcohol and Armaniyak
down a utility sink. Confiscated remaining bottles of wine and grain
alcohol in addition to 12 jars of what appeared to be prunes in
Armaniyck. Found another jar of xx prunes hidden in defendant's
handbag. Defendant appeared to be a little stewed up and swore at
deputies, after which she was taken to the station and booked without
further incident.

SHERIFF'S OFFICE
LOS ANGELES COUNTY, CALIFORNIA

———

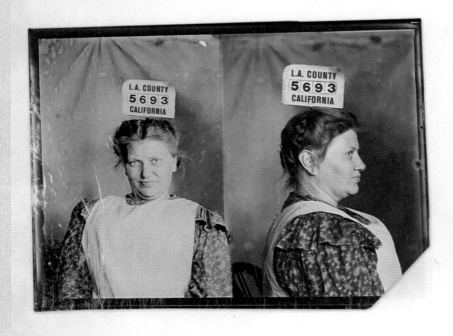

CH.07

259

Gallery No.	5693
Finger Prt. No.	3231
Rev. No.	
Nat. Det. No.	

Name Helga Vanderloop

Alias

Age 31 **Height** 5-8" **Weight** 125

Eyes Hazel **Hair** Brown **Complexion** Fair **Built** Large **Nativity** Holland

Occupation Cook, teacher

Crime Possession and distribution of intoxicating liquor in

Arrested 5/11/1924

Disposition **Date** **Judge**

Department of Fermentation | CH.08

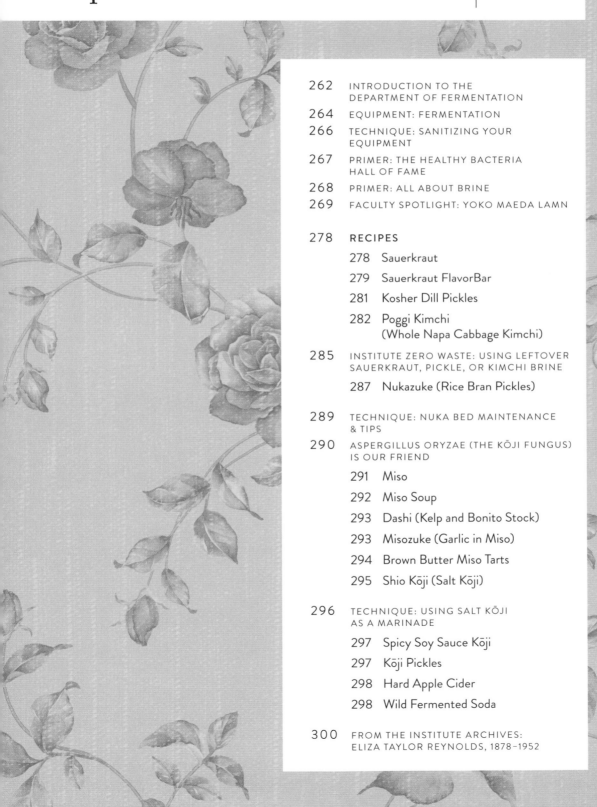

THE DEPARTMENT OF FERMENTATION

Fermentation, along with the bacteria that enable the process to take place, predates us humans. In fact, according to biologists, bacteria were the only inhabitants on the Earth for its first two billion years. Fermentation is essentially a metabolic process that converts sugars into acids, gases, and alcohol. It occurs in anaerobic (oxygen-starved) environments, breaking down nutrients in certain foods in a process that makes them easier for the human digestive system to assimilate.

According to master fermenter Sandor Katz, "In our bodies, bacteria outnumber the cells containing our unique DNA by more than ten to one." Katz goes on to observe, "The vast majority of these bacteria—a mind-boggling one hundred trillion in number—are found in our intestines."

Harnessing "good" bacteria to transform cabbage into sauerkraut, milk into yogurt, or fruit juice into alcohol is the goal of the home fermenter. These ancient transformations not only create environments that can preserve food without refrigeration but also produce aromatic compounds known as esters that are responsible for the unique flavors present in many fermented foods.

During the fermentation process, bacteria produce lactic acid, which creates a highly acidic environment. This acidity is important since the good bacteria we want to encourage are acid-loving and thrive quite nicely in an acidic environment. And any "bad" bacteria present? Well . . . not so much. Bad bacteria hate acidity, which kills them off. This leaves a host of flavor-producing bacteria with beautiful names, such as *L. mesenteroides* and *L. plantarum* (see Primer: The Healthy Bacteria Hall of Fame, page 267).

Good bacteria not only provide flavor to fermented products but also act as a probiotic, meaning they have a beneficial effect on our intestinal tract by contributing to its microbial balance. Making your own fermented products maintains these beneficial, live microorganisms, which are typically killed off during the high-temperature pasteurizing and canning processes common in many commercially made products. These include yogurt made from pasteurized milk, which is first inoculated with bacteria, then re-pasteurized to increase shelf life—an absurd practice that ends up killing off the live bacteria. Unrefrigerated commercial sauerkraut has also been pasteurized in order to keep it shelf stable without refrigeration. It is essentially a dead food.

We at the Institute encourage you to take back your microbiome by making your own fermented foods at home. We start you off with the basics; Sauerkraut (page 278), for example, requires only two ingredients: cabbage and salt. Once you've mastered that recipe, try our Sauerkraut FlavorBar for more variety and flavor ideas. Soon, you'll graduate to Kosher Dill Pickles (page 281) and Poggi Kimchi (page 282).

Thanks to Yoko Maeda Lamn, our Dean of Fermentation, this chapter is also full of intriguing (and delicious) Japanese ferments, like *Nukazuke* (Rice Bran Pickles). We also introduce *Aspergillus oryzae*, a.k.a. the kōji fungus, which is responsible for many different kinds of Japanese fermented products, including Miso (page 291) and *Shio Kōji* (page 295).

As you explore creating your own live, cultured foods, you'll discover that just as our bodies need caring and attention, so do our bacterial colleagues. In return, they will provide us with an abundance of unique flavors and good health.

FERMENTATION

Aside from an assortment of mason jars in different sizes (see page 77), you don't need any special equipment to try your hand at fermenting. However, there are a few specialized tools and containers that will definitely make the process go more smoothly.

CERAMIC CROCK

The simplest and most low-tech option for beginners is a glazed, straight-sided ceramic crock. Crocks can be found at hardware stores and flea markets, but be sure to choose one with a lead-free glaze. Glazes containing lead will leach out in acidic environments, such as those created by lactic acid bacteria during the fermentation process.

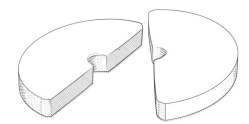

CERAMIC CROCK WEIGHTS

These weights are used to keep fermenting material submerged under brine. Although a sterilized plate or large stone, or a resealable plastic bag filled with salt brine will do the trick, many crocks already come with a pair of these weights. They can also be purchased separately, and their two-piece, half-moon design has the advantage of being easy to insert into a narrow-shouldered crock.

WATER CHANNEL CROCK

A traditional Eastern European invention, these crocks sport a remarkably simple water channel feature. A shallow moat on the lip of the crock is filled with water. The lid is placed on top with its edge resting in the water-filled channel, allowing carbon dioxide to bubble up and out through the water without letting undesirable elements in.

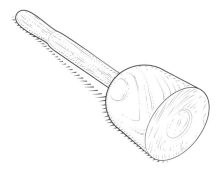

TAMPER

Not that your hand made into a fist won't do nicely, but a solid wood mallet-tamper can reach deep into a crock and make life a bit easier. Some are also sold as meat tenderizers.

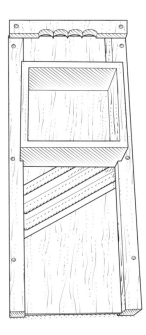

CABBAGE SHREDDER

When you've become completely addicted to making homemade sauerkraut, you'll want to begin making larger batches. That's where this tool comes in handy. Essentially an extra-large mandoline, this tool easily shreds whole cabbage heads, one after another.

GLASS GROWLER JUG

Cider will ferment in a 1 gl [4 L] glass growler, essentially a jug with a small thumb-handle on the neck. At the Institute, we use brands of unfiltered apple juice that are already packaged in these jugs when making cider. You can also purchase empty growlers from a brewing supply company and fill with juice according to your recipe.

RUBBER STOPPER

Also called a rubber stopper bung, these are inserted into the mouth of the glass growler. They have a small hole in the center for placing the airlock into. The apple juice jugs that we use accommodate a #6 stopper, sized at 1⅛ in [3 cm] top diameter and 1¹⁄₁₆ in [2.5 cm] bottom diameter. They come in smaller and larger sizes as well. Consult your brewing supply shop if you need help.

AIRLOCK

These are generally small plastic devices that allow carbon dioxide to escape from the glass jug, while keeping bacteria out. The two most common models are a three-piece, which, like its name, has three pieces, and an S-shaped model, which has two vertical chambers connected by a type of drain trap. Airlocks also come with a dust cap, which has perforations to allow the carbon dioxide to escape. Though typically attached to a rubber stopper for use in fermenting liquids in glass growlers, it's become increasingly common to find airlocks attached to mason jar lids for fermenting sauerkraut and other vegetables. These are available for purchase preassembled, but it's also easy to make one yourself by drilling a hole in a plastic mason jar lid and inserting a rubber grommet so that an airlock can fit tightly in the hole. While not necessary for success, feel free to use an airlock lid for ferments like Sauerkraut (page 278) and Kosher Dill Pickles (page 281) to help keep bad bacteria from getting in.

CONT'D

FERMENTATION, CONT'D

ANATOMY OF AN AIRLOCK

The *vented cap* (A) is filled with water. Expanding CO_2 travels up the *airlock stem* (B). Trapped by the *floating piston cap* (C), the CO_2 pushes its way through the water, finally exiting through the vented cap. Outside air or bacterial particles cannot enter through the airlock.

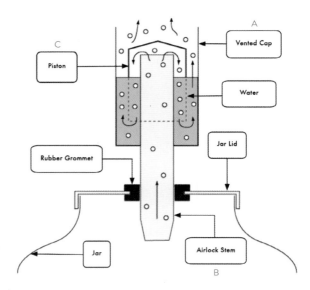

266

SANITIZING YOUR EQUIPMENT

For some ferments, such as hard cider (page 298), it is important to sanitize your equipment in advance to prevent unwanted bacteria from overwhelming the bacteria you are trying to cultivate.

SPECIAL EQUIPMENT

Large bucket or pot

1 Tbsp unscented bleach

In the bucket, make a sanitizing solution by combining the bleach and 4 qt [4 L] of water.

Dip each piece of equipment into the sanitizing solution, then allow to air dry on a dish rack or clean kitchen towel.

THE HEALTHY BACTERIA HALL OF FAME

GROW YOUR OWN

Bacterial cultures can be divided into different heat-loving categories and will either grow or die off depending on the ambient temperature.

Fermenters are interested in two of these categories of bacteria: mesophilic, which grow at moderate temperatures of 65°F to 113°F [18°C to 45°C], and thermophilic, which grow best at high temperatures ranging from 113°F to 252°F [45°C to 122°C].

Whether they are mesophilic or thermophilic, it is the lactic acid–producing bacteria (LAB), primarily *Lactobacilli*, that are the most important when fermenting foods. LABs have a very specific purpose—to multiply quickly in the fermenting environment. This causes the pH level to be reduced, making the environment acidic and thereby unsuitable for the growth of unwanted "bad" bacteria.

A deconstruction of the sauerkraut fermenting process is an excellent way to understand this intricate bacterial world.

As cabbage begins its journey to becoming sauerkraut, the first bacteria to kick off the fermentation process will be *Leuconostoc mesenteroides*. This lactic acid bacteria is mesophilic and thrives best in a 65°F to 72°F [18°C to 22°C], salty environment. In addition to producing lactic acid, *L. mesenteroides* also produces CO_2, alcohol, and acetic acid (vinegar), which contribute to the flavor of the sauerkraut. Its ability to produce large quantities of acetic acid inhibits the growth of undesirable organisms, such as molds and yeasts. Ironically, the increased acidity will eventually restrict *L. mesenteroides*'s own growth.

Next on the scene comes *Lactobacillus plantarum*, which continues the fermentation process. *L. plantarum* is also acid-loving and can grow quickly at temperatures of 72°F [22°C] and higher, or more slowly at lower temperatures. *L. plantarum* is the most popular LAB strain (at least in our circle), and is present in sauerkraut, pickles, cheese, and even meat. Its job is to consume natural sugars (carbohydrates) and produce lactic acid, which is responsible for the acidic taste of fermented food.

Finally, *Lactobacillus brevis* (a bacteria also used for souring beers) takes over the sugar consumption until there is no sugar left in the cabbage, spelling an end to the fermentation process.

SALT

Salting vegetables in preparation for fermenting serves multiple purposes. First, salt helps extract nutrients from vegetable cell walls, making it available as food for the lactic acid bacteria (LAB). It also draws out water from the cells, creating a moist environment for the LABs to thrive, and forming a brine to cover the vegetables and keep out unwanted oxygen.

Salt is also a mold and bacteria inhibitor, discouraging the growth of competing bacteria. In small amounts, the presence of salt is tolerated by *Lactobacillus*, the beneficial bacteria we want to encourage.

The more salt used, the slower the fermentation process will be. Using less salt will speed fermentation but, depending on the vessel being used, may create an environment more susceptible to unwanted molds. For a good starting point, begin with a 3 percent salt brine.

WATER

Most municipalities add chlorine and chloramine to treated tap water in order to kill off bacteria and other unwanted microorganisms. These additives can also kill the healthy bacteria we are trying to encourage when we ferment. Chlorine can be removed with carbon filters or by letting water sit out overnight. But chloramine, a combination of chlorine and ammonia, is much more difficult to remove. Check your city's water report to see if chloramine is present. If it is, using bottled water or a sophisticated home water filter is recommended.

TEMPERATURE

Bacteria are environmentally sensitive creatures and thrive best in very specific temperature zones. Keeping your ferments at an optimal temperature is one of the most important factors in achieving the best results. Depending on which bacteria you'd like to encourage and how much flavor you are trying to nurture, choose a location best suited for the temperature they like.

Most vegetable ferments prefer mesophilic bacteria, which can tolerate temperatures between 65°F and 72°F [18°C and 22°C]. The cooler the ambient temperature in which you store your fermenting vessel, the slower the fermentation process will be and the more flavor will have time to develop. Higher temperatures may encourage unwanted molds, but as long as the ferment is watched carefully, they will also speed the fermentation process and produce milder flavors.

Experiment with different locations in your home as well as fermenting at different times of the year.

3 Percent Salt Water Brine

2 Tbsp [30 g] kosher salt
1 qt [1 L] warm filtered water

Combine the salt and water, stirring to dissolve the salt. Allow to cool to room temperature before using.

YOKO MAEDA LAMN

Dean of Fermentation

In 2014, Professor Yoko Maeda Lamn, then an Institute student, took her first class with us. During class she mentioned that she leads a group miso-making workshop each winter for her church as a fundraiser. I was honored when she invited me to join her, though I basically invited myself. It turned out I was the only male and, besides Yoko, the only English-speaker. Interestingly, few of the women knew how to make miso, having grown up on easily accessible, store-bought, packaged varieties. Americans, it seems, are not the only ones who have relinquished many traditional skills to others. Yoko now teaches her recipe as part of our popular Miso Making class in addition to many other Japanese fermented recipes, including pickles, *amazake*, and *kōji*.

TIPS FROM THE PROFESSOR

Growing up in Japan, which uses metric measurements, I was nervous about converting my recipes to pounds and ounces when I began teaching at the Institute. When I discovered American bread bakers and coffee enthusiasts were already using scales and measuring in grams, it made me very happy. Not only is it easier to scale a recipe up or down, but using a scale also allows greater accuracy when measuring ratios of salt or kōji in recipes.

KOSHER DILL PICKLES (PAGE 281)

NUKAZUKE (RICE BRAN PICKLES) (PAGE 287)

MISO SOUP (PAGE 292)

MISOZUKE (GARLIC IN MISO) (PAGE 293)

BROWN BUTTER MISO TARTS (PAGE 294)

HARD APPLE CIDER (PAGE 298)

WILD FERMENTED SODA (PAGE 298)

Sauerkraut

One of the easiest vegetables to ferment is cabbage. It produces enough lactic acid bacteria (LAB) on its own to create an acidic environment hospitable to only "good" bacteria. The best-quality sauerkraut is produced at 65°F to 72°F [18°C to 22°C], which favors the growth and metabolism of the *Leuconostoc mesenteroides* LAB. Sauerkraut made within this range takes 18 to 20 days to ferment. In general, lower temperatures produce more flavorful sauerkraut at a slower pace, whereas higher temperatures, up to 96°F [36°C], produce sauerkraut more quickly, though with a less complex flavor.

YIELD: TWO 1 QT [1 L] MASON JARS

5 lb [2.3 kg] cabbage, core removed, finely shredded

2 oz [60 g] kosher salt

SPECIAL EQUIPMENT

Digital scale

1 gl [4 L] ceramic crock (see page 264) or glass mason jar

Wooden tamper (optional)

Two 1 qt [1 L] mason jars

In a large bowl, combine the shredded cabbage and salt. Use your hands to work in the salt and squeeze the cabbage, massaging to bruise and extract its juices, for about 10 minutes or until liquid begins to accumulate at the bottom of the bowl.

Working in batches, transfer the cabbage and juices to a 1 gl [4 L] crock or mason jar, pressing each layer down firmly with a wooden tamper or your fist before adding the next batch. Leave at least 2 in [5 cm] of headspace at the top of the crock to allow for expansion as the cabbage ferments.

If using a crock, use crock weights or place a small, clean plate over the surface of the cabbage, weighting the plate down with a sanitized stone or a sealed jar filled with water, in order to keep the cabbage submerged in its brine. Cover with a lid or a clean kitchen towel. If using a mason jar, use a smaller, sealed jar filled with water as a weight, placing it on the surface of the cabbage and covering the jar with a clean kitchen towel.

Check the sauerkraut daily for the first couple of days. If, after day 2, there is not enough brine released naturally from the cabbage to completely cover the sauerkraut, make a 3 Percent Salt Water Brine (page 268) and add it to the vessel until the cabbage is completely submerged.

Let the cabbage ferment at room temperature, ideally between 65°F and 72°F [18°C and 22°C], for up to 2 months (or even longer). Check the cabbage every 2 to 3 days for white froth that may form on the surface of the liquid. Use a fine-mesh strainer to remove and discard the froth, as well as any bits of cabbage that may have floated to the surface.

After 2 weeks, begin tasting the sauerkraut every few days, and when the flavor is to your liking, transfer it into two 1 qt [1 L] mason jars and refrigerate. The flavor will deepen as it sits. Use immediately for a brighter flavor and crisp texture, or after several months for a stronger flavor and softer texture. Sauerkraut will keep in the refrigerator for at least 6 months.

TROUBLESHOOTING

During fermentation, you may find white mold forming on the surface of the sauerkraut. This is usually caused by exposure to air, but may also be encouraged by higher ambient temperatures. To safeguard against this as best you can, make sure all the ingredients remain completely submerged under the brine, adding more 3 Percent Salt Water Brine if needed. If you do encounter some white mold, simply skim it off and discard it. If you encounter any colors of mold other than white, discard the entire batch, sterilize the container, and begin again.

SAUERKRAUT

Once you've made a batch or two of straightforward cabbage sauerkraut, you'll want to experiment with adding additional vegetables and flavors. This is your chance to dip into the Institute's FlavorBar and create your own recipe. The basic formula is simple: 4 lb [1.8 kg] of cabbage + 1 lb [450 g] other mixed vegetables, in any combination + 2 oz [60 g] salt + flavorings of your choice. Combine all of the ingredients and follow the instructions for making Sauerkraut (facing page).

CABBAGE (4 LB / 1.8 KG)

Green
Napa
Red
Savoy

SALT (2 OZ / 60 G)

Kosher salt
Pink Himalayan salt
Sea salt
Smoked salt

MIXED VEGETABLES (1 LB / 450 G)	PREPARATION
Apples	Shred, thinly slice
Beets	Shred or slice into thin batons
Bell peppers	Seed and slice into thin batons
Breakfast radishes	Shred or thinly slice
Broccoli	Cut into small florets; peel and thinly slice stem
Brussels sprouts	Small: use whole; Large: halve or quarter
Burdock root	Peel and thinly slice
Carrots	Shred or thinly slice
Cauliflower	Cut into small florets; peel and thinly slice core
Celery	Remove stringy ribs and thinly slice
Daikon radishes	Shred or thinly slice
Fennel	Bulb: thinly slice; Fronds: cut into short lengths
Ginger root	Peel and thinly slice
Jalapeños	Seed and thinly slice
Onions	Chop or thinly slice
Parsnips	Shred or thinly slice
Rutabagas	Shred or slice into thin batons
Turmeric root	Peel and thinly slice
Turnips	Shred or slice into thin batons

CONT'D

SAUERKRAUT, CONT'D

FLAVORINGS	AMOUNT (Start here and add more to taste)
Caraway seeds	1 tsp
Citrus zest (fresh or dried)	¼ tsp
Cumin seeds	1 tsp
Curry powder	¼ tsp
Dill seeds	1 tsp
Dried seaweed (shredded)	1 tsp
Fennel seeds	1 tsp
Ginger (fresh or dried)	¼ to ½ tsp
Harissa	2 tsp
Herbes de Provence	¼ tsp
Juniper berries	5 or 6
Nigella seeds	1 tsp
Oregano (fresh or dried)	1 tsp
Red pepper flakes	1 tsp
Savoy (fresh or dried)	1 tsp
Sesame seeds	1 tsp
Szechuan peppercorns	1 tsp
Tarragon (fresh or dried)	1 tsp
Tea leaves	1 tsp
Turmeric (fresh or dried)	¼ to ½ tsp
Thyme (fresh or dried)	1 tsp

FLAVORBAR

COMBINATION IDEAS:

green cabbage + Granny Smith apple +
caraway seeds + juniper berries

napa cabbage + daikon radish +
red pepper flakes +
ginger root

red and green cabbage + burdock root +
hijiki seaweed + carrot + sesame seeds

Kosher Dill Pickles

There are lots of misconceptions and mythologies around what constitutes a true kosher dill. Does a rabbi need to be present to certify its kosher-ness? Do you have to use kosher salt? I'm not here to settle these questions, but to me, all that matters is that the dills are fermented, as opposed to pickled in a vinegar brine. They must also contain garlic, and plenty of it, as well as fresh dill and a classic pickling spice mixture with both savory and sweet notes. The natural fermentation process provides the signature sourness associated with kosher dills, as well as plenty of probiotic benefits you won't get with vinegar pickles or fermented pickles that have been canned at high temperatures. **YIELD: 10 TO 14 PICKLES**

4 cups [1 L] warm filtered water
¼ cup [40 g] kosher salt
¼ cup [30 g] Basic Pickling Spice Mix (page 95)
6 garlic cloves, peeled
1 small bunch fresh dill
10 to 14 small pickling cucumbers, blossom ends trimmed (see Note on Cucumbers)

SPECIAL EQUIPMENT
2 qt [2 L] ceramic crock (see page 264) or glass mason jar

In a 2 qt [2 L] crock or mason jar, add the filtered water and salt, stirring until dissolved. Allow to cool to room temperature.

Add the pickling spice mixture, garlic, and dill to the crock, then add the cucumbers, wedging them against each other tightly in order to keep them from floating to the top. Place a small plate or other clean weight, such as a resealable plastic bag filled with a 3 Percent Salt Water Brine (page 268), on top. If necessary, add additional 3 Percent Salt Water Brine to keep the cucumbers submerged.

Cover the crock loosely with a lid or clean kitchen towel and leave in a cool place to ferment, preferably somewhere with temperatures between 55°F and 65°F [13°C and 18°C] (see Note on Temperature).

After 2 weeks, begin tasting the pickles every few days. Once they start acquiring a lightly soured taste, they are considered to be "half-sour" pickles and can be eaten immediately. For a classic "full-sour" kosher dill, allow the pickles to ferment for up to 4 weeks, or longer.

Once fermented to your liking, the pickles can be stored, submerged in brine, in an airtight container in the refrigerator for up to 6 months.

NOTE ON CUCUMBERS: Small Kirby cucumbers are the classic variety for kosher dills. Look for ones roughly the same size, generally 4 in [10 cm] long, so they ferment at an equal pace. Persian and Japanese cucumbers also work but will ferment differently due to their size and water content.

Before you pack them into jars, trim the blossom ends off the cucumbers, as they contain an enzyme that can inhibit the firmness of the pickles.

NOTE ON TEMPERATURE: Temperatures of 55°F to 65°F [13°C to 18°C] are ideal for achieving a slow and steady development of flavor. Avoid temperatures above 75°F [24°C], or the pickles will ferment too quickly and become soft and susceptible to mold during fermentation.

NOTE ON CONTAINERS: Feel free to divide this recipe between two 1 qt [1 L] mason jars rather than one 2 qt [2 L] crock or jar. Use regular rather than widemouthed jars, as their curved shoulders help keep the cucumbers submerged in the brine.

TROUBLESHOOTING
Depending on conditions, such as the variety of cucumber, temperature, etc., you may find a white mold forming on the surface of the brine. This is usually caused by the ingredient's exposure to air. To safeguard against this as best you can, make sure all the ingredients are completely submerged under the brine. It's inevitable that some of the pickling spice will float to the surface. This can be remedied by placing a layer or two of cheesecloth on the surface and weighting it down. If you do encounter

CONT'D

some white mold, simply skim it off and discard it. If you encounter any colors of mold other than white, discard the entire batch, sterilize the container, and begin again.

Poggi Kimchi (Whole Napa Cabbage Kimchi)

This recipe comes from Institute faculty member Hae Jung Cho. Her mother never made kimchi, so she developed the recipe from scratch, not having inherited one. There are literally hundreds of kimchi-making styles. The word *poggi* means "stuffed." In *poggi kimchi*, the cabbage is torn into quarters, brined in salt water, then stuffed with a chunky red chili, herb, garlic, and fermented fish seasoning paste called *sok* (literally "inside"). The kimchi is then packed into jars or crocks and left to ferment. (Traditionally, it was buried underground to maintain a consistent temperature.) Korean custom dictates that the cabbage quarters be left whole until just prior to serving, at which time a section is removed from the container and cut before being presented to guests, thus proudly displaying that the kimchi is homemade. The heat level of *gochugaru* (Korean red pepper flakes) can vary. We recommend a taste test when you open the package. If it's super-hot and you'd prefer a less fiery kimchi, use less than the standard amount indicated in the recipe. **YIELD: 2 QT [2 L]**

CABBAGE
1 large or 2 small heads Napa cabbage (about 5 lb [2.3 kg] total)
½ cup [80 g] kosher salt

SEASONING PASTE (SOK)
¼ bunch (2 oz [55 g]) Korean green mustard leaves
1 bunch (2 oz [65 g]) Korean chives (*buchu*)
1 bunch (5 oz [142 g]) Korean watercress (*minari* or water dropwort)
2 green onions, roots trimmed
1 Korean radish or large daikon, about 1½ lb [675 g]
¼ cup [70 g] salted, fermented shrimp (*saewoo juht*)
One 1 in [2.5 cm] piece fresh ginger, peeled and coarsely chopped

8 to 15 garlic cloves (about 1 head), peeled
½ white onion, chopped
¾ cup [85 g] gochugaru (Korean red pepper flakes)
2 Tbsp fish sauce

(See chart for ingredient substitutions following the recipe.)

NOTE: For vegan kimchi, omit the salted shrimp and fish sauce and add 4 tsp of additional salt to the seasoning mixture.

SPECIAL EQUIPMENT
Extra-large bowl or plastic tub for brining cabbage (see Tools, page 284)
Food processor or mortar and pestle
Thin kitchen or disposable food-handling gloves (see Tools, page 284)
2 qt [2 L] ceramic crock (see page 264) or glass mason jar
Wooden tamper (optional)
Kitchen shears (optional)

PREPARING THE CABBAGE

Remove any withered outer leaves from the cabbage and trim the root end, but leave it intact. Cut through the root end about a quarter of the way up. With your hands, rip the cabbage in half the rest of the way. Repeat with each half so that you end up with four separated quarters.

Rinse the cabbage under running water, then place it in an extra-large bowl and sprinkle the salt evenly over the leaves. Make sure that some salt gets in between the larger, thicker leaves. Pour enough water over the cabbage to cover. Place a clean plate over the cabbage to keep it submerged in the brine.

Leave the cabbage to soak for at least 6 hours or overnight. After soaking, drain the cabbage and taste a leaf. If you find it too salty, rinse under running water and let sit in a colander to drain. Otherwise, continue with the recipe.

MAKING THE SEASONING PASTE (SOK)

While the cabbage is draining, wash and trim the mustard leaves, chives, watercress, and green onions, then cut them into 2 in [5 cm] lengths and place them in a large bowl. Peel and julienne the radish before adding it to the bowl. Set aside.

In a food processor or a mortar and pestle, grind the shrimp, ginger, garlic, and onion together into a paste. Add the gochugaru and fish sauce and pulse or stir to combine.

Wearing gloves to avoid staining your hands (see Tools, page 284), add the mixture to the bowl of cut vegetables and mix with your hands. The sok should be moist and somewhat chunky. If it seems dry, add 1 or 2 Tbsp of water.

ASSEMBLING THE KIMCHI

Take one of the cabbage quarters and place it in the bowl containing the seasoning paste. Still wearing gloves, spread some seasoning paste between each layer of leaves, starting from the outermost leaf and working inward. Be sure to coat every bit of the cabbage so that the entire surface is stained red from the chili in the sok. Repeat with the remaining cabbage sections.

"PUTTING DOWN" THE KIMCHI

Transfer all of the cabbage sections to a 2 qt [2 L] crock or mason jar. Position the cabbage sections with the cut-sides down and folded over into neat packages.

If there is any seasoning paste left, put this on top of the cabbage in the container. Using a wooden tamper or your fist, tamp the cabbage down firmly to reduce air bubbles as well as encourage the release of liquid from the vegetables.

Leave at least 2 in [5 cm] of headspace at the top of the container to avoid overflow when the kimchi starts to ferment.

Poggi kimchi can be eaten the same day it is made, but the flavor will develop and change over time. If you like your kimchi less "ripe," serve immediately or cover tightly and transfer to the refrigerator right away.

If you prefer a stronger flavor, cover the container loosely and leave the kimchi at room temperature for 24 hours or up to 7 days, tasting daily until you are happy with the flavor, then cover tightly and transfer to the refrigerator. If the weather is cold, kimchi will ferment more slowly.

SERVING AND STORING

Wearing gloves, take out a cabbage section and use kitchen shears or a sharp knife to cut it into bite-size pieces, making sure to cut off and discard the root end. Serve with rice, soup, and *banchan* (side dishes) or invent your own kimchi dishes.

Store kimchi in an airtight container in the refrigerator for up to 6 months. During this time, the flavors will continue to develop, and the kimchi will get increasingly pungent and sometimes even effervescent. If it gets too intense for your taste, you can cut it up and make a kimchi stew, kimchi pancakes, or kimchi fried rice.

CONT'D

TOOLS

KOREAN KIMCHI GLOVES: Kimchi makers use thick, pink, elbow-length rubber gloves to prevent their skin from being stained red from the chili in the paste. I suggest you do the same. They're usually available in well-stocked Korean grocery stores, but if you can't find them, dedicate a pair of thin dishwashing gloves to the cause, or use disposable ones because they'll be stained red—permanently.

CABBAGE BRINING BOWL: Korean markets sell extremely large plastic bowls for soaking cabbages in salt brine. If making an extra-large batch of kimchi, a good alternative is a rope-handled plastic tub similar to one you'd fill with ice to use at a picnic.

KIMCHI INGREDIENT SUBSTITUTIONS

For some, especially those who do not reside near an Asian grocery store, sourcing the Korean ingredients and supplies for this recipe might prove challenging. But do not worry; here are suggestions for easy-to-find substitutions.

KOREAN INGREDIENT	SUBSTITUTION
Korean green mustard leaves	American mustard greens
Buchu, Korean chives	Chives, garlic shoots, or shallots
Minari, Korean watercress or dropwort	Watercress or celery leaves
Salted, fermented shrimp (*saewoo juht*)	Thai shrimp paste, or double the fish sauce
Gochugaru, Korean red pepper flakes	Red pepper flakes

USING LEFTOVER SAUERKRAUT, PICKLE, OR KIMCHI BRINE

Pickles, sauerkraut, and kimchi are gateway ferments, easy to learn how to make at home. Since we assume you'll be making repeated batches, you'll eventually end up with varying amounts of leftover brine. We know this and have come up with ways to not only use up the brine but also give you some inspiring project ideas.

#1 Use Leftover Brine to Start the Next Batch
Using the remaining brine from fermented pickles, sauerkraut, or kimchi is a great way to kick-start a fresh batch. The brine will be brimming with live, active bacteria eager to begin fermenting the fresh batch of vegetables. Add any amount, since even 1 Tbsp will add enough live bacteria to get things going faster.

#2 Salad Dressing
A classic vinaigrette is essentially acid + oil + salt + spices. A brine is just missing the oil. In a small bowl, whisk together 1 part brine + 3 parts oil. Add a squeeze of lemon and some fresh herbs, if desired. Done.

#3 Meat Tenderizer
Brine is a great way to tenderize meat prior to cooking via the process of osmosis. With a higher salinity than the meat, brine is able to diffuse into the cells of the meat, making it easier to absorb. The acidity of the brine also helps break down tough muscle fibers in meat, giving it a more tender bite once cooked. This is especially good when preparing chicken before deep frying.

#4 Michelada or Bloody Mary
Add a splash of brine to each serving in addition to, or in place of, Worcestershire or Tabasco sauce.

#5 Pickleback
A shot of (typically cheap) whiskey, followed by a shot of pickle brine. Possibly a frat-boy move, but when you've fermented the brine yourself and it follows a better whiskey, *kaboom*! Better yet, make a pickle brine Whiskey Sour: Combine ¼ cup [60 ml] pickle juice + ¼ cup [50 g] granulated sugar, heat until dissolved, and cool. In a cocktail shaker with ice, add 1 part pickle brine syrup + 1 part lemon juice + 2 parts whiskey, then shake and strain into a cocktail coupe glass.

#6 Brine Hard-Boiled Eggs
Combine 1 qt [1 L] brine + 12 hard-boiled eggs, shelled + 3 Tbsp spices (choose from dill seed, black peppercorns, allspice, cumin seed, and coriander seed) and marinate in the refrigerator for 3 days.

#7 Burning Man Gatorade
Pickles and pickle juice are a "thing" at Burning Man, the annual gathering that takes place at Black Rock City—a temporary metropolis erected on the Black Rock Desert Playa in Nevada. With temperatures there typically reaching triple digits with no shade, pickle juice is said to restore salts and electrolytes that your body sweats out. We found it was simply an excuse to do Picklebacks (see above).

CONT'D

USING LEFTOVER SAUERKRAUT, PICKLE, OR KIMCHI BRINE, CONT'D

#8 Boiling Pasta, Rice, or Beans
Add brine to the cooking liquid when boiling pasta, rice, or beans.

#9 A Splash Here and There
Wherever you would think of adding a squeeze of lemon to hummus, fresh salsa, or homemade mayonnaise, add a splash of brine instead to bring out the umami.

#10 Copper Cleaner
While we usually suggest using lemon juice and salt to clean copper pots, pans, and utensils, an acidic, salty brine works the same way, bringing a sparkle back to our prized utensils.

286

Nukazuke (Rice Bran Pickles)

Fermented pickles are such an integral part of the Japanese meal—even breakfast—that in Japan, entire stores specialize in selling them. *Nukazuke*, one of the most traditional methods used to pickle vegetables, produces a uniquely pungent flavor and pleasantly funky aroma, unattainable by any other method. Vegetables are fermented in a moist bed of rice bran (*nuka*), in which healthy, flavor-producing bacteria have been encouraged to grow. The rice bran bed, called a *nukadoko*, is fed vegetable scraps to jump-start its bacterial community. Once the nuka bed is ready, the vegetables are buried deep in the bed, where they can ferment anywhere from a few hours to overnight. The bed should be tended to on a daily basis by aerating the rice bran with your hands, then adding fresh vegetables and removing the old ones. A well-maintained nukadoko can carry on for years, with some Japanese households passing them down from generation to generation.

2 lb [900 g] *nuka* (rice bran), plus more as needed for adjusting consistency

½ cup [120 g] fine sea salt

1 qt [1 L] warm filtered water

One 4 by 4 in [10 by 10 cm, or 10 g] piece kombu (dried kelp), torn into large pieces

2 whole dried Japanese chiles

Handful of vegetable scraps for starting the fermenting bed (see Technique: Nuka Bed, page 289, for ideas on vegetables)

SPECIAL EQUIPMENT

1 gl [4 L] nuka pot (such as a nonreactive crock, deep baking dish, or mixing bowl made from ceramic, glass, or enamel-lined metal)

PREPARING THE FERMENTING BED

Working in batches if necessary, in a large sauté pan over medium heat, toast the nuka lightly until dry and toasty smelling. Stir frequently, being careful not to let it brown or burn. Transfer to a large bowl and cool to room temperature.

Meanwhile, in a large pitcher, add the salt and filtered water, stirring to dissolve. When the nuka has cooled, add the salt water in increments, mixing with your hands until the mixture resembles wet sand. You may not need all of the water. Squeeze a handful of the nuka in your fist, then let go. If the mixture retains its shape with the imprint of your fingers, it's ready. If it's too dry and crumbles, slowly add more salt water. If the mixture is too wet and mushy to hold its shape, add more rice bran.

Once you've achieved the right consistency, add the kombu, chiles, and vegetable scraps, mixing them into the nuka mixture with your hands.

Select your nuka pot. It should be sturdy, easy to dig into with your hands, and deep enough to accommodate several inches of nuka.

Place the nuka mixture in the pot, pressing firmly to remove any air pockets and making sure all vegetable scraps are submerged under the surface.

CULTURING THE FERMENTING BED

DAY 1
Cover the pot and keep at cool room temperature for 24 hours. Select a place with as little temperature variation as possible.

DAY 2
Aerate the mixture, stirring with your hands to help activate the bacterial growth. Depending on the size of your container, this can be achieved by simply sliding your hands down the sides of the pot, scooping the mixture up from the bottom, and bringing it to the top, repeating until well mixed. Alternatively, dump the contents of the pot into a large bowl, stir well, then return to the pot, tamping the mixture down to remove air pockets and keeping vegetable scraps submerged as you re-pack.

DAY 3
Aerate the pot with your hands, refreshing the vegetable scraps by removing the old ones (leaving the kombu and chiles in the pot) and replenishing with another handful of fresh vegetable scraps.

CONT'D

DAY 4

Aerate the pot with your hands, but do not remove or add any vegetable scraps.

DAY 5

Aerate the pot with your hands, refreshing the vegetable scraps by removing the old ones (leaving the kombu and chiles in the pot) and replenishing with another handful of vegetable scraps.

DAY 6

When ready, the nuka bed should have a strongly earthy aroma. Taste the vegetable scraps to see if they have developed a lightly sour, fermented flavor. If so, proceed to preparing daily pickles, or if not, continue to refresh vegetable scraps and aerate the mixture daily until they are ready.

PREPARING DAILY NUKA PICKLES

Fine sea salt

Assortment of vegetables, as desired (see below); every vegetable has a different preparation and can be peeled or left unpeeled

    Cabbage, cut into manageable pieces

    Carrots, scrubbed and cut in half lengthwise

    Celery, ribs removed, cut to fit

    Cucumber, ends removed, skin on

    Daikon, cut to fit or left whole, greens attached

    Gobo (burdock), scrubbed and dark spots peeled off, cut to fit

    Japanese eggplant, cut lengthwise into quarters but left attached at the crown; rubbed with salt inside as well as outside

    Japanese turnips, cut to fit or left whole, greens attached

    Okra, stems trimmed, dark spots removed, cap on

NOTE: Avoid pickling tomatoes or other excessively watery produce.

Massage each vegetable with a pinch of salt.

Bury vegetables in the nuka bed, allowing enough room to prevent them from touching each other, tamping down to avoid air pockets and making sure all vegetable surfaces are covered in nuka.

Smooth the top of the nuka bed and wipe the inside edges of the pot with a clean towel to remove any nuka clinging to the sides of the container.

Depending on the ambient temperature, size of the vegetables, and how active your pot is, the vegetables can take anywhere from a few hours to a couple of days to ferment.

Begin tasting the pickles after a few hours, and when they are to your liking, remove them from the pot, wipe or rinse the nuka off, and depending on the vegetable, squeeze gently to remove any excess moisture. Finished pickles should be limp but crunchy and have an earthy taste and aroma.

Nuka pickles are best eaten immediately, but can be stored in an airtight container in the refrigerator for up to 3 days.

Wheat bran can be used as an alternative to rice bran. Toasting brings out the bran's nuttiness but isn't necessary.

Vegetable scraps good for culturing the fermentation bed include carrot or daikon peels, cabbage cores, celery stalks, and broccoli or cauliflower stems. During the initial culturing period, avoid watery vegetables, such as cucumbers and eggplants, and always avoid tomatoes.

Over time, the kombu and chile will begin to break down in the nuka bed. Feel free to replenish them, and/or add additional flavorings to the fermenting bed at any time, such as slices of fresh ginger, dried shiitake mushrooms, or bonito flakes.

Softer vegetables, such as cucumbers, celery, and daikon greens, ferment faster. Harder, less watery vegetables, such as carrots and burdock, take longer.

Vegetables will ferment faster during hot weather, and slower in cooler seasons. During the summer, the nuka bed should be aerated twice a day.

If you forget to aerate the nuka bed for a day, it will probably survive, though a white bloom of mold may form over the surface. Scrape off the surface of the nuka bed and wipe the exposed sides of the container with sake or *shōchū*. If you neglect the bed for longer, especially if it's particularly hot, the nuka may develop an unpleasant, sour smell, which means it has spoiled and must be discarded.

If water begins to pool on top of the nuka bed, blot with paper towels and/or add dried soybeans, dried shiitake mushrooms, kombu, or fresh nuka (toasted or raw) to absorb the excess moisture. If the bed becomes too dry, add more salt water.

As the volume of the nuka bed shrinks or if it becomes too salty, add more nuka mixed with enough water to resemble wet sand, as you did when starting the bed. Because the daily pickles are rubbed with salt, usually no additional salt is needed.

If you feel the need to take a break from feeding the nuka bed, particularly during warm weather, you can move the container to the refrigerator to slow down the fermentation process. Remove any remnants of vegetables from the pot, wipe the exposed sides of the container's interior clean, and sprinkle a thick layer of salt over the top until the surface is completely covered. Cover with a lid and store in the refrigerator for 2 to 3 weeks or up to 2 months.

To wake up the nuka bed from hibernation, remove the lid and carefully scrape off and discard about 1 in [2.5 cm] of rice bran from the surface, as it will be too salty. Add fresh kombu and chiles and adjust the consistency of the bed by adding more rice bran, if very wet, or salt water, if too dry. Taste it first, and if it tastes very salty, you can use unsalted water instead. Reintroduce scraps of vegetables, as you did when initially starting up the bed, replenishing daily until the vegetable scraps taste good, then resume pickling.

ASPERGILLUS ORYZAE
(THE KŌJI FUNGUS) IS OUR FRIEND

Here at the Institute, we love nurturing bacteria, fungus, and yeast. We seem to always have crocks of sourdough starter, kimchi, or nuka pickling beds fermenting at any given time. If that wasn't enough, Yoko Maeda Lamn, our Dean of Fermentation, has turned us on to *kōji*, a powdered fungus also known as *Aspergillus oryzae* that is used to inoculate cooked rice and other grains, which can then be used to ferment a variety of foods. *A. oryzae* has been used for over two thousand years, and in fact, the Brewing Society of Japan decreed it the "national fungus" in 2006 for its importance in sake brewing, as well as in other traditional Japanese foods.

In this chapter we use kōji to make miso, salt and soy sauce kōji, and kōji pickles; however, kōji can also be used to make sake, soy sauce, shōchū, and mirin.

Kōji spores are grown on cooked brown or white rice, and sometimes other grains like barley, which is then dried for long-term storage. While it is possible to grow the *A. oryzae* fungus on rice or other grains yourself, it is much easier to purchase it in pre-inoculated and dried form, which is what we call for in this chapter. We use rice kōji, since that is the easiest variety to find. Kōji can be purchased online or at Japanese grocery stores (see Resources, page 340). When the dried rice kōji is added to larger quantities of cooked rice or other grains, it converts starches into sugar. When added to cooked soybeans during miso making or used as a marinade for meat, it causes proteins to break down, creating glutamic acid, responsible for the savory flavor that we know as umami.

Miso

Like all things Japanese, miso making has a long history and has developed its own set of rituals. While I respect tradition, I'm willing to modify things a bit in a nod to modern technology. (Hello, Mr. Food Processor!) This recipe is for a more classic miso, using soybeans and rice kōji, but miso can also be made with other bean and grain combinations, such as black beans or barley. Traditionally, miso is made using new-crop soybeans, which are whiter in color. They are harvested and dried the same year and require a shorter cooking time, whereas beans older than 1 year need to be cooked longer.

Miso styles in Japan vary from region to region, with salt levels playing an important role. Northern regions, including Tokyo, prefer a saltier "red" miso, whereas western areas, including Kyoto, prefer a sweeter "white" style, which is milder and less salty. This recipe is for a rustic "country" miso: a bit on the milder side and closer to a white than a red miso, though saltier and more robust. **YIELD: 8 CUPS [2 L]**

17½ oz [500 g] dried soybeans

17½ oz [500 g] dried rice kōji (see Aspergillus Oryzae Is Our Friend, facing page)

7 oz [200 g] fine sea salt

¼ cup [60 ml] sake, shōchū, or a neutral vodka

1 Tbsp yellow mustard powder (optional)

2 small, dried red chiles (optional)

SPECIAL EQUIPMENT

Digital scale

Potato masher, food mill, meat grinder, or food processor

3 to 4 qt [3 to 4 L] ceramic crock (see page 264)

Rinse the soybeans in plenty of water. Drain, then place in a nonreactive bowl or container. Pour in enough fresh water to cover the beans by 4 in [10 cm]. Cover the bowl with a clean kitchen towel and set aside to soak at room temperature for 12 to 18 hours.

After soaking, transfer the beans with their soaking water to a large pot and bring to a boil over medium-high heat. Reduce the heat to low and simmer for 4 to 8 hours, skimming off and discarding any scum that forms on top as they cook and adding additional water to cover, if needed.

To determine if the beans are cooked thoroughly, press one between your fingers. It should be soft and mash easily. If not, continue cooking longer. Another method to determine if the beans are done is to place one bean on a digital scale and press it down with one finger until the scale reads 500 g. The bean should mash easily between your finger and the scale surface at essentially 500 g of pressure per square inch.

Drain the cooked beans, reserving the cooking water, and set them aside to cool to 140°F [60°C].

While waiting for the beans to cool, in a large bowl, add the kōji and 6 oz [170 g] of the salt, mixing until thoroughly combined. Set aside.

Use a potato masher, food mill, meat grinder, or food processor to mash or grind the beans to a paste. Depending on your preference, beans can be ground to a smooth paste or left slightly chunky (see Note on Texture, page 292).

Add the ground soybeans to the kōji-salt mixture and massage the ingredients together with your hands until they are thoroughly incorporated. The mixture should resemble a soft but pliable dough, not too crumbly, not too wet. To test for the proper consistency, grab a handful of the mixture and gently squeeze your hand into a fist, then release. You should see smooth indentations of your fingers in the paste. If not, add the reserved bean cooking water in 1 tsp increments to adjust the consistency of the paste.

Wipe the inside of a 3 to 4 qt [3 to 4 L] crock with a clean cloth dipped in 2 Tbsp of the sake.

Pack the soybean mixture into the prepared crock by forming a handful of paste into a ball and then pitching it forcefully into the bottom of the crock. With the palm of your hand, firmly press the ball to flatten it against the crock, eliminating any air bubbles. Repeat with the remaining mixture, pitching each consecutive ball into the crock, slightly

CONT'D

overlapping the previous ball and pressing each one to flatten and remove air pockets. When all of the paste has been transferred, smooth the top surface, mounding it slightly higher in the center.

Sprinkle the remaining 1 oz [30 g] of salt over the surface, gently rubbing it into the paste, then drizzle the remaining 2 Tbsp of sake evenly over the top.

Cover the surface of the paste with a sheet of plastic wrap slightly larger than the width of the crock, pressing down firmly to remove air pockets. Make sure to press the plastic wrap into the corners.

Sprinkle the mustard powder and dried chiles, if using, on top of the plastic wrap to discourage mold formation.

Cover the crock with a lid and store in a cool, dry, dark place, preferably at 68°F to 86°F [20°C to 30°C], for 6 months to 1 year, depending on how strongly fermented you prefer the miso.

Begin tasting after 6 months, and when the fermented flavor is to your liking, transfer the miso to an airtight container and store in the refrigerator, where it will keep for at least 1 year. If you encounter a small amount of white mold on the surface, particularly around the edges, gently scrape it away with a spoon and discard. The remainder of the surface may have formed a soft, gelatinous skin that can either be skimmed off and discarded, or stirred and incorporated back into the body of the miso.

NOTE ON TEXTURE: Yoko prefers her miso with a chunky texture because this indicates that it is homemade—a badge of honor—but others might prefer a smoother consistency. To regulate the texture, soybeans may be finely ground early on, before the fermenting stage, or chunky, fully fermented miso may be pushed through a fine-mesh sieve when just a small amount of smooth paste is needed. For some recipes in this book, like Miso Soup (following) and Misozuke (facing page), we use the two textures interchangeably; for others, such as the Brown Butter Miso Tarts (page 294), we prefer a smooth texture.

Miso Soup

Miso, at least to Westerners, is primarily known for its starring role in soup. In Japanese culture, miso soup holds an almost mystical place, inspiring poetry and boasting healing properties similar to the West's chicken soup. A traditional Japanese breakfast would not be complete without miso soup and we wholeheartedly approve. **SERVES 4**

2 tsp dried wakame seaweed
4 cups [1 L] Dashi (recipe follows)
4 Tbsp [70 g] Miso (page 291)
8 oz [226 g] silken tofu, cut into ½ in [12 mm] cubes
1 green onion, finely chopped, for garnish

In a small bowl, cover the wakame with 2 cups [500 ml] of water and soak for 10 minutes.

Meanwhile, prepare fresh dashi, or return previously made dashi to a gentle simmer in a medium saucepan over medium-high heat.

Place 1 Tbsp of the miso in a ladle or small mesh strainer and set it directly into the simmering dashi, using chopsticks or a small spoon to blend the miso and dashi directly in the bowl of the ladle, until it is thoroughly incorporated. Repeat with the remaining miso, 1 Tbsp at a time.

Add the tofu to the soup, stirring gently and being careful not to break the pieces.

Drain the wakame and add to the soup, then return to a simmer and cook just until heated through, but not boiling.

To serve, pour into four bowls and garnish with the green onion.

Dashi (Kelp and Bonito Stock)

YIELD: 4 CUPS [1 L]

One 6 by 6 in [15 by 15 cm, or 20 g] piece kombu (dried kelp)
2 cups [20 g] dried bonito flakes

SPECIAL EQUIPMENT
Butter muslin or a paper coffee filter (optional)

In a medium saucepan over medium heat, add the kombu and 5 cups [1.2 L] water. Turn off the heat just before it boils. Remove the kombu and set aside.

Return the pan to medium heat and add the bonito flakes, heating just until the dashi reaches a boil. Immediately turn off the heat and allow to rest for 2 to 3 minutes, undisturbed.

Strain the dashi through a fine-mesh sieve without pressing or squeezing the solids, or, if a clearer stock is desired, line the sieve with a piece of damp butter muslin or a paper coffee filter and strain again. Discard or reserve the solids for another use (see Note). Dashi is best used immediately, while at its most fragrant, but can be stored in an airtight container in the refrigerator for up to 3 days.

NOTE: Leftover kombu and bonito flake solids from making dashi can be discarded or, preferably, reused to make a batch of "Second Dashi"; place the solids in a medium saucepan, add 2½ cups [625 ml] filtered water, and simmer for 10 minutes, then turn off the heat and add an extra handful of dried bonito flakes. Allow to rest for 2 to 3 minutes before straining. Use as you would regular dashi.

Misozuke (Garlic in Miso)

Misozuke, any pickle fermented in miso, is a Japanese delicacy. This version has all the mellow, full-flavored attributes of roasted garlic with the added benefits and flavors resulting from the fermentation process. Eat these delicious miso-encrusted garlic cloves right out of the jar, or use them as you would roasted garlic. Be sure to save the miso and use it for garlic-infused miso soup, miso-marinated fish, or in a salad dressing. **YIELD: 10 TO 20 GARLIC CLOVES**

1½ cups [415 g] Miso (page 291)
2 Tbsp mirin (Japanese sweet rice wine)
Whole, peeled garlic cloves, from 1 to 2 heads of garlic

In a small bowl, combine the miso and mirin, mixing thoroughly.

Spread a thin layer of the miso mixture across the bottom of a shallow, 4 to 5 cup [1 to 1.2 L] glass,

ceramic, or food-safe plastic container. Add a layer of garlic, making sure the cloves do not touch each other and are completely surrounded by miso along the sides of the container.

Cover the garlic with a second layer of miso, pressing to remove any air pockets.

Repeat the procedure of layering and pressing with as many garlic cloves as will fit in your container, making sure that all cloves are covered with miso.

Cover the container and allow to ferment for 1 to 3 months at room temperature, preferably at 60°F to 72°F [16°C to 22°C]. Begin tasting the garlic after 1 month. It should have a mellow, slightly sweet flavor. If it doesn't, continue to ferment at cool room temperature, tasting every few weeks.

Once the flavor is to your liking, the garlic cloves are ready to be used immediately, or sealed tightly and moved to the refrigerator for long-term storage, where the garlic will continue to ferment slowly in the miso and deepen in flavor, up to 1 year.

The miso bed may be reused many times for subsequent batches of pickles. After several batches, if the fermentation starts to slow down, add a few tablespoons of fresh miso, mixing thoroughly, to jump-start the fermentation process.

VARIATIONS

ASPARAGUS:
Trim the ends and shave the tough stems of raw asparagus with a vegetable peeler. Cut the stalks into 2 in [5 cm] lengths.

BURDOCK ROOT OR CARROT:
Trim and peel, or scrub the skin with a stiff vegetable brush. Slice crosswise into 2 in [5 cm] lengths, then cut lengthwise into uniform ½ in [12 mm] thick sticks.

CAULIFLOWER:
Cut into 1 to 2 in [2.5 to 5 cm] florets. The core can be peeled and cut into ½ by 2 in [12 mm by 5 cm] sticks.

Brown Butter Miso Tarts

While researching traditional Japanese miso makers online, we discovered a company that, in addition to their line of miso, sells small, individual miso tarts, sprinkled with sesame seeds. They were photographed so beautifully, but the minimal English description (and the fact that they didn't ship to America) left us to interpret what we thought they would taste like ourselves. We love these so much, we can only imagine that we've matched, if not exceeded, the inspiration. **YIELD: SIX 4½ IN [11.5 CM] TARTS**

TART SHELLS

½ cup [110 g] Brown Butter (page 181), chilled until solid (see Note)

½ cup [100 g] granulated sugar

Pinch of kosher salt

1 large egg

1½ cups [210 g] all-purpose flour

MISO FILLING

2 large eggs, at room temperature

½ cup [100 g] granulated sugar

¼ cup [70 g] smooth Miso (page 291, see Note)

1 tsp Vanilla Extract (page 41)

1 tsp lemon zest

¼ cup [35 g] all-purpose flour

½ cup [110 g] Brown Butter (page 181), melted and cooled until warm but not hot to the touch (see Note)

Black sesame seeds, for garnish

SPECIAL EQUIPMENT

Stand mixer or hand mixer

Bench scraper (optional)

Six 4½ in [11.5 cm] tart pans

MAKE THE TART SHELLS

Twenty to 30 minutes before you plan to start, remove the chilled brown butter from the refrigerator and allow to soften slightly at room temperature, then cut into 1 in [2.5 cm] chunks.

In the bowl of a stand mixer fitted with the paddle attachment, or using a hand mixer, cream the brown butter, sugar, and salt on medium speed until fluffy and lightened in color, about 2 minutes. Scrape down the sides of the bowl, then add the egg, mixing until well combined. Scrape down the bowl again and add the flour and 1 Tbsp water, mixing on low speed, just until incorporated.

Transfer the dough to a sheet of plastic wrap laid on a work surface and gently shape the dough into a 1 in [2.5 cm] thick disk, then wrap tightly with the plastic wrap and chill in the refrigerator for at least 2 hours or overnight.

When ready to bake the shells, preheat the oven to 325°F [160°C]. Remove the dough from the refrigerator, unwrap it, and place it on a lightly floured work surface. Using a bench scraper or knife, divide the dough into six equal pieces. Working with one piece at a time, shape the dough into a small disk and use a rolling pin to roll it into a circle ⅛ in [3 mm] thick, dusting lightly with flour as necessary to prevent sticking. Chill the dough for brief intervals as needed if it becomes too soft while you're working.

Place a tart pan on top of the dough and cut a circle around the pan about 2 in [5 cm] wider than the base.

Carefully transfer the circle of dough to the tart pan, gently easing it into the bottom edges of the pan and being careful not to pull or stretch the dough. Lightly press into place, patching any tears with additional dough, then use a knife to trim the overhanging dough even with the top of the pan.

Repeat with the remaining dough portions. Refrigerate all six shells for 15 minutes before proceeding.

Prick the bottom of each tart shell five or six times with a fork. Place the shells on a baking sheet and transfer to the oven. Bake for 18 to 20 minutes, rotating the sheet halfway through the baking time, until the shells are light golden brown.

Transfer the shells to a wire rack to cool completely.

FILL AND BAKE THE TARTS

Increase the oven temperature to 350°F [180°C].

In the bowl of a stand mixer fitted with the paddle attachment, or using a hand mixer, combine the eggs and sugar and beat on medium speed until thick and lightened in color, about 3 minutes.

Scrape down the sides of the bowl, then add the miso, vanilla, and lemon zest and beat until smooth. Scrape down the bowl again and add the flour, mixing on low speed just until incorporated, then add the melted butter and mix just until absorbed. Be careful not to overwork the batter.

Divide the miso batter evenly between the tart shells and lightly sprinkle black sesame seeds over the surface of each tart. Place the filled tarts on a baking sheet, transfer to the oven, and bake for 23 to 25 minutes, rotating the sheet halfway through the baking time, until the tops are chestnut brown and spring back when lightly pressed. Transfer the tarts to a wire rack to cool.

Serve warm or at room temperature. Tarts can be transferred to an airtight container and stored at room temperature for up to 3 days.

NOTE ON BROWN BUTTER: In this recipe we use brown butter in two states: chilled solid for the tart shells, and warm and melted for the filling. Though they can be prepared separately, another option is to make the entire amount in advance, chill it, and then melt only the butter needed for the filling. Four sticks (1 lb [450 g]) of butter will yield enough brown butter for the entire recipe, with a small amount left over—lucky you!

NOTE ON MISO: If using homemade miso, following our recipe on page 291, make sure to strain or purée it until completely smooth before using in this recipe. If using store-bought, we recommend a mild white miso paste.

Shio Kōji (Salt Kōji)

Here, salt kōji is a creamy condiment that, when added to meat, seafood, or vegetables before cooking, brings out a deeper range of flavors than plain salt would. Kōji produces enzymes that transform starches into sugars. It also causes proteins to break down, creating glutamic acid, that umami flavor we crave. **YIELD: ABOUT 2 CUPS [500 ML]**

1⅓ cups [220 g] dried rice kōji (see Aspergillus Oryzae Is Our Friend, page 290)
¼ cup [60 g] fine sea salt
1⅓ cups [330 ml] filtered water

SPECIAL EQUIPMENT

1 qt [1 L] mason jar
Instant-read thermometer
Blender (optional)

In a 1 qt [1 L] mason jar, add the kōji and sea salt, mixing with your hand or a wooden spoon to combine. Set aside.

In a small saucepan over medium-high heat, bring the filtered water to 140°F [60°C], then add to the kōji mixture and stir well to combine.

Cover loosely and store at room temperature, stirring the mixture thoroughly once a day for 7 to 10 days.

Salt kōji is ready when the mixture has thickened slightly and has a salty-sweet smell, with the rice grains appearing smaller in size.

Salt kōji may be used as is, or puréed in a blender if a smoother texture is desired. Use immediately or store in an airtight container in the refrigerator for up to 6 months.

USING SALT KŌJI AS A MARINADE

To gauge the amount of salt kōji to use, weigh whatever is being marinated and then use 10 percent of that weight. That's a ratio of 10 to 1, so for every 3.5 oz [100 g] of food, use 1½ tsp [10 g] salt kōji.

Baste the food with salt kōji and marinate for 20 minutes or up to overnight.

Salt kōji can burn with high heat, so avoid high-heat grilling or roasting, especially with longer-cooking meats.

MARINADE IDEAS

• Rub a whole chicken with salt kōji and marinate in the refrigerator, uncovered, for up to 48 hours before roasting. Roast at 350°F [180°C] for 60 to 90 minutes, until the internal temperature at the deepest part of the thigh reaches 165°F [74°C].

• Spread salt kōji on fish fillets and refrigerate for 1 to 4 hours or overnight. Bake, broil, or pan grill, being careful to avoid high heat, which may burn the salt kōji.

• Coat drained, firm tofu with salt kōji, wrap in plastic wrap, and marinate in the refrigerator for 1 week. Serve cold with a garnish of toasted sesame seeds, sliced green onions, grated ginger, or wasabi.

OTHER WAYS TO USE SALT KŌJI

• Add salt kōji to vinaigrettes: 1 part blended salt kōji + 3 parts olive oil + 1 part vinegar.

• As a salt substitute, use 2 tsp salt kōji for every 1 tsp salt.

• Make salt kōji pickles (see facing page for the recipe).

• Make salt kōji–baked French fries: Cut potatoes into fries, taking note of the total weight, coat with oil, then spread on a baking sheet in a single layer and bake at 350°F [180°C] for 20 minutes. Remove from the oven and add salt kōji at 10 percent of the weight of the potatoes, tossing to coat. Sprinkle with freshly ground black pepper, then return to the oven and bake for 15 to 20 minutes more, until crisp and golden brown. Watch closely to prevent burning.

Spicy Soy Sauce Kōji

Swapping salt for soy sauce takes shio kōji a step further. With the addition of jalapeños, it becomes more of a sauce than a marinade due to its intensity. Professor Lamn calls this her *San Sho Zuke*, or Three-Ingredient Sauce, because, well, there are three ingredients, and also because they are used in equal amounts, making it easy to scale up or down. Blended with oil and vinegar, it makes a great salad dressing, but it can also be served on rice, tofu, or grilled fish, preferably with a garnish of toasted sesame seeds, sliced green onions, and a squirt of fresh lemon juice. **YIELD: ABOUT 2 CUPS [500 ML]**

1 cup [200 g] dried rice kōji (see Aspergillus Oryzae Is Our Friend, page 290)

1⅓ cups [200 g] jalapeños, stemmed, seeded, and finely diced (from about 8 or 9 jalapeños)

¾ cup plus 1 Tbsp [200 ml] soy sauce

SPECIAL EQUIPMENT

1 qt [1 L] mason jar

In a 1 qt [1 L] mason jar, add the kōji and jalapeños, stirring to combine.

In a small saucepan over medium-high heat, bring the soy sauce to 140°F [60°C], then add to the kōji mixture and stir well to combine.

Cover loosely and store at room temperature, stirring the mixture thoroughly once a day, for 2 to 3 weeks.

Soy sauce kōji is ready when the mixture has thickened slightly and has a salty-spicy smell, with the rice grains appearing smaller in size.

Use immediately or seal the jar tightly and store in the refrigerator for up to 3 months.

Kōji Pickles

Both Salt Kōji and Spicy Soy Sauce Kōji make excellent pickling mediums for vegetables. This recipe is not only quick, but is easily scaled up or down. First, weigh the vegetables you would like to pickle, then use 10 percent of the vegetables' weight in kōji. **YIELD: 1 LB [450 G]**

1 lb [450 g] vegetables, such as Japanese cucumbers, daikon, Japanese turnips, carrots, burdock, or cabbage

3 Tbsp [45 g] Shio Kōji (page 295) or Spicy Soy Sauce Kōji (left)

Cut the vegetables into even chunks and place in a medium bowl.

Add the kōji to the bowl, massaging it into the vegetables by rubbing gently. Cover the bowl and refrigerate for 3 to 4 hours or overnight.

Remove the vegetables and serve. It is not necessary to rinse off the kōji.

FLAVORBAR

KŌJI PICKLE IDEAS:

Add thinly sliced ginger, citrus zest, or chopped Japanese shiso (perilla) to the mixture when adding the kōji. Other mix-ins could include rice vinegar and sesame oil, 1 tsp or more to taste. Garnish with red chili powder and/or toasted sesame seeds.

cucumbers + turnips + salt kōji + ginger

cucumbers + shiso + spicy soy sauce kōji + sesame oil + toasted sesame seeds

cabbage + salt kōji + lemon zest + toasted sesame seeds

burdock + spicy soy sauce kōji + sesame oil

daikon + carrots + salt kōji + rice vinegar + sesame oil

Hard Apple Cider

While craft beer brewing has recently been enjoying a long-overdue resurgence, years ago Daniel Kent, the Institute's Dean of Spirits, was already on to the next logical progression: hard cider. With very little specialty equipment needed, this recipe is an easy entry point for the home cider maker. This recipe calls for a 1 gl [4 L] jug of store-bought apple juice; if you can find a brand sold in a glass bottle, you won't need to purchase a growler (see Equipment, page 265). For another variation, consider swapping in pear juice for the apple juice to make perry, a delicious pear hard cider. **YIELD: NINE 12 OZ [355 ML] BOTTLES**

1 gl [4 L] unfiltered apple juice

¾ tsp dry ale yeast

1 cup [250 ml] filtered water

3 Tbsp honey

SPECIAL EQUIPMENT

1 gl [4 L] growler or glass jug (if not purchasing juice in a 1 gl [4 L] glass bottle), sanitized*

Funnel, sanitized

#6 rubber stopper, sanitized

1 brewing airlock, sanitized

2 gl [8 L] food-safe container, sanitized

Nine 12 oz [355 ml] glass bale-top bottles, sanitized

FERMENTATION

If using a growler, use a funnel to pour 15 cups [3.5 L] of the apple juice into the growler. Drink the remaining 1 cup [250 ml] of juice or reserve for another use. If using a glass apple juice jug, simply pour out 1 cup [250 ml] of juice, leaving the remaining 15 cups [3.5 L] in the jug.

Insert a rubber stopper into the mouth of the growler, holding your thumb tightly over the hole, (or recap the jug), and shake for 1 minute to oxygenate the juice.

---

* In order to prevent unwanted bacteria, it is important to sanitize any tool that comes in contact with the cider. See sanitizing instructions, page 266.

Remove the stopper or lid and add the dry yeast, then insert the stopper. Fill the airlock with water to the indicated level (approximately half full) and attach it to the stopper.

Leave your cider in a warm, dark place to ferment where the temperature will remain relatively stable, around 70°F [21°C]. After about 2 days, you should notice little bubbles appearing on top of the cider. After 5 days, bubbles should be noticeable in the airlock. When no new bubbles are forming in the jug or airlock, after 3 to 6 weeks, the cider is ready for bottling.

BOTTLING

When the cider is ready, decant into a 2 gl [8 L] food-safe container and set aside.

In a medium saucepan over medium heat, combine the water and honey, stirring with a sanitized utensil until the honey is completely dissolved. Remove from the heat and allow to cool.

Pour the honey water into the cider and mix thoroughly with a sanitized utensil.

Using a funnel, fill the bale-top bottles with the cider mixture, leaving 1 in [2.5 cm] of headspace in each bottle, and secure the lids.

CONDITIONING

Leave the bottles in a warm, dark place where the temperature will remain relatively stable, around 75°F [24°C], for 5 days, then transfer the bottles to the refrigerator and allow them to age for 2 weeks before opening and drinking. Store bottled cider in the refrigerator for up to 6 months.

Wild Fermented Soda

Fermented soda is made with your own live, wild starter, fermented using only fresh ginger and sugar, charmingly referred to as a "ginger bug." Using a neutral-tasting sugar such as white sugar will allow the flavor of the ingredients to shine. Using a less refined sugar, such as evaporated cane sugar, turbinado, or brown sugar, is fine, but be aware, they will impart a stronger molasses flavor.

Honey is also an option, but will also add its own flavor to the soda. Splenda, or any other artificial sugar substitute, cannot be used since the fermentation process needs actual sugar to convert to CO_2. **YIELD: ONE 16 OZ [500 ML] BOTTLE**

GINGER BUG STARTER

1 Tbsp fresh, unpeeled, and finely chopped ginger, plus more for feeding

1 Tbsp granulated sugar, plus more for feeding

Filtered water

GINGER SODA

7 Tbsp [105 ml] strained active Ginger Bug Starter

⅓ cup [80 ml] fresh lemon juice

4 tsp fresh ginger juice (see Note)

2 Tbsp granulated sugar

Filtered water

Fresh mint or a stalk of lemongrass, for garnish (optional)

SPECIAL EQUIPMENT

½ pt [250 ml] mason jar

Funnel

16 oz [500 ml] glass bale-top bottle

TO MAKE THE GINGER BUG STARTER

Place the ginger in a ½ pt [250 ml] mason jar. Add the sugar, then fill the jar with filtered water, leaving 1 in [2.5 cm] of headspace at the top. Stir to combine, then cover the jar and set aside at room temperature.

After 24 hours, add an additional 1 Tbsp diced ginger and 1 Tbsp sugar, stirring to combine. Continue adding fresh ginger and sugar daily for 5 to 7 days, discarding some of the liquid as needed to make room for the additional feedings.

Toward the end of the week, the "bug" should fizz strongly when the sugar is added, indicating that it is active and ready for soda making.

To use the starter for soda, strain out the ginger pieces and use the liquid only. Save any remaining liquid and the ginger pieces to keep your ginger bug going; replenish with fresh ginger, sugar, and filtered water.

TO MAKE GINGER SODA

Using a funnel, place the starter, lemon juice, ginger juice, and sugar into a 16 oz [500 ml] bale-top bottle. Top with filtered water, leaving 1 in [2.5 cm] of headspace, and secure the lid.

Leave the soda to ferment at room temperature (around 70°F [21°C]) for 5 days, then transfer to the refrigerator until well chilled.

Serve over ice, garnished with a sprig of mint or a stalk of lemongrass, if desired.

NOTE ON MAKING GINGER JUICE: Finely grate an unpeeled, 3 to 4 in [7.5 to 10 cm] piece of fresh ginger root, then transfer to a fine-mesh sieve set over a small bowl. Press and scrape the grated ginger with the back of a spoon to extract the juice.

NOTE ON MAINTAINING GINGER BUG: If making soda regularly you may need to discard some of the ginger pieces in your ginger bug periodically. Continue to feed the bug daily, or else store in the refrigerator for up to 3 months. The bug can be reactivated by returning it to room temperature and resuming the feedings.

VARIATION: CITRUS SODA

Follow the Ginger Soda recipe (above), adding 1 cup [250 ml] fresh citrus juice (such as Meyer lemon, grapefruit, or tangerine) in place of the lemon and ginger juice. Serve garnished with a slice of fresh citrus, if desired.

ELIZA TAYLOR REYNOLDS, 1878–1952

Memorializing what must have been a somber day for the Institute, this Los Angeles Times obituary for the Institute's founder and first director, Eliza Taylor Reynolds, contains an ironic plot twist involving, of all things, pickled carrots. (A variation of Taylor Reynolds's actual recipe can be found on page 96.) Despite the rumors, it turned out that the late director didn't succumb to botulism: The coroner's report found no evidence of C. botulinum and determined that she had died "of natural causes."

Los Angeles, October 12, 1952—Eliza Taylor Reynolds, the Founder of Southern California's Institute of Domestic Technology and its Director for 22 years, has died. She was 74.

While Mrs. Taylor Reynolds's daughter, Mrs. Henry Archer, told the *Los Angeles Times* that her mother's death was unexpected and sudden—the result, she worried, of her mother's possibly having eaten tainted canned goods of her own making—the County Coroner's office has yet to declare the official cause of death, which is pending the results of a toxicological report. There is no suspicion of foul play.

Born Eliza Maisie Taylor in 1878 to Bertrand and Mildred Taylor of Cave Springs, Kansas, Mrs. Taylor Reynolds came to Los Angeles with her family as a young woman in 1891, following the closure of her father's health resort and his subsequent attempt to stake a claim in the Oklahoma Territory, which also ended in disappointment. Mrs. Taylor Reynolds, an educator and author known for her boundless enthusiasm and dedication to ensuring that the fading food preparation methods of earlier generations would be preserved into this century, founded the Institute of Domestic Technology in 1911. Head-quartered in downtown Los Angeles, the Institute still offers classes in such old-fashioned "domestic technologies" as pickling and canning. A series of instruction pamphlets written by Mrs. Taylor Reynolds spread the Institute's influence across the country and garnered her the respect and admiration of homemakers across the country. Mrs. Taylor Reynolds was nevertheless known to be cautious when discussing her legacy. "Despite all of my efforts to the contrary, I wouldn't be at all surprised if, a mere ten years from now, the number of home cooks capable of putting up a decent jar of pickled carrots will have dwindled to nothing," she told the *Saturday Evening Post* in 1934. Given her retirement the previous year, this may have been a subtle dig at her immediate successor, Miss Melinda McCracken. Nonetheless, Miss McCracken, who herself stepped down as the Institute's Director in 1941, was lavish in her praises following Mrs. Taylor Reynolds' sudden death, eulogizing her as a "tireless pioneer to whom the future will one day owe a tremendous debt." That said, it appeared that Mrs. Taylor Reynolds's comment of long ago had stung, as Miss McCracken added, "The entire staff at the Institute—past and present—can't help but wonder if our esteemed Founder had somehow failed to follow her own meticulous instructions when preparing what turned out to be the fatal jar of pickled carrots." This interpretation of events was disputed by the Institute's current Director, Mr. Theodore J. Hoover III. "The idea that someone with Eliza's expertise could have botched a simple water bath canning is, quite frankly, absurd," Hoover asserted. "She would definitely know better than to use a sharp, metal instrument to measure the headspace. I am confident that the cause of death will be correctly attributed once all the facts are known." (Author's Note: The canning term "headspace" refers to the empty area between the contents of a jar and its lid.)

Predeceased by her husband, Mr. Edgar Reynolds, Mrs. Taylor Reynolds is survived by her daughter, Nellie Reynolds Archer, who will assume ownership of the Institute, as well as two grandchildren, Edgar Jr. and Maxine. Funeral services will be held at Forest Lawn Cemetery in Glendale, California. In lieu of flowers, the family requests that donations be made to The Institute of Domestic Technology and the "Women's Food Safety League" (WFSL), an organization whose mission it is to popularize the food preparation guidelines promulgated by the United States Food and Drug Administration.

22 ★ Los Angeles Times
Part I—SUNDAY, OCT. 12, 1952

54 Red Feather Youth Enrolled in Chest Drive

Fifty-four Los Angeles area children will have a part in the forthcoming Community Chest campaign.

They are Red Feather Kids. You will be able to spot them at any gathering of Chest volunteers because they will be wearing bright blue hats with a brilliant Red Feather speared through the crown.

The hats were designed especially for the Red Feather Kids by Eddie Tirella of Saks Fifth Avenue, Beverly Hills, and donated by the store. They will wear them at all public appearances.

To Receive Awards

"These are typical American boys and girls, 10 to 15 years of age, selected for this honor by 26 of our 160 health and welfare services," said Garner A. Beckett, campaign chairman.

The 54 Red Feather Kids were chosen from fields of candidates offered by the Chest's character-building youth services. Each of them will get a Red Feather Kid

Eliza Taylor Reynolds, Founder of Institute for Preserving Lost Domestic Arts

Eliza Taylor Reynolds, the Founder of Southern California's Institute of Domestic Technology and its Director for 22 years, has died. She was 74.

While Mrs. Taylor Reynolds' daughter, Mrs. Henry Archer, told the Los Angeles Times that her mother's death was unexpected and sudden – the result, she worried, of her mother's possibly having eaten tainted canned goods of her own making – the County Coroner's office has yet to declare the official cause of death, which is pending the results of a toxicological report. There is no suspicion of foul play.

Born Eliza Maisie Taylor in 1878 to Bertrand and Mildred Taylor of Cave Springs, Kansas, Mrs. Taylor Reynolds came to Los Angeles with her family as a young woman in 1891, following the closure of her father's health resort and his subsequent attempt to stake a claim in the Oklahoma Territory, which also ended in disappointment. Mrs. Taylor Reynolds, an educator and author known for her boundless enthusiasm and dedication to ensuring that the

Institute of Domestic Technology in 1911. Headquartered in downtown Los Angeles, the Institute still offers classes in such old-fashioned "domestic technologies" as pickling and canning. A series of instruction pamphlets written by Mrs. Taylor Reynolds spread the Institute's influence across the country and garnered her the respect and admiration of homemakers across the country. Mrs. Taylor Reynolds was nevertheless known to be cautious when discussing her legacy. "Despite all of my efforts to the contrary, I wouldn't be at all surprised if, a mere ten years from now, the number of home cooks capable of putting up a decent jar of pickled carrots will have dwindled to nothing," she told the Saturday Evening Post in 1934. Given her retirement the previous year, this may have been a subtle dig at her immediate successor, Miss Melinda McCracken. Nonetheless, Miss McCracken, who herself stepped down as the Institute's Director in 1941, was lavish in her praises following Mrs. Taylor Reynolds' sudden death, eulogizing

appeared that Mrs. Taylor Reynolds' comment of long ago had stung, as Miss McCracken added, "The entire staff at the Institute – past and present – can't help but wonder if our esteemed Founder had somehow failed to follow her own meticulous instructions when preparing what turned out to be the fatal jar of pickled carrots." This interpretation of events was disputed by the Institute's current Director, Mr. Theodore J. Hoover III. "The idea that someone with Eliza's expertise could have botched a simple water bath canning is, quite frankly, absurd," Hoover asserted. "She would definitely know better than to use a sharp, metal instrument to measure the headspace. I am confi-

Department of Dehydration | CH .09

THE DEPARTMENT OF DEHYDRATION

Dehydrating has been around for thousands of years. Today, we tend to look at preserved food through the lens of two different eras. In the Before Refrigeration Era (B.R.E.), foods were dried or cured out of necessity in order to store an abundant supply of summer produce through the rest of the year. After the introduction of the electric refrigerator as a common household appliance—marking the beginning of our modern Refrigerator Era (R.E.)—the newfound ability to keep ingredients fresh for extended periods of time led many dried foods to be dismissed as "hiking foods" or in-case-of-emergency pantry items. That's not to say they can't be great snacks on a hike, but there are so many more possibilities for these underutilized power tools in the kitchen workshop.

From a scientific perspective, dehydration is about removing water to reduce the possibility of unwanted mold growth and bacteria, but from a culinary perspective, dehydrating is about concentrating flavor. Chef-y chefs around the globe are now discovering the impact that dehydrated ingredients can have on modern cuisine, and dehydrators are turning up in restaurant kitchens alongside sous-vide setups.

We use an electric Excalibur dehydrator at the Institute for its reliability and even heating, and the time ranges given in our recipes are based on its results. We also offer alternative methods for dehydrating in an oven, as well as outdoors under the sun. The timing of these last two methods can vary dramatically based on the model of your oven or the temperature and humidity of your environment, but we encourage you to experiment until you get your preferred method down and are happy with the results.

The simplest gateway into the exploration of home dehydrating is to begin by replacing any ancient jars of herbs or spices in your pantry with freshly dried ones (see page 331). You'll notice the difference right away.

Drying fruit is another easy way to explore dehydrating and is not so far removed from the practices of our B.R.E. ancestors. Yes, we can now purchase dried fruit in sealed bags at the store, but the best fruits are the ones grown and harvested in season, or better yet, in our own backyards. Many of us have had moments when we stared at a beautiful farmers' market flat of apricots or "suffered" from a bumper crop of homegrown tomatoes, without knowing what to do with all of them. Such bounty needs to be preserved, and in a way that will make it useful throughout the year. We present ideas for using that bounty throughout this chapter—try Fruit Leather (page 333), Sun-Dried Tomato Pesto (page 322), or even cake (page 328)! And don't forget the food-swap possibilities of dehydrating neighborhood fruit in exchange for other foods or services.

Drying meat is another essential B.R.E. method of food preservation. For our ancestors, storing protein-rich foods meant the difference between life and death during lean times. Today, we can enjoy dried meat in snack form as Beef Jerky (page 332), seasoned with a home-made spice rub made from other dehydrated ingredients.

Our latest experiments at the Institute have involved dehydrating vegetables, mushrooms, fruit peels, and even kimchi until they are bone-dry, then grinding them to a powder. We call these Pantry Powders (page 324) and consider them our next-gen herb and spice drawer. They can be used as a concentrated essence to add extraordinary flavor to a dish with just a small amount. Because they are dry and finely ground, they work especially well in lending flavor to baked goods, and do not affect consistency or chemistry due to their insignificant volume and zero-moisture content. They are also wonderful companions for savory cooking. Think of them as flavor intensifiers and add a dash of onion powder to a stir-fry, mix some kelp powder into a meat loaf, or sprinkle mushroom powder over a roast.

Our exploration into Pantry Powders hasn't stopped with powdering single ingredients. We also dehydrate flavor powerhouses like miso and sauerkraut—think of them as Pantry Powders 2.0—and use them to punch up spice mixes, vinaigrettes, marinades, and meat rubs. They have expanded our flavoring arsenal tenfold and are now as indispensable in our kitchens as traditional spices.

Our hope is that you will dive into exploring dehydration with an open mind, unlocking the flavor potential of unlikely but powerful flavor bombs already residing in your kitchen.

DEHYDRATION

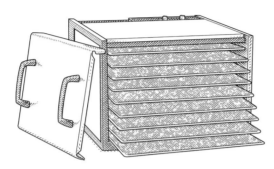

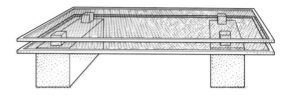

ELECTRIC DEHYDRATOR

Electric dehydrators are designed to make life easier, and when you've decided you're ready to dive deep into dehydrating, these workhorses are the way to go. They're portable, relatively lightweight (at least lighter than an oven), and many have timers and can do double duty as a bread proofer or an incubator for yogurt. The benefits of these appliances are their ability to dry at an even temperature and, in models that feature built-in fans, remove moisture from the dehydrating environment. Many of the lower-priced models are designed with trays that stack above the heating source, necessitating that the trays be rotated regularly since the ones closer to the heat source will dehydrate faster than those above. We're partial to models that have a rear-mounted motor and fan that blows evenly over all the trays, providing better distribution of heat and therefore more efficient drying. The drying times given throughout this chapter are based on using an electric dehydrator with a rear-mounted fan, which we found to be the most consistent method for measuring time and temperature.

WINDOW SCREENING

When drying food outdoors (see facing page), window screens or wood frames stretched with screening should be placed on cinderblocks or bricks to safely keep ingredients off the ground and allow for airflow around the food. To avoid potential moisture from the soil, situating the screens on a paved surface is best. Screens also need to be safe for contact with food. The best choices are stainless steel, Teflon-coated fiberglass, or plastic. Avoid galvanized metal hardware cloth, which is coated with cadmium or zinc and can leave harmful residues on the food. Also avoid copper and aluminum screening, which tend to discolor and corrode. Cover food to be dehydrated with a second screen, fine netting, or cheesecloth to keep bugs and critters at bay. Turn the ingredients daily to encourage even drying.

HANGING MESH DRYING RACK

Collapsible, multitiered mesh hanging drying racks are convenient for sun drying (see facing page) where outdoor space is at a premium. Choose a model that completely encloses the ingredients (by way of a zipper or Velcro) to keep out insects.

— TECHNIQUE —

OVEN AND OUTDOOR SUN DRYING

OVEN DRYING

The oven method is a great way to experiment with dehydrating before investing in a dedicated electric dehydrator. Try a few recipes, and if you are enthusiastic about dehydration and plan to do a lot more, then take the plunge and buy an electric dehydrator. If you want to dehydrate only occasionally and when the mood strikes you, then oven drying may be the way to go.

SPECIAL EQUIPMENT

Parchment paper (optional)

Electric fan

Set the oven to the desired dehydration temperature, usually 125°F [50°C] or 135°F [55°C]. Use the convection setting if you have it. If your oven doesn't go this low or if you know it runs hot, set it to the lowest possible temperature. Close the oven door and allow to preheat for at least 10 minutes.

Prepare the food to be dehydrated according to the recipe. Drying trays can be made using a wire cooling rack placed on top of a baking sheet. You may need to line the racks with parchment to prevent small pieces of food from falling through if the rack holes are large.

Once the oven is preheated, place the trays of food to be dehydrated on separate racks in the oven, allowing as much air circulation around each tray as possible. Prop the oven door open 2 to 3 in [5 to 7.5 cm].

Place an electric fan set to low speed at the side of the oven so that it blows air through the propped door, allowing the moist air to escape.

Use the drying times in this chapter as a starting point and follow the visual and textural cues to know when your ingredients are done. Depending on the temperature of your oven, ingredients may take slightly more or less time to dehydrate. If you find that your ingredients are dehydrating much too quickly, the oven is probably running too hot and you risk baking, rather than dehydrating, your ingredients; lower the temperature or prop the door open wider. If your ingredients are dehydrating much too slowly, raise the temperature by 10°F to 15°F [5°C to 8°C] but continue to keep the door propped open.

OUTDOOR SUN DRYING

There's something satisfying about harnessing the power of the sun to preserve food. This primal form of food preservation is time honored, and for good reason: It works. What this method lacks in temperature and timing control, it makes up for in simplicity. The considerations are essentially the same no matter how you go about it. The ingredients need to be placed on something that allows for airflow around them (see Window Screening and Hanging Mesh Drying Rack, facing page), and should be covered with a fine netting or cheesecloth to protect from insects and birds. An outdoor temperature of 85°F [29°C] with dry, breezy weather is ideal. The dryer the climate, the better, since drying outdoors requires low to no humidity. Due to longer drying times with this method, the ingredients may need to be taken indoors at night to avoid nocturnal wildlife as well as evening moisture, then returned outdoors during the day until finished.

DEHYDRATION 101

PREPARING INGREDIENTS

Wash and dry the fresh ingredients well before dehydrating.

Prior to dehydrating, it is important to create uniform pieces that dry evenly at the same rate. A mandoline slicer will create perfectly even slices from thick to paper-thin. A box grater is good for shredding, and a vegetable peeler can create long, thin ribbons. Hand slicing is also an option, using a sharp knife and carefully making uniform cuts.

When filling trays, leave at least ½ in [12 mm] of space between pieces to allow for air circulation. When dehydrating onions, separate out the rings before dehydrating.

DEHYDRATING TIMES

The time ranges given in this chapter's recipes are simply guidelines, and are calibrated for an electric dehydrator. Many factors will determine how long it takes to dehydrate an ingredient: ambient humidity and temperature, how densely packed the ingredients are, freshness and size of the ingredients, and dehydrating method used. Experiment with your particular setup to get a sense of where you fall in the range.

If using other dehydrating methods, such as oven drying, your times may be longer or shorter than those given in the recipes. For sun-drying, times will be much longer.

DEHYDRATING TIPS

When using any dehydrator, rotate trays during the dehydration period to promote even drying.

Smells may cross over between foods, influencing flavor. Separate aromatic ingredients like garlic and onions from more delicately flavored ones and dehydrate in separate batches.

If you find that some foods are sticking to your dehydrator trays, grease the trays lightly with a neutral oil or place a lightly oiled piece of parchment or a nonstick silicone drying sheet on the tray before adding ingredients.

For all recipes except jerky, the dehydration process can be placed on hold for a few hours or up to overnight. Leave the food in the dehydrator or oven, and, when ready, resume dehydrating at the same temperature. Note that this may extend the total dehydration time, as ingredients can rehydrate with ambient humidity.

STORAGE & CONDITIONING

Once foods have reached your desired level of dehydration, bring them to room temperature and then immediately package them in airtight containers. If left to sit out, even in the dehydrator once it stops running, moisture from the air can cause foods to rapidly rehydrate.

Dried food is often "conditioned" before consumption by placing all the pieces from a given batch into a single airtight container. This is particularly helpful when dehydrated pieces are of different sizes and thicknesses. After several days, the hydration level of the pieces should equalize, so that they all have the same level of moisture and, therefore, texture.

Store dehydrated foods in airtight containers, preferably in the dark and at a cool room temperature. Clear glass containers or resealable plastic bags are ideal because you can easily see inside. Check on foods the first few days after storing and watch for signs of moisture, such as condensation or fog, inside the storage vessel. This is an indicator that the food was not fully dehydrated and will spoil more quickly. If this happens, return the pieces to the dehydrator until fully dry.

Silica or oxygen-absorbing packets can be used to extend freshness, and are especially good for very dry foods such as Pantry Powders (page 324).

Recipes indicate how long dehydrated foods will last when properly prepared and stored under ideal conditions. Of course, mold and off-putting smells are indicators of spoilage, and those foods should be discarded.

HANA VAN DER STEUR
Dean of Dehydration

Professor Hana van der Steur is not only the Dean of Dehydration but also the Institute's Assistant Director. In addition to running the Institute's Dehydration Lab, she is our boots-on-the-ground cookbook administrator, also charged with recipe testing and development. An avid baker, Hana has helped develop many of the book's baked goods, including this chapter's Carrot Cake (page 328), and when not at the Lab, she can usually be found preparing a loaf of sourdough bread or frosting a birthday cake for a friend. Her inquisitiveness into flavor, and how to use it, has equipped her perfectly to head up our dehydration experiments.

What's been particularly beneficial about having her involved with all of the Institute's departments is that she recognizes how much crossover is possible between techniques. She's dehydrated many of the Department of Fermentation's recipes, such as miso, sauerkraut, and kimchi, with great success. The same goes for items in the Pantry Department, and she concentrated the flavor of ketchup into a "fruit" leather, ready to use on burgers or a BLT. There are many more flavors yet to be captured through dehydration, and we hope that Hana's approach will inspire you to explore your own dehydration journey.

TIPS FROM THE PROFESSOR

Dehydration is not an exact science—there are too many variables involved, making it difficult to create precise formulas for when a particular ingredient will be "done." As a baker, I appreciate precision, but I also love how the dehydrating process defies exactitude. Embrace this uncertainty with the spirit of experimentation. Don't sweat the timing—just check at regular intervals and use tactile cues, provided in the instructions, to tell when your ingredients are ready. Create your own timing charts that work for your particular dehydration setup and take notes in order to replicate your successes or gain a better understanding of what to try next time.

Take this experimental spirit a step further and try dehydrating unexpected ingredients like olives, or underappreciated vegetables like parsnips, and then take creative liberties in how you use them—parsnip powder spice cookies, anyone?

DEHYDRATED CITRUS WHEELS (PAGE 321)

LINGUINI WITH SUN-DRIED TOMATO PESTO (PAGE 322)

Garlic

Mushroom

Kombu

Onion

Tomato

Carrot

Beet

CARROT CAKE (PAGE 328)

DEHYDRATING HERBS (PAGE 331)

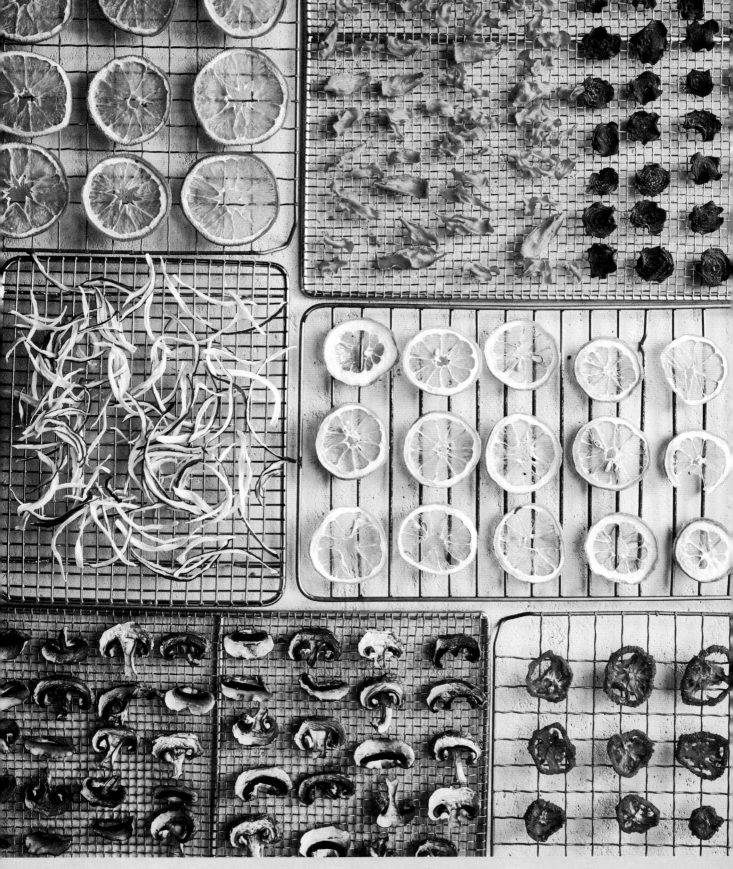

BEEF JERKY (PAGE 332)

FRUIT LEATHER (PAGE 333)

DEHYDRATING FRUIT

One of the foods most associated with dehydration is fruit. Whether it's citrus, stone fruit, melon, or tomatoes, dried fruit is a great pantry item to have on hand since it's not only a healthy snack but also a go-to ingredient for baked goods and a topping for granola or yogurt.

The best fruits to use are ones that are in season, preferably picked just at their peak of ripeness. Organically grown fruit is also a first choice for us since we're drying and consuming the peels, which may harbor lingering pesticide residue or cosmetic waxes.

We have outlined the basic steps needed in order to get started drying fruit, grouping some of our favorites into categories that have similar preparations and times. It's important to note that the process of dehydrating can vary greatly depending on the water content of the fruit, ambient humidity, style of dehydrator or dehydrating method, and thickness of each slice. Times and temperatures given are meant only as guidelines and are calibrated for an electric dehydrator with relatively low ambient humidity. Keep an eye on the fruit during the process, testing it at hourly intervals to check on its progress.

Follow our preparation guidelines, then spread the fruit on a dehydrating tray in a single layer and dehydrate at the temperature indicated, using the timing suggestions as a starting point. When finished dehydrating, dried fruits should be conditioned (see page 309) before storing in an airtight container at cool room temperature for up to 6 months.

WASHING FRUIT

When using unpeeled fruit, sourcing organic is best in order to avoid any waxes or concentrated pesticide residue. If using conventional fruit, soak first in a solution of baking soda and water (1 Tbsp baking soda for every 4 cups [1 L] water), then scrub with a stiff brush and rinse thoroughly.

PRETREATMENT

Some fruits, such as apples, tend to oxidize and turn brown on their surface shortly after they're cut. This is purely cosmetic and won't affect the taste, but a pretreatment dip in a diluted mixture of lemon juice will prevent this. In a medium bowl, mix ½ cup [125 ml] lemon juice with 2 cups [500 ml] water. Working in batches if necessary, dip the fruit slices in the solution for 2 minutes, draining well before proceeding with the recipe.

TROUBLESHOOTING

No matter how uniform we've made the slices, some pieces of fruit always seem to dehydrate faster than others. Check their progress regularly and remove pieces that dry more quickly.

If you overshoot and dry fruit beyond the pliable point, you can steam it briefly to bring back some of its moisture and chewy texture. Conditioning (see page 309) will also help even out texture.

Dried Apples & Pears

PREPARATION: Use a mandoline slicer or a sharp knife to cut whole fruit into uniform slices, ⅛ to ¼ in [3 to 6 mm] thick. The core and seeds can be removed if desired, but we like the way they look—and the ease of leaving them in.

DEHYDRATION: 135°F [55°C] for 4 to 12 hours, until dry and leathery but still slightly tacky and pliable. If "chips" are desired, dehydrate longer until crisp and brittle.

USES: Dried apples and pears are a great addition when dropped into a mug of hot apple cider.

Dried Citrus Wheels

PREPARATION: Use a mandoline slicer to cut the citrus fruit crosswise into thin, uniform ⅛ in [3 mm] slices and remove any seeds. Leaving the peel on will make the fruit much easier to cut, and it is surprisingly easy to eat a whole dehydrated orange or mandarin slice, peel and all. If using a knife, a slightly thicker (up to ¼ in [6 mm]) slice will make the job easier.

DEHYDRATION: 135°F [55°C] for 4 to 10 hours, until the peel is crisp and brittle and the flesh is dry and leathery but still slightly tacky.

USES: We love these dehydrated citrus wheels, which come out looking like stained glass and make a great decoration for the top of a cake. Dried lemon slices are an elegant addition to a glass of tea.

Dried Figs

PREPARATION: Remove the stems and leave the fruit whole, or use a sharp knife to cut the fruit in half or in quarters. Look for Brown Turkey, Black Mission, or Calimyrna varieties.

DEHYDRATION: 135°F [55°C] for 20 to 30 hours, until dry and leathery but still tacky and pliable.

Halved or quartered figs will dry much faster than whole figs.

USES: Dried figs are a welcome accompaniment to a cheese plate, and they make a delicious and unusual topping for pizza.

Dried Melons

PREPARATION: Use a sharp knife to cut the melon in half and remove the seeds and rind. Cut into uniform slices, ⅛ to ¼ in [3 to 6 mm] thick.

DEHYDRATION: 135°F [55°C] for 10 to 14 hours, until dry and leathery but still slightly tacky and pliable.

USES: Dried watermelon and cantaloupe are so sweet that they can satisfy that craving for candy.

Dried Stone Fruit

PREPARATION: For apricots and plums, use a sharp knife to cut the fruit in half or in quarters. Remove the stems and pits from cherries. For nectarines and peaches, cut the fruit into ¼ in [6 mm] slices. Discard the pits, or save apricot pits for Amaretto (page 250).

DEHYDRATION: 135°F [55°C] for 8 to 16 hours, until dry and leathery but still slightly tacky and pliable.

USES: Dried apricots make an appearance in a number of our recipes; see Shrikhand (page 170) and Carrot Cake (page 328).

Dried Tomatoes

PREPARATION: Yes, tomatoes are a fruit. Meatier tomatoes are ideal for drying. Use a sharp, serrated knife to cut the fruit lengthwise into uniform slices, ½ in [12 mm] thick. Smaller tomatoes, such as Roma, may be left halved, but will take much longer to dry. Seeds can be left intact.

DEHYDRATION: 135°F [55°C] for 12 to 16 hours (or up to 24 hours for halved Romas), until dry and leathery but still slightly tacky and pliable.

USES: See recipe for Marinated Dried Tomatoes (page 322).

Marinated Dried Tomatoes

Whether dried in the sun, in an oven, or in a dehydrator, tomatoes take to olive oil and spices like peanut butter takes to jelly. Preserving a summer's worth of home-grown or farmers' market tomatoes makes the off-season a bit less melancholy. We stuff our faces each summer with as many fresh tomatoes as we can, then we spend a few days canning more of them for sauce or juice (page 99) before drying the remaining harvest. The final voyage for our little red beauties is in a marinade, which we use on toast or transform into pesto (right). **YIELD: 1 PT [500 ML]**

8 oz [225 g] dried tomatoes (page 321)
½ cup [125 ml] olive oil, plus more to cover
3 Tbsp fresh lemon juice
3 or 4 garlic cloves, minced
1 tsp dried oregano (page 331)
1 tsp dried thyme (page 331)
¼ tsp red pepper flakes
Sea salt
Freshly ground black pepper

SPECIAL EQUIPMENT
1 pt [500 ml] mason jar

In a medium saucepan over medium-high heat, bring 3 cups [750 ml] of lightly salted water to a boil. Blanch the dried tomatoes for 1 minute to soften them. Use a slotted spoon to transfer them to a colander to drain.

In a medium bowl, whisk together the olive oil, lemon juice, garlic, oregano, thyme, and red pepper flakes. Add the tomatoes and toss well to coat. Season with salt and pepper to taste.

Pack the tomatoes into a 1 pt [500 ml] jar and pour the remaining marinade over them. Top with additional olive oil to cover.

Seal the jar tightly and refrigerate for at least 3 days to allow the flavors to meld before using. To serve, allow the tomatoes to sit at room temperature until the olive oil, which will have solidified in the refrigerator, becomes liquid again.

Marinated tomatoes may be stored in an airtight container in the refrigerator for up to 2 weeks.

Linguini with Sun-Dried Tomato Pesto

This dark red version of the classic green basil pesto is a great way to use oil-packed dried tomatoes, whether dried and packed yourself or store-bought. Combined with the umami-power of Pecorino Romano cheese, they lend a deep, meaty flavor to this vegetarian sauce. Linguini pasta works well here, giving more surface area for the pesto to cling to, but any other pasta will work as well. **SERVES 4 TO 6**

¼ cup [30 g] pine nuts
2 large garlic cloves, peeled
½ cup [120 g] Marinated Dried Tomatoes, drained, roughly chopped, and firmly packed (left)
¼ cup [10 g] chopped fresh Italian parsley, plus more for garnish
¼ tsp dried oregano (page 331)
¼ tsp red pepper flakes
¼ cup [60 ml] olive oil
⅔ cup [65 g] grated Pecorino Romano cheese
1 lb [450 g] linguine pasta, fresh (page 136) or dried
Kosher salt
Freshly ground black pepper

SPECIAL EQUIPMENT
Food processor

In a dry, heavy skillet over medium heat, toast the pine nuts, shaking the pan frequently, until fragrant, about 5 minutes. Transfer to a plate to cool briefly.

In a food processor with the motor running, drop the garlic cloves through the feed tube. Process until the garlic is minced, about 10 seconds. Add the tomatoes, pine nuts, parsley, oregano, and red pepper flakes. Pulse until the mixture forms a paste, scraping down the sides as needed. With the machine running, drizzle in the oil, followed by ½ cup [125 ml] of water, blending just until smooth. Add half of the cheese, pulsing to incorporate, then set aside.

To cook the pasta, bring a large pot of heavily salted water to a rolling boil. Add the linguini and boil until al dente, 1½ to 2 minutes for fresh pasta, or follow the package directions for dried. Remove from the heat and drain, reserving 1 cup [250 ml] of the cooking water.

Return the pasta to the pot and add the pesto, tossing together until the pasta is coated. Add some of the reserved cooking water, ¼ cup [60 ml] at a time, until the sauce thins a bit. Season with salt and pepper to taste, then garnish with parsley and the remaining Pecorino Romano and serve.

MAKE AHEAD: Transfer the pesto to a storage container and cover with a thin layer of olive oil. Seal tightly and store in the refrigerator for up to 2 weeks. Return the pesto to room temperature before using.

PRO PLATING TIP: To create a beautiful swirl of pasta on each plate, use a two-pronged meat fork to twirl a portion of pasta around in the pot. Carefully lift and slide the noodles off the fork, arranging the swirl of pasta neatly on the plate.

PANTRY POWDERS 101

We are obsessed with dehydrating ingredients bone-dry, then grinding them into powders. We're not just talking the usual herbs and spices, but roots, vegetables, fruit, and fungi—not to mention unexpected ingredients like miso and sauerkraut. You'll be surprised how concentrated the flavors are with these powders, so begin your exploration in small doses; you can always add more as needed.

SPECIAL EQUIPMENT

Electric dehydrator (optional)

Spice grinder

ADDITIONAL HELPFUL EQUIPMENT

Mandoline slicer

Box grater

Vegetable peeler

Food processor

Parchment paper or nonstick silicone drying sheets

Offset spatula

PREPARING PANTRY POWDERS

Prepare fresh ingredients as indicated in the recipes following, then spread on a dehydrating tray in a single layer and dry in a dehydrator, or use another dehydrating method (see page 307).

Dehydrate at the temperature indicated for each ingredient, using the timing suggestions as a starting point. Ingredients are ready to be powdered when they are completely bone-dry and brittle. They should snap crisply when folded in half, with no rubbery give. Cool to room temperature, then pulverize in a spice grinder until fine and powdery.

Use immediately or transfer to an airtight container and store in a cool, dark place for up to 3 months.

TIPS

- When preparing ingredients, we prefer using a mandoline slicer, box grater, vegetable peeler, and sometimes a food processor to create small, thin, uniform pieces, which make for the fastest drying times and most consistent results. Slicing by hand with a sharp knife works, too, but make sure to slice as thinly and evenly as possible to achieve the same effect.

- We recommend using an electric dehydrator rather than an oven for making powders, due to the long dehydration times needed.

- Spread ingredients out on the dehydrating trays, leaving at least ½ in [12 mm] of space between pieces to allow for better air circulation.

- When dehydrating pastes or ingredients with very small pieces, line dehydrator trays with parchment paper or nonstick silicone drying sheets.

- If your dehydrator has a powerful fan, small pieces may blow around as they dry out. Lay a weighted piece of parchment or a second nonstick silicone drying sheet directly on top to hold them in place.

- If dehydrating a paste (such as miso) or other food prone to clumping (such as sauerkraut), spread it out across the drying sheet as thinly as possible using the back of a spoon or an offset spatula. Halfway through dehydrating, crumble it with your fingers to break up and disperse any clumps.

- An electric spice grinder is essential to achieving a fine powdery finish, but clean it well in between uses to prevent flavors from mingling. The lid can be washed with hot, soapy water and dried thoroughly before using, but to clean and deodorize the bladed interior, grind a handful of uncooked white rice until powdery. Discard and repeat until the powdered rice appears pure white and has no flecks of color. Unplug the grinder and wipe the interior with a clean towel.

Beet Powder

PREPARATION: Scrub and trim the beets, then use a mandoline slicer to cut into very thin, uniform slices, 1/16 in [1.5 mm] thick. Or use a box grater to coarsely grate.

DEHYDRATION: 125°F [50°C] for 4 to 8 hours.

USES: As an all-natural food coloring.

Carrot / Parsnip Powder

PREPARATION: Scrub and trim the carrots or parsnips, then use a vegetable peeler to make thin ribbons. Or use a mandoline slicer to cut crosswise into very thin, uniform slices, 1/16 in [1.5 mm] thick. Or use a box grater to coarsely grate.

DEHYDRATION: Carrots: 125°F [50°C] for 4 to 8 hours. Parsnips: 125°F [50°C] for 2 to 4 hours.

USES: Carrots: As an all-natural coloring for Cream Cheese Frosting (page 329). Parsnips: In sweet or savory baked goods.

Citrus Peel Powder (Oranges, Lemons, Limes)

PREPARATION: Using a vegetable peeler or a sharp paring knife, carefully remove the outermost layer of peel from the citrus fruit, leaving behind the white pith. Use a knife to scrape off any white pith clinging to the peel for the most intensely colored (and least bitter) powder.

DEHYDRATION: 125°F [50°C] for 2 to 4 hours.

USES: Use anywhere you would use fresh zest. Oranges: Baked-goods topping. Lemons: Vinaigrette. Limes: Mix with an equal amount of salt and rim margarita glasses.

Garlic Powder

PREPARATION: Peel and thinly slice individual cloves of garlic.

DEHYDRATION: 125°F [50°C] for 3 to 4 hours.

USES: A pantry staple. Mix with butter and spread on bread for garlic toast; vinaigrettes (page 37); Fermented Ketchup (page 32); Mustard (page 28).

Ginger Powder

PREPARATION: Peel the ginger, then slice crosswise into 1/8 in [3 mm] pieces.

DEHYDRATION: 125°F [50°C] for 4 to 6 hours.

USES: A pantry staple. Use in baked goods, such as gingerbread or Carrot Cake (page 328).

Miso Powder

PREPARATION: Spread an even layer of miso paste onto a dehydrator tray lined with lightly oiled parchment paper or a nonstick silicone drying sheet. The layer should be as thin as possible without showing any transparent spots.

DEHYDRATION: 125°F [50°C] for 18 to 22 hours. You can speed the process by peeling the layer of miso off the parchment and breaking it into smaller pieces halfway through the drying time. When done, the miso should be completely dry and brittle, cracking cleanly rather than bending when folded.

USES: Instant miso soup: 1 Tbsp powder per 1 cup [250 ml] of hot water or Dashi (page 293); seasoning for popcorn, oven fries, chips.

Mushroom Powder

PREPARATION: Most aromatic when made with all shiitake mushrooms, but you can blend shiitake and cremini. Clean the mushrooms and remove the stems. If using shiitakes, place the whole caps gill-side down on a dehydrator tray. If using cremini, cut into ½ in [12 mm] slices.

DEHYDRATION: 125°F [50°C] for 6 to 8 hours (sliced cremini) or 8 to 12 hours (whole shiitakes).

USES: Umami Cocaine (page 328); Fermented Ketchup (page 32).

Onion Powder

PREPARATION: Peel and halve onions, then cut into ¼ in [6 mm] slices. Separate the layers before dehydrating.

DEHYDRATION: 125°F [50°C] for 14 to 18 hours.

USES: A pantry staple. Dry rubs; Fermented Ketchup (page 32); Mustard (page 28).

Sauerkraut / Kimchi Powder

PREPARATION: Using a food processor, pulse Sauerkraut (page 278) or Kimchi (page 282) several times until all large chunks have been reduced to small, roughly uniform pieces. Transfer to a colander set over a bowl and drain well, using your hands to squeeze out as much liquid as possible. Reserve the brine for another use, such as Fermented Ketchup (page 32). Spread the sauerkraut or kimchi onto a dehydrator tray lined with parchment paper or a nonstick silicone drying sheet.

DEHYDRATION: 125°F [50°C] for 8 to 12 hours.

USES: Bloody Mary garnish; salad dressing; seasoning for popcorn, oven fries, chips.

Tomato Powder

PREPARATION: Firm Roma, baby, or other meaty tomatoes are ideal. Use a sharp knife to cut tomatoes lengthwise into uniform slices, ½ in [12 mm] thick. Seeds can be left intact.

DEHYDRATION: 135°F [55°C] for 14 to 20 hours.

USES: Dry rubs; soups; flavoring for Mayonnaise (page 35); Domestic Seasons Italian Dressing Mix (page 39).

Umami Cocaine

Not illegal, and your new secret weapon in the kitchen. A concentrate of flavor from two of the most powerful umami kingpins: mushroom and kombu. We use UC to add a savory backbone and as a vegan-friendly alternative for meaty flavor. When used in soups, stews, braises, pastas, sauces, meatballs, or other savory dishes, it will deepen and round out umami flavor. To scale this recipe up or down, just use a ratio of 2 parts shiitake and 1 part kombu by weight. **YIELD: ABOUT ½ CUP [30 G]**

8 medium [20 g] dried shiitake mushrooms, sliced in half and stems removed (see Note)
One 4 by 4 in [10 by 10 cm, or 10 g] piece kombu (dried kelp)

SPECIAL EQUIPMENT
Spice grinder

Working in batches, use a spice grinder to pulverize the shiitake mushrooms. Pulse until fine and powdery, then transfer to a small bowl and set aside.

Tear the kombu into 8 smaller pieces, then place in the spice grinder and pulse until fine and powdery. Add to the bowl.

Stir the shiitake and kombu powders well to combine. If any large chunks remain, sift the mixture through a fine-mesh sieve and discard the larger bits or regrind. Transfer Umami Cocaine to an airtight container and store in a cool, dark place for up to 3 months.

NOTE ON MUSHROOMS: Dried shiitake mushrooms may be purchased from your local Asian grocery store, or dehydrated at home (page 308).

Carrot Cake

Carrot cake has a reputation as a somewhat "healthy" dessert. I assume the presence of a vegetable helps with that perception. My sister's amazing 1970s wedding featured a carrot wedding cake. (She was also barefoot and had foraged flowers in her hair.) I've loved carrot cake ever since, but now feel it's due for a bit of an update. Dean of Dehydration Hana van der Steur took on this challenge by punching up the cake's flavor with a healthy dose of cardamom and orange peel powder, in addition to traditional spices like cinnamon, ginger, and nutmeg. Dehydrated carrot powder adds both color and the startlingly concentrated sweet-fresh taste of carrots to a classic cream cheese frosting. Adding dried apricots and cherries brings the cake into fruitcake-adjacent territory while still remaining light and moist, a power play in our opinion. **SERVES 12**

NOTE: Use a box grater rather than a food processor to grate the carrots for the best texture. Crème fraîche is a baker's best friend and yields a moist and tender result. The cake can be dressed down with simple frosting, or dressed up with carrot powder frosting and carrot curls.

CARROT CAKE
¾ cup [90 g] raw walnut halves or pieces
2 cups [280 g] all-purpose flour
1½ tsp baking powder
1 tsp baking soda
1 tsp kosher salt
1 tsp ground cardamom
½ tsp Ginger Powder (page 326) or ground ginger
½ tsp Orange Peel Powder (page 326) or 1 tsp orange zest
¼ tsp ground cinnamon
⅛ tsp freshly grated nutmeg
1 cup [200 g] granulated sugar
1 cup [180 g] packed brown sugar
¾ cup [180 ml] sunflower oil
½ cup [120 g] Crème Fraîche (page 177)
1 tsp Vanilla Extract (page 41)
4 large eggs, at room temperature
3 cups [300 g] coarsely shredded carrots
¼ cup [40 g] dried apricots (page 321), finely chopped
¼ cup [35 g] dried cherries (page 321), finely chopped

CARROT CURL DECORATIONS

1 to 2 large carrots

2 cups [400 g] granulated sugar, plus more for sprinkling if desired

CREAM CHEESE FROSTING

Two 8 oz [226 g] packages cream cheese

1 cup [220 g] unsalted butter

3½ cups [420 g] powdered sugar, sifted

1 tsp Vanilla Extract (page 41)

½ cup Carrot Powder (page 326), sifted, plus more for decorating (optional)

SPECIAL EQUIPMENT

Three 8 by 2 in [20 by 5 cm] round cake pans

Parchment paper

Stand mixer or hand mixer

Offset spatula

MAKE THE CAKE

Place a rack in the center of the oven and preheat the oven to 325°F [160°C]. Butter and flour three 8 by 2 in [20 by 5 cm] cake pans, line them with parchment paper, and set aside.

Spread the walnuts on a baking sheet and bake in the oven for 7 to 10 minutes, until fragrant and lightly toasted. Transfer to a plate and cool to room temperature, then finely chop the nuts and set aside.

In a medium bowl, add the flour, baking powder, baking soda, salt, cardamom, ginger powder, orange peel, cinnamon, and nutmeg and whisk to combine. Set aside.

In the bowl of a stand mixer fitted with the paddle attachment, or using a hand mixer, beat the sugars, oil, crème fraîche, and vanilla together on medium speed until smooth. With the mixer still running, add the eggs, one at a time, and continue to beat until well incorporated, scraping down the sides of the bowl as needed.

With the mixer on low, add the flour mixture ½ cup [70 g] at a time and blend just until incorporated, with some streaks of flour still visible. Scrape down the sides of the bowl and add the carrots, walnuts, and dried fruit, blending just until incorporated.

Divide the batter evenly among the prepared cake pans, smoothing the surfaces with an offset spatula. Transfer to the oven and bake for 35 to 40 minutes, or until a toothpick inserted into the center of the cakes comes out clean and the cakes spring back when lightly pressed in the center.

Cool the cakes on a wire rack for 15 minutes before removing from the pans. Peel off the parchment paper and return the unmolded cakes to the wire rack to cool completely before frosting.

MAKE THE CARROT CURLS

Lower the oven to 200°F [95°C] and line a baking sheet with parchment paper.

Use a vegetable peeler to peel long, even strips of any width down the length of the carrot(s). Reserve 15 to 20 of the best-looking strips and set the rest aside for another use.

In a medium saucepan, combine the sugar and 2 cups [500 ml] water. Bring to a boil over medium-high heat, stirring occasionally, until the sugar dissolves.

Add the carrot strips, lower the heat to medium, and simmer for 8 to 10 minutes, stirring occasionally, until the strips are soft and turning translucent around the edges.

Remove the strips from the syrup and transfer to a fine-mesh sieve to drain thoroughly before arranging in a single layer on the prepared baking sheet, leaving at least 1 in [2.5 cm] between the strips.

Bake the strips for 30 minutes, or until dry but not brittle. They should still be flexible and slightly tacky.

CONT'D

Wind carrot strips, one at a time, in a loose spiral around the handle of a wooden spoon. Slide each curl off and return to the baking sheet. Sprinkle lightly with granulated sugar if a "sparkle" effect is desired. If the carrot strips do not hold their shape, return to the oven for a few more minutes before trying again.

Transfer the curls to the oven and bake until dry and crisp, 30 to 45 minutes more. Cool completely on the baking sheet before using.

MAKE THE FROSTING

Remove the cream cheese and butter from the refrigerator and soften at room temperature until both are pliable but still cool.

In the bowl of a stand mixer fitted with the paddle attachment, or using a hand mixer, cream the butter on medium speed until smooth.

With the mixer still running, add the cream cheese in small increments until thoroughly blended, scraping down the sides of the bowl as needed.

With the mixer on low speed, add the powdered sugar in ½ cup [50 g] increments, followed by the vanilla, then increase the speed to medium and beat until smooth.

Add the carrot powder, if using, beating until thoroughly combined and the frosting turns a speckled orange color.

Use immediately.

ASSEMBLE THE CAKE

Place a dollop of frosting on a large, flat plate, then place one of the cake layers on top, centering it on the plate. Spread ½ cup [120 g] of the frosting over the top of the cake, using an offset spatula to spread it evenly to the edges.

Place a second layer of cake on top and repeat with another layer of frosting.

Place the final layer of cake on top upside down, so that the bottom of the cake layer faces up (thus ensuring a flat top).

Spread a thin layer of frosting over the entire cake, so that all surfaces are covered. This is the crumb coat, and will prevent crumbs from showing on the frosted cake exterior. Place the cake in the refrigerator for 15 minutes to chill.

Remove the cake from the refrigerator and add another, thicker layer of frosting over the entire cake, holding an offset spatula at a 90-degree angle and running it around the sides of the cake to create a smooth surface.

Decorate the cake with the carrot curls and a light dusting of additional dehydrated carrot powder, if desired, and serve.

DEHYDRATING HERBS

If you read our Pantry Department chapter rant about replenishing your spice cabinet often, you'll know that herbs lose their potency over time. A good way to guarantee a constant supply of "best use"–date herbs is to dry bunches of fresh ones yourself. If you can grow them, too, even better.

PREPARATION

For each of the dehydrating methods that follow, prepare the herbs by washing and thoroughly drying them on a clean, dry dish towel or in a salad spinner, depending on how fragile they are. Keep herbs on their stems for easy handling and pick them over carefully, discarding any wilted leaves.

STORAGE

Once dry, snip or pull the leaves from their stems and store herbs in airtight containers in a cool, dark place for up to 6 months. Store leaves whole and lightly crush them just before using. Take the time to label each container with the herb's name and date dehydrated.

PAPER BAG METHOD

So low-tech we can't think of a way to complicate it even if we wanted to. Herbs + paper lunch bag = done.

SPECIAL EQUIPMENT

Paper lunch bags

Gather the herbs into small bundles by type of herb, then tie the ends together with twine. Place each bundle in a paper bag, stem-end up, and tightly secure the bag around the bundle with string or a rubber band. Hang the bundles in a warm, well-ventilated spot for 7 to 10 days, checking on their progress periodically, until the herbs are completely dry, brittle, and easily crumbled.

ELECTRIC DEHYDRATOR METHOD

The fastest way to dry herbs is in an electric dehydrator, which can dry thyme in less time than it takes to go to the store to buy some.

SPECIAL EQUIPMENT

Electric dehydrator

Parchment paper or nonstick silicone drying sheet(s)

Spread the herbs on a dehydrator tray lined with parchment paper or a nonstick silicone drying sheet. Stems may be left intact, which helps prevent the leaves from blowing around (depending on how powerful the dehydrator fan is). Herbs may also be weighted down by placing a second silicone dehydrator sheet on top. Dehydrate at 125°F [50°C] for 1 to 2 hours for delicate herbs like parsley and thyme, and 3 to 4 hours for heartier herbs such as rosemary and sage, or until the leaves are completely dry, brittle, and easily crumbled.

Beef Jerky

One of the foods most associated with dehydration is jerky, especially beef jerky. While any lean meat will "jerk," beef is tasty, easy to source, and safe when dehydrated at 160°F [71°C] or higher. We've borrowed a BBQ dry rub technique, curing the meat in a dry mixture of salt and spices. Not only is it delicious, but drying times are also a little faster without the added moisture of a wet marinade.

YIELD: ABOUT ½ LB [225 G]

One 1 lb [450 g] flank steak, trimmed

1 Tbsp coarsely ground black pepper

1 Tbsp brown sugar

1 Tbsp kosher salt

2 tsp smoked paprika

1 tsp ground fennel

1 tsp ground coriander

1 tsp red pepper flakes

1 tsp Garlic Powder (page 326)

1 tsp Onion Powder (page 327)

1 tsp Umami Cocaine (page 328, optional)

SPECIAL EQUIPMENT

Electric dehydrator (optional)

Pat the steak dry with paper towels, transfer to a plate, then place in the freezer, uncovered, until firm but still pliable, about 1 hour. This will make the meat easier to slice.

Meanwhile, place a wire rack on a rimmed baking sheet and set aside. In a large bowl, combine the remaining ingredients and mix well.

Remove the steak from the freezer and use a sharp chef's knife to slice it into ¼ in [6 mm] thick strips. Slice the meat with the grain for a tougher, chewier texture or against the grain for a more tender texture.

Add the steak strips to the bowl containing the spice mixture and toss until evenly coated.

Place the coated strips on the wire rack, leaving ¼ in [6 mm] of space between each strip, then refrigerate, uncovered, for 12 to 24 hours.

Remove the steak strips from the refrigerator and allow to come to room temperature, about 30 minutes on the counter, before dehydrating. Pat them dry with paper towels if any surface moisture is present.

If using a dehydrator, transfer the strips to dehydrator trays and dry for 4 to 8 hours (or longer) at 160°F [71°C], until dry to the touch, pliable, and leathery. Jerky should crack but not break when bent. If using the oven, preheat to the lowest setting, preferably 200°F [95°C] or below (but no lower than 160°F [71°C]). Follow directions for oven dehydrating (see page 307) and dehydrate for 3 to 4 hours or until done, as indicated above.

When jerky is ready, blot with paper towels to remove any rendered fat on the surface and allow to cool completely. Jerky can be served immediately or stored in an airtight container at room temperature for up to 2 weeks, or in the refrigerator for up to 1 month.

Fruit Leather

Fruit leathers are dried sheets of puréed fruit that can be rolled up into convenient snack batons and slipped into lunch boxes, backpacks, purses, or briefcases. At the Institute, we take the leathers of our youth to the next level, using this basic recipe as a springboard for mixing fruits and flavors, adding liqueurs, spices, and anything else hanging around the pantry. See our FlavorBar ideas following the recipe. Our go-to fruit is anything in season, but our favorites include apricots, nectarines, peaches, plums, cherries, and any type of berries. We also love "leatherizing" bananas, applesauce, pears, persimmons, pineapples, and even ketchup (see Variation, page 334). Choose ripe or even very ripe fruit, and remove stems, pits, and any blemishes. Leave the skins on or remove them; it's up to you. If you don't have a dehydrator, try using the oven; see page 307 for instructions. **YIELD: 3 ROLLS**

3½ cups [550 g] pitted and finely chopped fruit
1 Tbsp fresh lemon juice
1 Tbsp brown sugar or honey (optional)

SPECIAL EQUIPMENT
Parchment paper or nonstick silicone drying sheets
Blender
Offset spatula
Electric dehydrator (optional)

Line three dehydrator trays with parchment paper or nonstick silicone drying sheets and set aside.

In a blender, combine the fruit, lemon juice, and sugar, if using, and purée until smooth.

Pour one-third of the purée onto a prepared tray, tilting the tray and using an offset spatula to spread it around until it's distributed across the entire surface. The purée should be about ⅛ in [3 mm] thick at the center and ¼ in [6 mm] thick at the edges, since the edges of the fruit leather will dehydrate faster than the center. Repeat with the remaining trays.

Dehydrate the purée at 135°F [55°C] for 4 to 6 hours, or longer, until the surface is dry and leathery to the touch, but still pliable. Give the leather a final test by peeling it up 1 in [2.5 cm] or so along one edge; it should peel up easily without sticking to the parchment or drying sheet.

When the leather is ready, and working while it's still warm, peel the leather completely off the parchment, then transfer to a fresh piece of wax paper or plastic wrap and roll it into a baton, rolling the paper around the leather to keep it from sticking to itself.

Store fruit leather in an airtight bag or container at room temperature for up to 2 weeks, in the refrigerator for up to 6 months, or in the freezer for up to 1 year.

CONT'D

VARIATION: TOMATO KETCHUP LEATHER

YIELD: FOUR 4 IN [10 CM] SQUARE PIECES

Follow the instructions for fruit leather (page 333), but use 1 cup [250 g] Fermented Ketchup (page 32) or store-bought ketchup instead of chopped fruit and flavorings. Line a dehydrator tray or baking sheet with parchment paper or a nonstick silicone drying sheet, then spread the ketchup into an 8 by 8 in [20 by 20 cm] square and dehydrate according to the recipe, 2 to 6 hours, testing every 2 hours until dry enough to peel off the sheet. Once dehydrated, cut into four 4 in [10 cm] squares to use on burgers or BLTs.

FLAVORBAR

—

FRUIT LEATHER IDEAS:

Go forth and experiment! Using 3 cups [700 g] of puréed fruit as a guide, start by adding 1 tsp extract or spirits and ¼ tsp of each dried spice. Stir to combine, then taste. Adjust the flavoring until it pleases your palate. Go slow—remember that you can always add more, but it's hard to take away if you add too much.

applesauce + cinnamon

pear + cloves + nutmeg

strawberries + vanilla extract

apricot + dates + brandy

banana + strawberries + vanilla extract

peaches + lavender

blackberries + orange zest

pineapple + rum

RAIDERS OF THE LOST RECIPE BOX

Having disappeared for decades, this beat-up metal file box containing Institute founder Eliza Taylor Reynolds's original recipes was finally located in, of all places, a commune in Summertown, Tennessee. It was believed to have been passed down by Taylor Reynolds's daughter, Nellie, as a precious family heirloom to her own daughter, Maxine. However, Maxine—who changed her name to "Galadriel," after moving to San Francisco soon after her mother died in 1967—appeared to have simply vanished. It was Maxine/Galadriel's daughter, Jane, who alerted us to the box's discovery when she unearthed it from among her late mother's possessions while cleaning out her yurt. Jane—who changed her name from "Solstice"—graciously donated it to the Institute. With its dog-eared tabs and faded index cards, this miraculously preserved treasure trove of recipes forms the centerpiece of the archives and is the basis for many of the recipes in this book.

WALDORF TRIANGLES

6

Lightly beat 6 egg yolks, then slowly beat in 1/2 cup of granulated sugar. Add 2 tablespoonfuls of orange juice. Add a 1/2 cup of sifted flour, sifting again with a teaspoonful of baking powder and pinch of salt.

Pour the mixture into buttered Waldorf Triangle pans and bake in a moderate oven.

After the cakes are turned from the pan, cover the sides with boiled frosting and sprinkle with finely chopped pistachio nuts.

ABOUT THE AUTHOR

Trained as a Certified Master Food Preserver in 2011 by the University of California Cooperative Extension and the County of Los Angeles, Joseph Shuldiner is a writer, food consultant, and cook. He is also the founder of the Institute of Domestic Technology, which promotes the lost domestic arts, teaching students the essential foodcrafting skills they need to make their own ingredients and food choices.

Among the group of prominent "makers" currently influencing LA's food culture, Joseph established the Altadena Farmers' Market, an alternative, certified market, in 2012. Along with fellow cookbook author Kevin West, he cofounded Headspace Consulting,

which reenvisioned public spaces by populating them with creative chefs, food-makers, and farmers. Together, Joseph and Kevin contributed to the visionary reinvigoration of the 1917 historic landmark Grand Central Market in downtown Los Angeles, which has since become an international food destination, called one of the ten best new restaurants of 2014 by *Bon Appétit*.

Joseph is the author of *Pure Vegan: 70 Recipes for Beautiful Meals and Clean Living* (Chronicle Books, 2012). A native Angeleno, Joseph lives with his husband, Bruce, and their cat, Oscar, in LA's Highland Park.

ACKNOWLEDGMENTS

First, I'd like to acknowledge my parents, Max and Sarah Shuldiner, both of whom, in their own ways, respected my insatiable childhood curiosity about how things are made and tried valiantly to help me find the answers I sought in a world before Google. I so wish they could be here to see this book, in which I think they'd recognize the spirit of their inquisitive eleven-year-old.

Next, although it is undoubtedly a cliché for an author to thank his or her spouse by saying, "This book would not exist without you," in the case of my husband, Bruce, it's actually true. His helpful suggestions, edits, and, most of all, willingness to be a listener and sounding board were only surpassed by his nuts and bolts assistance with everything from running around town finding obscure ingredients I needed to tasting recipes in development over and over again. Above all, his unshakable belief in me—in those moments when I may not have entirely believed in myself—was, and has been, one of the greatest gifts I have received from him in our over thirty years together.

I'd also like to thank my early collaborators and co-instructors at the Institute, Stephen Rudicel and Gloria Putnam. The origin of the Institute of Domestic Technology was, in large part, the result of my participation in their groundbreaking, under-the-radar farmers' market at the Zane Grey Estate, Stephen's

family's beautiful historic property in Altadena. It was there that I put together what was to become the Institute's first iteration: the Urban Farmer's Market University. Gloria and Stephen's hard work, expertise, and influence during its formative years contributed immeasurably to the Institute's long-term success, and I will be forever indebted to them.

Thanks also to Daniel Kent, who, in addition to serving double duty as the Dean of Caffeine and the Dean of Spirits, was for many years my right-hand man at the Institute. From Daniel's formidable supply-schlepping to his witty, informative teaching, his brains and brawn have left an indelible impression on the Institute.

Honorable mention must also be made to Daniel's successor, my essential, irreplaceable, and long-suffering assistant (and Dean of Dehydration) Hana van der Steur. Without Hana's beyond-the-call-of-duty perseverance and uncanny eye for detail, the recipes in this book would be far less cogent, clear, and easy to follow.

I also owe a debt of gratitude to Greta Dunlap, my farmers' market mentor and colleague, for her support and generosity in sharing the depth and breadth of her knowledge with me when I was first starting up my own farmers' market, an experience that has found its way into this book in so many ways.

336

All of my "Deans" deserve my sincere thanks as well, not only for graciously accepting their positions on the Institute's faculty but also for sharing their formidable knowledge and experience with me and with all of the Institute's students. Thank you to David Asher, Daniel Kent, Nan Kohler, Yoko Maeda Lamn, Zach Negin, Rashida Purifoy, Hana van der Steur, and Kevin West.

I also offer my heartfelt thanks to my agent, Laura Nolan, for her deep understanding of this book as well as her careful guidance during its realization. Special mention is also due to Camaren Subhiya, my editor at Chronicle, for her keen insight and limitless patience throughout the editing process.

Thanks as well to my sister-in-law, Wendy Heidari, who generously allowed me the use of her space in Los Angeles for the Institute's test kitchen (or "The Lab," as it came to be known).

I'd also be remiss if I didn't thank these friends, colleagues, and supporters for their inspiration, encouragement, and assistance: Alexandra Agajanian, Colleen Dunn Bates, Laura Bennett, Elizabeth Bowman, Hae Jung Cho, Nancy Donavan, Monica Ford, Clémence Gossett, Harriet Hayes, Sarah Hymanson, Leslie Ito and the staff at the Japanese American Cultural and Community Center, Andy Kadin, Sandor Katz, Karen Klemens, Eric Knutsen, Sara Kramer, Jordan "Uri" Laio, Joshua McIver, Ernest Miller, Carol Moore, Jessica Mortarotti, Michael O'Malley, Carmi Paulson, Nicole Rucker, Jonathan Salvador, and Jered Standing.

I'd also like to thank the Institute's many students, whose desire to learn traditional foodcrafting techniques has been a revelation, and whose passionate embrace of our class offerings provided the inspiration for this book. Our army of dedicated recipe testers was largely drawn from these same ranks of dedicated students. The generous donation of their time and effort in testing and commenting on the scores of recipes in this book assured that each and every recipe was thoroughly vetted and subjected to scrutiny by multiple pairs of eyes. Every successful loaf of bread and jar of jam you prepare with the help of this book is due, in large part, to their efforts.

My thanks are also due to Laura Im, who, as our capable Recipe Testing Liaison, provided the vital link between our over 100 volunteer testers and the Institute.

And finally, to all of my illustrious predecessors, the former directors of the Institute of Domestic Technology: It has been my honor to follow in your footsteps. Above all, I owe a debt of gratitude to the founder of the original IDT, Eliza Taylor Reynolds. I'd like to imagine that she would be pleased to learn that her Institute and her legacy live on.

RECIPE TESTERS

STAR PUPILS

Veronica Anderson
Cynthia Barron
Blumberg Family
Deena Bowman
Brenda Burke
Maggie Kymn Chang
Mandy Barton Clark
Sandra Crouch
Victoria Curtis

Kristen Desmond
Pamela Dilley
Victoria A. Elsberry
Rachel Garcia
Lindsey Hill
Alice Hom
Charlene Huston
Annjanette Isorda
Elsa Jacobson
Lynn Katano

Kristen Keegan
Jeanette Moreno King
Janel Kranking
Stephen Lamb
Heather MacFreier
Allen Manning
Kelley McIntosh
Nic Meek-Whitehead
Shari Morita

Natalie Ige Muldaur
Julie Normand
Kyoko Oguri
Kelli O'Leary
Melissa Palmer
Christa Peitzman
Sara Pelton
Christine Krause Pham
Diane Plaskow

Lelia Scheu
Mary Scheu
Luis Solares
Adina Sullivan
Laci Ulrich
Chauvon Venick
V.R. Marianne Zahn

HONOR ROLL

James Aarons
Marcia Baker
Lelah Baker-Rabe
Mari Bennett
Patty Burnstein
Malika R. Cohen
Hunter Curra
Sara DeLeeuw
Angelo J. Di Fusco
Alia DiOrio
Michele DuVall

Carmen Grammer
Dawn Harvey
Cheri Herrboldt
Mona Soo Hoo
Courtney Hopkins
Kristine Kaiser
Rena Kashmere
Lauren A. Kaufman
Wasima Khan
Tom Krenzke
Shannon Lanus

Sarah LaVoie
Sandra Lourenco
Candy Mako
Katie Bergin Mankiewicz
Kirk McCarty (and Silverado High School)
Gulen McKeever
Brenda Northcutt
Deborah Nucatola
Karen Ostler

Joel Palmer
Liz Pedroza
Shelley D. Perpall
Michelle Pierce
Dyane Razook
Maura Redmond
Caitlin Robertson
Wendy Roskin
Michon Roth
Mary Jane Saintignon
Sharon Sarpong

Terry Sauer
Chanda Singh
Marci Stepman
Shira Tarrant
Jenna Thomas
Helen Veth
Robert Wallace
Brian Weiss
Rena Wheeler
Britany Wilcher
Lane Wong

DEAN'S LIST

Jeanne Ackerman
Bryce Butcher Altounian
Keri Bacic
Katie Bowman
Christian Bushnell
JD Cantarella

Alexandra Charlemagne
Dana Dantzler
Magda Diaz
Susan Dretzka
Mary Feliton
Gina Grossi

Nicole Hausman
Alexandra Holbrook
Kerry Jacobs
Mark & Karen Joseph
Roland Kato

Morgan Kays
Kasey Knose
Mary Ellen Leggio
Deirdre Marlowe
Marisa Martinez
Yoko Masumura
Peter & Kim Pendergest

Maria Angeles Perez
Andreas Sautter
Kyle Taborski
Emilie Tarrant
Mark Zedella

RESOURCES

PANTRY

Dandelion Botanical
(herbs, spices, and salts)
877-778-4869
www.dandelionbotanical.com

Penzeys Spices
(spices)
800-741-7787
www.penzeys.com

The Spice House
(spices)
312-676-2414
www.thespicehouse.com

Wild Terra
(spices/herbs)
323-739-9300
www.wildterra.la

CAFFEINE

Fresh Roasted Coffee LLC
(unroasted green coffee beans)
570-495-4300
www.freshroastedcoffee.com

PICKLES, PRESERVES & FERMENTATION

Cultures for Health
(kōji and other fermentation
starters)
www.culturesforhealth.com

General Bottle Supply
(bottles and jars)
800-782-0198 (Los Angeles, CA)
800-788-9596 (Oakland, CA)
www.bottlesetc.com

Hakko
(kōji, miso making crocks)
www.hakko.online

Kawashima: The Japan Store
(kōji, Japanese cooking utensils)
81-42-510-2593
www.thejapanstore.jp

Laura Soybeans
(soybeans)
515-583-2198
www.laurasoybeans.com

NW Ferments
(kefir grains, airlocks, etc.)
1-844-558-2752
www.nwferments.com

SKS Bottle and Packaging, Inc.
(mason jars)
518-880-6980 Ext. 1
www.sks-bottle.com

GRAINS

Anson Mills
(whole-grain milled flour)
803-467-4122
www.ansonmills.com

Grist & Toll
(whole-grain milled flour)
626-441-7400
www.gristandtoll.com

DAIRY

New England Cheesemaking
Supply Co.
(cheesemaking supplies)
413-397-2012
www.cheesemaking.com

The Cheesemaker
(kefir grains, cheesemaking
supplies)
414-745-5483
www.thecheesemaker.com

MEAT

The Sausage Maker
(sausage casings)
888-490-8525
www.sausagemaker.com

SPIRITS

Blue Mountain Organics
(apricot kernels)
540-283-9589
www.bluemountainorganics.com

Lhasa Karnak
(cinchona, wormwood, spices)
510-548-0380
www.lhasakarnak.com

NY Spice House
(apricot kernels)
516-360-9008
www.nyspicehouse.com

DEHYDRATION

Excalibur
(dehydrating equipment)
800-875-4254
https://excaliburdehydrator.com

TOOLS & EQUIPMENT

Cuisinart
(mixers, blenders, ice cream
makers, etc.)
800-726-0190
www.cuisinart.com

Lodge Cast Iron
(cast-iron cookware)
833-563-4387
www.lodgemfg.com

JAPANESE INGREDIENTS

Marukai
(kōji, nuka, and other japanese
ingredients)
www.marukai.com

Nijiya Market
(kōji, nuka, and other japanese
ingredients)
www.nijiya.com

South River Miso Company
(kōji and other Japanese
ingredients)
413-369-4057
www.southrivermiso.com

MISC

Melissa's/World Variety Produce
(specialty produce)
800-588-0151
www.melissas.com

SELECTED BIBLIOGRAPHY AND RECOMMENDED READING

PICKLES AND PRESERVING

Morris, William C. "Low or No Sugar in Jams, Jellies and Preserves." The University of Tennessee Institute of Agriculture, 2014. https://extension.tennessee.edu/publications/Documents/SP325-F.pdf.

University of Wisconsin. "pH Values of Common Foods and Ingredients." Clemson Cooperative Extension: College of Agriculture, Forestry and Life Sciences, 2009. www.clemson.edu/extension/food/food2market/documents/ph_of_common_foods.pdf.

U.S. Department of Agriculture. "Complete Guide to Home Canning and Preserving, 2015 revision." National Center for Home Food Preservation, 2015. https://nchfp.uga.edu/publications/publications_usda.html.

West, Kevin. *Saving the Season: A Cook's Guide to Home Canning, Pickling, and Preserving*. New York: Alfred A. Knopf, 2013.

GRAINS

Baker, Josey. *Josey Baker Bread: Get Baking – Make Awesome Bread – Share the Loaves*. San Francisco: Chronicle Books, 2014.

Boyce, Kim. *Good to the Grain: Baking with Whole-Grain Flours*. New York: Stewart, Tabori & Chang, 2010.

Medrich, Alice. *Flavor Flours*. New York: Artisan, 2014.

DAIRY

Asher, David. *The Art of Natural Cheesemaking: Using Traditional, Non-Industrial Methods and Raw Ingredients to Make the World's Best Cheeses*. White River Junction, Vermont: Chelsea Green, 2015.

Karlin, Mary. *Artisan Cheese Making at Home: Techniques & Recipes for Mastering World-Class Cheeses*. Berkeley, California: Ten Speed Press, 2011.

Mendelson, Anne. *Milk: The Surprising Story of Milk Through the Ages*. New York: Alfred A. Knopf, 2018.

SPIRITS

Morgenthaler, Jeffrey. *The Bar Book: Elements of Cocktail Technique*. San Francisco: Chronicle Books, 2014.

Parsons, Brad Thomas. *Bitters: A Spirited History of a Classic Cure-All, with Cocktails, Recipes, and Formulas*. Berkeley, California: Ten Speed Press, 2011.

Teacher, Matt. *The Spirit of Gin: A Stirring Miscellany of the New Gin Revival*. Kennebunkport, Maine: Cider Mill Press, 2014.

FERMENTATION

Andoh, Elizabeth. *Kansha: Celebrating Japan's Vegan and Vegetarian Traditions*. Berkeley, California: Ten Speed Press, 2010.

Flynn, Sharon. *Ferment for Good: Ancient Food for the Modern Gut: The Slowest Kind of Fast Food*. South Yarra, Australia: Hardie Grant Books, 2017.

Hachisu, Nancy Singleton. *Preserving the Japanese Way: Traditions of Salting, Fermenting, and Pickling for the Modern Kitchen*. Kansas City, Missouri: Andrew McMeel Publishing, 2015.

Karlin, Mary. *Mastering Fermentation: Recipes for Making and Cooking with Fermented Foods*. Berkeley, California: Ten Speed Press, 2013.

Katz, Sandor Ellix. *The Art of Fermentation: An In-Depth Exploration of Essential Concepts and Processes from around the World*. White River Junction, Vermont: Chelsea Green, 2012.

Katz, Sandor Ellix. *Wild Fermentation: The Flavor, Nutrition, and Craft of Live-Culture Foods*. White River Junction, Vermont: Chelsea Green, 2016.

DEHYDRATION

Dickerman, Sara. *Dried & True: The Magic of Your Dehydrator in 80 Delicious Recipes and Inspiring Techniques*. San Francisco: Chronicle Books, 2016.

Gangloff, Tammy, et al. *The Ultimate Dehydrator Cookbook: The Complete Guide to Drying Food, Plus 398 Recipes, Including Making Jerky, Fruit Leather & Just-Add-Water Meals*. Mechanicsburg, Pennsylvania: Stackpole Books, 2014.

MISC

America's Test Kitchen. *DIY Cookbook: Can It, Cure It, Churn It, Brew It*. Brookline, Massachusetts: America's Test Kitchen, 2012.

Coyne, Kelly, and Erik Knutzen. *Making It: Radical Home Ec for a Post-Consumer World*. New York: Rodale, Inc., 2011.

Coyne, Kelly, and Erik Knutzen. *The Urban Homestead (Expanded & Revised Edition): Your Guide to Self-Sufficient Living in the Heart of the City*. Port Townsend, Washington: Process Media, 2010.

Kauffman, Jonathan. *Hippie Food: How Back-to-the-Landers, Longhairs, and Revolutionaries Changed the Way We Eat*. New York: William Morrow, 2018.

McGee, Harold. *On Food and Cooking: The Science and Lore of the Kitchen*. New York: Scribner, 2004.

Pollan, Michael. *Cooked: A Natural History of Transformation*. New York: Penguin Books, 2013.

Pollan, Michael. *The Omnivore's Dilemma: A Natural History of Four Meals*. New York: Penguin Books, 2006.